Jan Anders Andersson

I0167905

Money,
and
the Art
of Losing Control

A story about friendship on the road
or just a matter of time

1st printed edition
All rights reserved
© 2012 J A CoMedia
ISBN 978-91-980330-4-5
Cover and photo: J A Andersson

Preface

This is a story about a human enterprise on the planet Earth in the end of the year 2011. It draws a connecting line between simple diverse matters like the biggest fictional massmurder in the history of literature, Cosmological Evolution, Money, Time, Thermodynamics, Love, The Funniest Joke in the World, the Meaning of Life, Gravitation, Violence, the Holy Grail, and Trails of Truth and Friendship.

The book is written for your pleasure and entertainment. It is a road story but not a map. It is also a book about itself. Why it is worth the effort of communicating and cooperating with each other at all.

The conclusions that are presented in this book are not intended to be believed in, as they can cause a serious impact upon your conception of the world, but you may try it at your own risk, and pleasure.

Acknowledgements

No book is the work only of its author.

I owe much to the works of Robert M Pirsig, Anthony McWatt, Stephen Hawking, Sture Dahlström, Bodil Jönsson, Arto Paasilinna and Brian Greene.

I must thank the people at the *Metaphysics Of Quality Discuss*[1] forum whom I have terrorized with my stupid stories and strange ideas.

Many thanks to Anthony, Marsha, Daina, Barbro and Sally for reviewing the manuscript and for your valuable comments.

---

1 http://www.moq.org/

The Swedish Road to the MOQ

If you enjoy the films of Ingmar Bergman and the books of Robert Pirsig, you'll enjoy this book. It's often forgotten that much of Pirsig's second book, *Lila. An Inquiry into Morals* was written in a wood cabin on the Swedish coast. *Money and the Art of Losing Control* expands on the rather bleak atmosphere of the former to the knife edge of credibility. In a country that is cold and dark for much of the year, it should come of no surprise that the Swedish approach to life has developed an underlying black humour with a touch of stoicism and the rather uninhibited Scandinavian view (at least for my reserved English eyes) of human sexuality. You will not have to read too far in Mr Andersson's book to find all of these elements; often in combination.

Keeping in mind the caveat at the beginning of *Zen and the Art of Motorcycle Maintenance* about it not being much concerned with motorcycle maintenance or Zen, you will be disappointed if you are looking to *Money and the Art of Losing Control* as a precise guide for making money. However, in the same way that Pirsig's book is a "meta-book" about motorcycle maintenance (in the sense of finding the best attitude of mind before engaging in this type of endeavour), you will likewise find Mr Andersson's book helpful in developing the right attitude for money making… Oh, and on the way (as we travel through the snowy Swedish forests with the happy couple of John and Elsa), it is also worth noting that included in the narrative are some useful insights about the good life as viewed through the prism of Robert Pirsig's "Metaphysics of Quality".

Dr Anthony McWatt[2]

May 2012

---

2 http://robertpirsig.org/PhD.htm

1 - Dissect the Evolution

John held the steering wheel with his left hand and pressed his right foot gently on the accelerator to keep the car straight at around 50 mph. He was alone in the car and on the road. At the end of the straight he could see a bend to the right. He looked forward to what he would find there.

It was Thursday at the beginning of November. John had been driving all day long, with only a few stops at his customers' offices in different cities and to eat some fast food. The wheels were running. The engine made a low tone which told him that it worked fine. His dark green Volvo estate wagon was a 1996 model and 15 years old. He had driven this car as far as six times around the whole world.

The radio was the original from when the car was produced and it had a cassette player. John was listening to a German promotional cassette that he had found in a flea market, *Stereo Spectacular 3*, which demonstrated the advantages of stereo recording. It was Kurt Edelhagen playing 'My Prayer'. John liked to listen to this kind of exaggerated stereo effect. He heard the sound of a wild technician freaking out on the soundboard.

"What if time is running backwards?" he was thinking. He was wondering about his sight and his eyes. At a petrol station half an hour earlier he had realized that his eyes had got used to the upcoming road. When he stopped the car, the front view seemed as if it was leaving him, giving a feeling that the car was moving backwards though he knew that it was standing still. He knew that the eyes were trying to compensate for light and colour, but movement?

He gave his eyebrows some massage. He had heard that it would help when his eyes were getting tired. But he thought that this error must be happening in his brain not in his eyes.

John passed a fire beside the road. Someone had set fire to a heap of rubbish. He drove through the smoke. The smell of wet cardboard, hay and used dirty textiles triggered his memories of smelling sensations. There was something else, like rubber. He wasn't sure.

There was thin ice on the ponds. The trees stood bare and naked. The crowns were filled with branches and twigs in a maze pointing around to the horizon. Another winter coming again in an endless wheel of change.

"No, time cannot run backwards. The petrol was burning in the engine. That is a process that cannot run in the wrong direction. It is impossible that the engine should run backwards collecting all the exhaust fumes in the air along the road and making them into petrol and clean air. And what energy would then drive the car backwards if the tank was filled during the drive instead of emptied?" he was thinking.

"It is impossible to build up new tyres with a perfect pattern from the small parts of rubber that were left on the thousands of miles of the roads he had been driving."

He was getting older.

John was 46 years old and a father of three kids, now teenagers and preparing to leave home for higher education. His wife was at home and working on her career as an artist. John was an enterprise consultant who specialized in energy cost management services, assisting the people responsible for it in industries to get better control of their costs for energy. Very good business concept, as all companies have energy costs – costs for electricity, gas and oil for heating and processes. Normally, it had been about huge amounts of money so it was not too hard to make a living from it. But he knew that he was not the only one that wanted to make his living in this little niche. He had to work hard to keep in the lead, even inside his company.

He was dressed in a suit and tie to convey a serious impression to his customers. Polished shoes and a new black overcoat to protect against the coming cold season. At home he preferred to walk around in black jeans and worn T-shirts. His mobile phone, a completely outdated Sony Ericsson P900, lay in its holder and showed the calendar and who he was to visit next on this day. Between the seat and the gearbox tunnel he had placed his new iPad, on which he had his customer database, a presentation file of the business and his own music collection.

In the back of the car he had a big cardboard box with a computer and a printer. His sister had called some days earlier and asked if he could fix a computer for Elisabeth, her former weaving teacher. She lived in Livelong, a city that John used to pass on his trips. Elisabeth's granddaughter had moved to New York to study and she wanted to use email to keep in contact with her. Elisabeth was 86 years old and had not learned how to use a computer yet and John was well known for training people in computer skills.

"No problem," he had answered, "just let me do it when it fits my travelling schedule." He had looked around on eBay and other sites and found a used iMac with all the software included that was cheap.

It was not late, about 5 pm, so now it was ideal to visit Elisabeth and hand over the computer. He went through a forest. "Sometimes you can't see the forest because of the trees," he thought. It was a traditional saying, about how we sometimes can't see what is between all the facts that are showing, blinded by too much information. "Too much light has a blinding effect and can be used as a strategy against enemies if you are chased. Too little light makes you unable to outline the truth. But if you get perfect light but too many details then it can be hard to see the connections, what it is between the trees." He was thinking planlessly as he was driving. Most of his concentration was on the driving while the rest of his half-conscious mind was playing around with small, easily definable pieces.

He went straight on at a roundabout on the way into the city. As usual he took a tour around the streets to learn the local road geography. It was a typical small town in the country with shops and restaurants. People were driving around and walking in and out of the shops.

When he arrived at the right address he parked the car outside the block of flats and brought out the box from the rear. It was heavy with all the equipment: computer, printer, keyboard and cables.

He went to the door and looked up her name on the list. He had to put down the big box to be able to press the digits. He pressed 245B and 'Call' to ask her to open the main door.

"Elisabeth."

"Hi – I am John who is delivering a computer to you. What floor do you live on?"

"Don't you know that? Well it's on Floor 3. Just step in and I'll leave the door open."

A green LED light flashed and a beep was heard and he understood that the lock was released.

It took him a while to get through the doors with the heavy box. The elevator door springs nearly knocked him over. But on the third floor he could see an open door in the middle of the corridor. John stepped through it, put the heavy box on the floor and closed the door. He could smell a warm mix of wool and linen. The door led straight into the kitchen where Elisabeth was sitting at the table with another woman. John could see that there was a bigger room inside the kitchen with antique furniture, a big clock on the wall, cardboard boxes filled with all sorts of material.

Elisabeth had short grey hair and was wearing a light wool jumper, necklace and pearl eardrops. The kitchen was small but well equipped with a refrigerator and a freezer, microwave oven and coffee machine. Cups and plates in the sink and small wooden handmade tools. John could see a sugar bowl on the table that was made from birch tree. The kitchen table was covered by a thick white cloth with blue stripes. Elisabeth smiled in a friendly manner at him as John said "hello" to the women.

Because she had been teaching textiles all her life she had a lot of material and leftovers that she was offering to younger women. The woman in her apartment was there to buy some material. They sat at the table in the kitchen with a cup of coffee and asked John to sit down for a cup. John took off his overcoat and sat down at the end. Elisabeth and the other woman Maja, did not actually know each other very well. It was apparent that they had never met before. John realized that when

Elisabeth tried to introduce her to him. In fact, this small business was a way for her to get in contact with others, and preferably with people sharing her own interests, to break up her solitude.

"My name is Elisabeth but you can call me Elsa! What was your name again?"

"Maja."

"My name is John. John Smith at your service. Nice to meet you ladies."

Elsa smiled at them and put her hands together. "Oh it's so nice to have two visitors at once. Now we can have a pleasant talk as new friends do."

"So what are we going to talk about?" Maja asked. No interest in John or the computer in the box on the floor.

"Tell us about your first love affair," Elsa said as she poured coffee into John's cup. "A person's first love affair is always interesting."

"Why do we have to speak about love?"

"Don't you like to talk about love? Are you unhappy?" Elsa looked sharply at Maja.

"Are you happy with your life?" Maja countered.

"Yes, I'm happy. I am 86 years and I am happy with my life and I'm prepared to stay happy for the rest of my life."

"Does that mean that you are happy with your sex life as well?"

"Yes!" Elsa answered briefly. "Because I am done with my sex life. I've outlived three men, that's good enough. I have spent 50 years of my life in relationships with men. Now I am happy with living alone so I can take my own decisions without interference by any man. I wake up every day at the time of my own deciding. I plan my day as I like it and I am very happy about that. I do not have to listen to

11

some loud stupid football game on the radio. I do not have to experience the smell of a dirty man hanging around in the kitchen waiting for food. I do not have to argue about this or that. Still I have got friends to hug and easy work to do all day long. I eat when and what I like. I am absolutely a happy woman."

"That does not sound correct to me," Maja said, maybe a bit frustrated, "because I think that there is nothing absolute and especially no absolute happiness, it's just an illusion."

"Hmm," John said. "That reminds me of Grg, he was an absolutely unhappy man."

"Who?" Elsa looked sharply at him.

"Grg. One of the sons of Tor, the God of the Vikings. It's kind of a long story but I can tell you a short version before the coffee gets cold in your cups."

No one objected so John began to tell the story of Grg:

"Grg was angry at his parents because they tried to tell Grg that he was lazy and did not seem to take life seriously enough. It was a big godlike quarrel. In fact Grg got totally furious, he felt the berserk inside him wake up and so he yelled to his parents Tor and Siv:

"'You can take that big shiny world of yours out there and stick it up your arse! I know that we are Gods! What do I care about some "world out there"! We are Gods and we can do just what we want with it!

"'I am not going to change myself to fit the world out there! The world shall change based on us! You are talking about it as if it is yours only and I can tell you that I hate it!

"'I HATE your world!'

"Just when he had said that he saw that for a second he would be able to grab Mjölner, Tor's hammer, that

12

lay on the table in front of Tor. Quick as a snake his hand swept over the table and grabbed the hammer. Bang!"

John slammed his hand on the table. Both Elsa and Maja jumped up.

"With one big powerful stroke he killed Tor and also crushed the table and the wooden bench he was sitting upon. With four more violent blows he wiped out his mother, their home and house and all the cattle around them. 'Bang, Bang, Bang and Bang!'

"You know that Mjölner does not only put the heavy metal of the hammer head on its target. It also works by thunder and lightning, flashes of high voltage electricity that kill and destroy."

John waved his arms around so Elsa and Maja had to duck.

"With his home now in ruins and with both his parents slain, Grg ran away roaring. 'I shall destroy it all! Your whole world and all!'

"Grg continued to run around all day and by nightfall he had banged all the humans and animals in Europe into small pieces of trembling death. He burned the soil and drove all living beings in Africa to the south with his hammer and when they could not go further south, he kicked them all into the sea to drown. Madagascar was completely crushed in one beat from the big hammer, turtles and all.

"He continued his work until next morning in Asia, Russia and China. All living men and animals were dead from his hammer work. In the afternoon the American continents were done and all humans, all animals, fish and birds were smashed into wet pulp by his tireless arms.

"That night he took a deep rest and looked over his act of destruction. He recognized that the deep sea was still full of fishes and whales and small plankton that were hard to nail with his hammer. So the next morning he punched Mjölner straight through the crust of the planet Earth so that hot lava ran out in big eruptions and heated up the sea to boiling point, that way killing all that was still alive in the water and on some distant small islands in the Pacific. The whole atmosphere was then so hot that at noon there was no water left at the bottom of the deepest depth of the sea. All the water was boiled into steam and now the atmosphere was completely filled with water and clouds.

"Grg sat down on the remains of Finland and let the hot steam surround him, reminding him of the sauna at home. He took off all his clothing and when he realized that they were made by his mother he cried out again and threw them all into a big volcano so they were destroyed by the hot lava.

"Naked he sat and let the rain fall upon him until he fell asleep again.

"The next day when he woke up most of the steam in the sky had cooled down and had begun to fall back to Earth as rain. Huge floods continued the destruction of the land. The vast water washed away the dirt from the rocks and all the remains of the living were transported out into the seas for their final resting place.

"As the clouds vanished he could see through a blue hole in the grey that the sun was still hanging in the sky. Now the turn came of the sun. Grg gathered all his force and with a giant scream he threw his hammer at it. But it was too far away. Mjölner lost its power and had to return to Grg again with its objective unfulfilled.

Mjölner was drilled to return to its owner after being thrown so it didn't worry Grg. After a while he would once again have the hammer in his hand.

"Grg was still looking at the sun waiting to see the sun being destroyed by the hammer. Unfortunately the sunlight blinded him so he did not recognise Mjölner on its way back and just by accident the hammer struck him straight on his right knee.

"'Ouuaaagh!'

"A shock like the shot of a cannon hit his knee and disabled his right leg and he fell down. The pain spread up through his body and he could hear a clear bright tone ring in his right ear. His pulse was rising. His breath was strained and uneasy and he could not move his leg. Grg was paralysed by the shock and all his muscles were tensed to the maximum in a fruitless effort to escape the pain.

"For the first time in his life he felt himself to be powerless. He could not fight back against the pain that held him down on the ground. He could not move his leg because any little movement intensified the pain. He grabbed the hammer. Yelled at it as he tried to break the shaft in vain. He tried to use his teeth and broke off a tooth. Finally and in deepest anger he threw it away towards the sun again, but while sitting on the ground this time. That was a bad position for a throw so of course the throw was too weak, and Mjölner changed its direction again to return to his disabled master.

"This time the hammer came from behind as the throw was totally ineffective. Grg could not catch it because he did not see it. Now the hammer came from behind and hit Grg on his neck and broke it. This time the hammer hit left Grg totally paralysed. It sounded like another gunshot to him; a hot burning stream ran

15

up the back of his head while he fell to the ground on his left side.

"Thus he was lying and could not do anything anymore. He started to cry as he realized that this must be it. He was incapable of destroying the whole world. He was incapable of saving himself as well. He understood that this would be the end of his life but not of the world. He could not destroy Mjölner itself, the tool he was using against the world that he knew.

"He began to think about his possibilities. He was thirsty but could not drink. He was totally helpless. He tried to move his arm but nothing happened. His left eye was sore as it was filled with grain and mud and he could not move his head, only blink. The eye flooded with tears to get rid of the dirt. He could still breathe and he tried to shout but there was nobody around to hear him. There was no longer anyone around that could help him.

"He was the last one alive on the Earth and he understood that he would die soon too. He thought about Lena, one of the girls on his farm that used to be his. All the times they had been together, her warmth, her musky smell and how sweet it was to share sex with her in her fur-coated bed both day and night. Now she was dead. Time would go on but with no living being left on the Earth. Everything but the hammer was destroyed. He realized that at one point there would not be anything left of his body, just some bones. There was no one left to carry the memory of his or anyone's life and deeds on the Earth. It was too late to regret what he had done."

"Where did you read that?" Elsa looked up from the table.

"I did not read it. I made it up in my mind just now!"

John was being honest; he just made it up for fun. Sometimes he just could not stop his brain from fooling around. Afterwards he would see the meaning of it.

"It was a way to explain how Descartes, the philosopher of the 17th century who froze to death in Stockholm, how he found that thinking is a real thing and absolutely existed by questioning anything that he could think of. At the end, when he called into question the question itself, he found that the question was real. The question was the tool he used to test if anything in the world was real. By doing so the question itself must be a reality. The question itself must exist to be questioned. This way Descartes found proof that thinking must really exist for it to be possible to put the question of whether thinking is real or not. Cogito ergo sum in Latin. I think, therefore I am."[3]

"I've studied philosophy since 1944 so I have heard that before a couple of times. That does not have to do with if I'm happy or not."

"So how do you define happiness then?"

"Just as I said. When I can do what I like without anyone disturbing me," she said. "That's what men do at most. Disturb!"

Elsa looked at John but he was well trained in keeping up a dialogue with someone that did not have the same opinion. He smiled back and looked friendly to Elsa.

"I was thinking about the story of Grg, how he did not believe in the world so he destroyed it. I think that you have to have an impression of the world as real to be able to treat it as something to be happy about. If the world is just a fake, an illusion, why bother?"

---

3 http://en.wikipedia.org/wiki/Cogito_ergo_sum

"I know for sure when I'm happy. I do not have to explain everything in a philosophical way. But you're damn right that you have to be sure of what's right and wrong for you. After so many years I know what I like and don't like. A man is not the first thing I think of when I want to fill my time and be happy."

Maja took a long breath and sighed deeply. John could feel that she was not very happy.

"Well, I think you're right about that, but despite that, I think you are too old for me and I am here just to deliver a computer so you can keep in contact with your granddaughter."

Maja prepared to leave. She seemed to realise that there was not much more she could get from Elsa.

"Are you hungry? I can make some food for you while you are installing the computer."

John admitted that he could eat a bit, as fast food doesn't last. He began to think about the rest of today's work. He was still about a two-hour drive from home. It would be late again.

Maja said "Thank you!" and left. Elsa started preparing something to eat. John opened up the cardboard box. He pulled out all the fillings of wrinkled newspaper and pieces of Styrofoam that were placed so as to protect the parts from damage. The printer was placed upside down beside the monitor. He pulled out the printer and placed it on the kitchen table. Then he pulled out the computer, an already archaic piece of computer design: the iMac Globe.

Mutations are interesting. Most of them are doomed to disappear and the rest may have a chance to succeed. We need them all, however, because without mutations there will be no evolution at all.

Steve Jobs was inspired to create this design while he looked at a sunflower. The design of the iPhone is copied by every smartphone designer but the iMac Globe didn't find any followers. Comic-strip artists had problems making jokes about this design. The best John had seen was from a TV show where they used this model. The lower part of the computer that was used on stage was covered with a pattern which made it look like a monitor mounted on an Earth-globe.

John was thinking that this computer design was like a symbol of how the intellectual level was related to the physical world. The intellectual level was the fourth evolutionary level described by Robert M Pirsig in his book *Lila. An Inquiry into Morals*, a book where the Metaphysics of Quality and terms like dynamic and static Quality were discussed. Reality in regards to Quality and Patterns. The metaphysical perspective is called the highlands of the soul, reality looked at from a distance or from above. Pirsig was better known for his first book, *Zen and the Art of Motorcycle Maintenance*. That book had interested John for decades.

To achieve a metaphysical perspective we must do the hard work to mentally climb up something. From there, the way down will be enjoyable as we can easily carry the new perspective with us.

Quality is a morality that affects evolution. The results of Quality that we can experience are Values and Patterns. It is hard to understand the mechanisms behind the weather as it is always changing but we all know the particular patterns of a clear day, rain, winter or storm. We know how the sea looks – the chaotic surface that turns into waves from the force of the wind, creating a rhythmic sound that helps us to relax on the beach.

Pirsig divides evolution into levels. Throwing dice is basically a physical matter. The maths behind the bounce of the dice on the table is at the physical level. Which side it shows is of no value to the physical condition. The value of the throw is on a level above the purely physical level.

Statistical probability for the value shown is at a level above the purely physical. The sum of a pair of dice can show values from 2 up to 12.

VALUE	1	2	3	4	5	6
1	2	3	4	5	6	7
2	3	4	5	6	7	8
3	4	5	6	7	8	9
4	5	6	7	8	9	10
5	6	7	8	9	10	11
6	7	8	9	10	11	12

The probability is equal for all 36 possible combinations. The sum of 1 or less is impossible to achieve, as well as 13 or more. From this table it is easy to see that there are 6 possible combinations that give the sum of 7 but only one possible combination each for 2 and 12. This means that if you throw the dice 360 times it is highly probable that you will get a sum of 7 on 60 throws and the sum of 2 on about 10 throws.

If someone then creates a game out of this these probabilities are transformed into real objects. Every sum creates a result in the game. The game will be a reality on a level above the mathematics of the statistical possibilities behind each throw. The maths in the game can be totally different from the maths of the dice. Seven is the same value in the game for any of the combinations. A different kind of morality. A new level of morality using the former but with its own purpose.

The players can build a new level in their turn. They can build teams that use strategies, a team rationale, to win the game against other teams. These strategies are naturally dependent on the statistical probabilities and the rules of the game, but at a new level above the rules of the game, because the teams are free to create and choose their own strategies.

John looked at the strange computer design again. The lower part of the computer symbolized our physical planet Earth, while the flat screen mounted on a shaft on the top of the globe was holding the intellectual information that was in some way independent from the physical world. "1", "2"or "3" on the screen doesn't affect the electronic components in the lower part of the machine. The design of the computer reminded John about how the conditions for intellectual concepts are independent from the conditions for the physical world to exist. Whatever joke presented itself on the screen, the machine would never laugh.

John was thinking that a computer must be the pinnacle of the human-made machines and systems for managing information. From the earliest creation of sound and signs used by primitive beings to share information and communicate, to the spectrum of human languages and information networks that are used today in the global society.

John was not an especially religious person. He was mostly interested in how things were constructed and what made them work without any spiritual help from outside.

He wanted to know how the world, the whole universe was constructed. What kind of conditions there were that separated the possible from the impossible. He was sure that there had to be a complete system of conditions behind it all. He did not believe in an almighty, all-knowing, individual entity that was permanently managing the whole universe. It must be some kind of general system in the background, so basic and logical that it was also the source of itself.

After reading Lila John understood that the conditions behind evolution on Earth, the moral code of values, the conditions that separate the possible from the impossible, have four levels. An inorganic, an organic, a social and an intellectual level.

The inorganic level forms the conditions for physics and chemistry, geology, electrons and molecules. Atoms and particles following the guiding values that from the very beginning at the Big Bang have given us structures like hydrogen, oxygen and coal, water, carbon dioxide and alcohol.

One of the most fascinating results of these conditions is how the two oxygen atoms of the water molecule are placed at a special angle to each other so that the water molecule is in fact like a magnet with a positive end (the hydrogen end) and a negative oxygen end. Water molecules use this magnetic force to create chains that hold the water together to form drops by its surface tension. Magnetic force holds the water molecules together and by that every process that uses water is affected.[4]

This little fact makes water the perfect fluid for the evolution of the organic level. The organic level, however, does not follow physical and chemical laws. Organic phenomena are processes and the code for every process follows rules other than the codes for inorganic beings. The organic level is dependent on the inorganic level but the organic level follows another set of rules or moral code. The code that makes organic processes better than purely physical and chemical processes. It was totally impossible to think that physical and chemical morality by itself should be able to create chestnuts or hummingbirds. The better the process, the higher the probability of surviving in the global competition of space and energy. "Survival of the fittest" as it was termed by Charles Darwin[5].

Every biological species has its unique strategy for survival. What all species have in common is reproduction by mitosis[6], which results in identical

4 http://en.wikipedia.org/wiki/Water

5 Darwin; "On the origin of species by means of natural selection,..."

6 http://en.wikipedia.org/wiki/Mitosis

copies. This means that the species can overcome individual ageing and stand the test of time.

The next level, above the biological, is the social. The rules for the success of a social group are different from the biological where pure competition is the key factor. The main factor which gives a group power to survive is cooperation. The better a group cooperates, the higher the probability that the group will survive and progress. By sticking together in groups and taking care of children and the sick, the group gets stronger. Individuals in a group have specialized functions in the group, like soldiers, nurses or teachers. Differences and specialized capabilities give strength to the group as a whole. Concrete is strongest when the grain in it is of mixed size and format.

Sexual reproduction gives the advantage of more varied individuals which makes a species less vulnerable to extinction from inferior monocultural bacteria. Sexual reproduction also give more mutations per time unit and thereby a higher rate of evolutionary tests of new processes.

Fishes, bees and antelopes survive thanks to their group strategy, which most of the time lets some representative individuals survive even after massive virus attacks.

The fourth level of conditions that determine the world is that of the rules for the intellectual level. The intellectual level is about truths and lies, the art of war and politics, concepts of music and maths, money and business systems, stories and tales. All that we have in our mind about our selves and our life, seen at a distance from ourselves, as reflected in a mirror. The breeding ground for philosophy. Intellectual morality is independent from the biological and the social level. That is why the pencil is mightier than the sword. We can shoot the pianist but not the music. John Lennon is dead but his music will continue.

We are dependent on the chemistry and biological processes in our body to stay alive even if most of it is out of our control. Still it is hard for the atoms or our cells to decide what we want to happen with our own mind and thinking. We believe in the wind that forces trees to shake but it is still hard to understand how ideas can force people to act.

Physics and chemistry have been around since the Big Bang. When human biology evolved social processes and humans were given time to think and make models in their mind about the surrounding reality, intellectual models of physics began to be useful.

One early representation of this is presented by the inventor Al Jazari's Elephant Clock[7], an early machine that was constructed to process information.

One interesting thing for human individuals regarding their intellectual standard is how to understand and overcome the physical barriers between their minds. It is still impossible to connect our brains physically in order to listen to one another's thoughts. It is natural to think differently and individually but very scary because everyone's thoughts are kept secret from others. One strategy to avoid this social unrest stemming from secret individual thoughts is to behave like everyone else. To be normal.

---

7 http://en.wikipedia.org/wiki/Al-Jazari

That is why normal decent behaviour can be considered a human evolutionary disorder. Because it was difference that made social groups stronger against pure biological monocultural processes through evolution. Until individuals realized that thoughts are free and can be kept secret from other members of the group. Then it became convenient to be afraid of being special and not like other people. The difference and the individuality turn into something evil. The imagined advantage from being a mass of identical individuals in a big group forces people to prefer to think that what they know by themselves is all there is to know and that this is also known by everyone else in the group as common sense.

People love to discuss TV series, nature programmes and sports that they have been watching. They like to have the same picture of the world. TV is a perfect preacher to the crowd. TV has taken over the preacher's role in the temple to explain the state of the world to the people. Today journalists are doing the job that the former religious heads did. The difference is that the priest may have felt some responsibility for the picture he delivered to his parish.

This is also what happens in countries with strong religious organisations. As TV and media come into the home, the TV-watching people's picture of the world will change, sooner or later. From the beginning there used to be a government-controlled channel. But soon the state realized that one channel can be very dangerous because if all viewers get the same information it can cause riots and unrest. With more than one TV channel there are more programmes running and less risk that all people will agitate for a single cause.

The state still try to control the media but TV production is expensive, so an occasional foreign production sneaks into the country. As soon as the cheap soaps are broadcast and seem to be very popular from the beginning the fall of the state begins.

The cheap soaps look harmless to begin with, often produced in a country not so far away culturally. People look at the foreign people and laugh and cry at it. And, they also watch their acting and clothing, what kind of things they are using and how shiny their teeth are. And no smell! People want to feel normal and look decent and like others. They look at the people on the screen and then at themselves. The difference is obvious and beyond dispute. When they see people on TV with better clothes and shinier cars they begin to feel jealous, uneasy and angry. They also want to be clean, rich and normal.

The need for social affirmation. The need for normal behaviour and thinking, common codes for decency and properness are crucial for the members in a social group. Shame on all kinds of indecency! Anyone that does not share this type of common knowledge is regarded as abnormal, uncivilized or just stupid.

Information technology has made it easier to access information, but John was not sure that it has made it easier to be a human. It seemed to him that the more information is standardized and technologicalized the harder it is for humans to communicate and understand each other. Blinded by the mass of information, humanity is beginning to have a hard time even understanding itself.

In the 17th century Thomas Hobbes wrote:

"For such is the nature of men, that howsoever they may acknowledge many others to be more witty, or more eloquent, or more learned; Yet they will hardly believe there be many so wise as themselves; **For they see their own wit at hand, and other mens at a distance.**" (Bold by author.)

Leviathan ch XIII.[8]

That is why literature is so great. Literature brings people closer to understanding each other. A book is a mirror of the world. It shows how the author sees the world around him. It is a map of his concepts and the matter connected to it that is known to the author. It is the portal for the 'Return of the Monster of Difference'.

Literature and the written word are the magnifiers of the author's mind and work as a bridge to the reader. Any speaker or listener is using language. Language is the carrier of the intellectual level that let human culture grow up in the soil of the social level.

"This computer is just another attempt by humanity to cross this border." John was thinking about how little he knew about what was in other people's minds and whether there was something he really needed to know. The main question for him was if there really was anything left that could make him laugh.

It took him about ten minutes to put the parts together and start up the computer. There was an ethernet cable already mounted in the apartment's phone jack and there was a free hole in the electric

---

8 Hobbes; "Leviathan or The Matter, Forme and Power of a Common Wealth Ecclesiasticall and Civil"

socket in the wall. The computer already had a user configuration. He started to work with the main settings and created a new user account for Elsa and marked it as a standard account but he needed a password for it.

"What kind of password do you want for your computer?" he asked.

"What is that? I just want to use my computer to be able to use email and Internet."

"Well you must have a identity in the net too, just like your postal address and a key to your apartment."

"Can I choose whatever I want?"

"Yes. Something that is easy for you to remember."

"Well, take my second name, Margarete, if it is possible."

"Sure, no problem. It is a little short but it will work."

John filled in the rest of the information needed to set up the email account from the papers from the Internet service provider. He connected the printer to the computer and filled it with some paper and pressed the button for the ink-head cleaner. He restarted the computer to be sure that everything worked as desired.

"Wong." The start-up sound told him that the computer was ready to deal with the digits. It reminded him of the first chord of the song about 'Her Majesty' from the Beatles album *Abbey Road*. As a pun to the lawyers of Apple Records, its creator Jim Reekes called this sound a 'Sosumi' instead of a 'Chime'[9]. That was because Steve Jobs once promised Apple Records that Apple Inc. should not have anything to do with music.

"Music is what happens in your brain when you are listening to organized sound. How can someone try to

9 http://en.wikipedia.org/wiki/Jim_Reekes

illegalize something that is happening in your brain? Who's in it only for the money?" he was thinking.

John hesitated – should he introduce Elsa to the blessings of the Internet? Or should he rather try to catch up on old-fashioned dialogue with the lady and meet her mind?

His choice led him into a spectacular trip where he would experience the lights that would really guide the rest of his life.

2 - Dinner Game

"Dinner is ready!"

John was stunned by the wonderful scent that spread through the kitchen when Elsa opened the oven. She had roasted a chicken! Filled with almonds, ginger and raisins boiled in rum swimming around in the broth. Plates with fried rice, salad, bread and cheese. A bottle of red wine was opened. That was one of John's weaker points. He could not resist good cooking.

He had other weak points too – saying no to people, fear of being alone in a standpoint. It felt like a duty but he also liked to please other people and make them happy. Sometimes this would cause problems because it could cost him money. It could cause conflicts with other people who had received other promises from him. He had a bad conscience, sometimes, that tormented him when he remembered times when he had done things to friends that were not the best. Sometimes when he tried to compensate for earlier mistakes it made things even worse. So he was not surprised that some people were dreaming of a second chance in a new life beyond death. John, however, did not believe in reincarnation. He preferred to save the small memories of goodness in his life and tried to forget the rest. This dinner seemed to be a good one to save, so he left his gruesome pondering and forgot everything else but the chicken, and Elsa.

Elsa opened a bottle and John was surprised. "Are we going to drink cognac to the chicken?"

Elsa laughed and poured some cognac over the hot chicken in the casserole. In the next second she threw a lit match on it so the chicken was set alight with blue and yellow flames.

"Bon appétit! I like to eat good food and this is what I wanted to eat today! Happiness is important for me. Don't try to stop me."

"I won't," John said. "I am all yours now. You seem to be a lady of my own tastes!"

"Cheers then." Elsa poured the rest of the cognac in the wine glasses and John was obliged to meet her toast. The strong aperitif warmed its way down. John had already forgotten that he was supposed to drive home after dinner. The chicken and the rice were so delicious.

"I heard from your sister that you were some kind of salesman, is it a good job?"

"It's all about confidence." John answered after he had swallowed a mouthful of rice and sauce with a strong scent of ginger. "I have tried many jobs and I have learned that no rhetoric is better than when I myself believe in what I am saying and selling. If I think that the thing to sell is good, something that I think is of good quality for the customer, then my mind is open and full of arguments to convince the people I meet. When I know that what I sell is something of value. I just can't make money on things that I do not believe in because that makes me feel like a liar and the money I would make from lying would be worthless to me."

"One of my men was a priest and he did not believe in God personally but he told me that he had to choose to believe to be able to do his job. He was paid to act confident."

"I could never do that," John answered, while he took some more cognac. "I can't compromise my own conscience. To me that sounds as if he was paid to be a liar. Even if I know that my brain is lying to me all the time and makes me believe things that I can't understand."

"Like what?"

"When I am dreaming at night, for example, or when I am watching TV." John was well aware that there were a lot of things in the world that he did not understand or get time to think over completely. When he was watching sports on TV he enjoyed himself imagining that he was one of the players in the game. Kicking in the air. He knew perfectly well that that was not true but the fancy made it more fun to watch the game.

John was a bit ashamed about having this kind of fantasy. He moved on to a less embarrassing topic to protect his self-confidence.

He continued. "When I look at TV or film my brain is lying to me to make me believe that I am looking at something really happening. In reality there are just 24 still pictures per second shown in a row that make me think there is a real event going on there. When I am asleep I usually dream silly dreams but all that I am dreaming is my brain making me feel that I am doing all the things that I mostly wish to do."

"So what is it that you would like to do? What are your dreams?" Elsa poured more of the red wine into his glass.

"Oh, I dream a lot about sex, travelling, flying and meeting nice people and things like that. Anything that would make me happy, I think." John felt the alcohol loosening his fears a bit and he felt that he could speak honestly about what he felt about things.

"I am an old woman. I have done most of the things that I've dreamt of. I am still happy with my life. I do

33

not have the same preferences any longer but sometime I dream that I was younger, ha, ha. I am happy when I am awake and I am happy in my dreams."

"I was born in Denmark, 1925," Elsa continued. "We were a happy family, but we had no money! It is so much about money today. My grandfather was a merchant in cattle. He travelled around in the country and bought young cattle, sending them to Hamburg in Germany. At that time there were no railways so he had to drive the herd himself just as an American cowboy all the way across the country. With the money he made on this business he bought the farm where I was raised.

"We did not have money but we had cows, pigs and chickens. We had land that gave us the crops we needed. We had no electricity or telephone. I and my brother helped with all we could on the farm and nearly every day we learned something more about how to live. Like stripping the feathers from chickens for cooking. Working in the garden and feeding the animals. My father had some money that he used when he bought things that we could not make ourselves at home. But everyday life was not at all about making money to buy things.

"On Saturdays me and my mother and the maid were baking and cooking all day, so our home was better equipped than a modern café. On Sunday we used to have many visitors because we had many relatives and friends in the neighbourhood. Sunday was the day of rest so there was not much of anything to do other than making visits to exchange information and playing games after attending church."

"Sounds like you had a nice childhood."

John saw Elsa change in front of him. At first he had just seen a grey-haired old woman in a little kitchen and now he saw a woman with a long history. A woman who had gone through many decades of life.

The red wine was delicious with the chicken, light and sweet. He was not drunk but could feel the alcohol running around in his veins.

"No it wasn't. My mother was terrible. She was a religious fanatic and tried to make me believe in God, but I refused. I remember when I was six years and heard the confession of faith and I just knew in my heart that it was a big lie. We sang a lot of songs at home all the time. It was these hymns with religious implications about sins and hell and what would happen if you did not keep pace with what the Bible said. My mother scared me to death from even taking one single dance step. I am still so frightened of dancing and can't move one single inch to the sound of music."

"So how can you say that you're living a happy life then?"

"Oh there is so much more in life to enjoy so I can do well without dancing. My father bought a radio. It was in the 1930s and we could listen to Niels Bohr's lectures about quantum mechanics. We also heard Adolf Hitler screaming in the box. My mother was afraid of the radio. She called it the 'Evil Forces of the Spiritual Heavens'. The radio had to be put in a small room that she never went into.

"But one Sunday when we were waiting for grandfather, who had gone to the railway station to pick up the newspaper from the 3 pm train, my father was listening to the radio in the little room – we called it the radio room – and the door was open. Suddenly my mother could hear a priest preaching the words of

God from a church somewhere. Then my mother changed her opinion about the evil machine. But she was still afraid of it so she placed a chair just outside the door so she could listen to the mass every Sunday. She never went into that room again as long there was a radio in there."

"So you liked the radio?"

"My father didn't allow me to touch it. At night he would listen to music, music from all over the world. That was so fantastic! I sat in the room beside my father. I didn't dare to move and disturb him but I think I remember every song I heard and they are all kept down in my heart. The sound was not such high quality and there was a lot of interference. But at that time everyone tried to sing and play as beautifully as possible. It's not like the screaming rock stars we can hear today calling for attention. Today the broadcast is perfect but the performances are terrible."

"And you are still happy?"

"But for chrissake, I can shut it off if I don't like it! That makes me happy."

"And it makes the broadcasters unhappy if you do not want to listen to them." John was a bit drunk now so he decided not to drink more. He wanted to be able to continue listening to her story. All his life he wanted to be happy but he could not give a clear answer as to what he meant by happiness. He could say when he felt fine and OK sometimes, but happiness was harder to get.

John continued. "It seems to me that one's happiness depends on some others' unhappiness. And if both should be happy it is something in-between, where both parts have half of it. General happiness for all seems to me to be just a grey mash.

"Once I won a big sum of money. Just when I won I was rather excited but later when I looked at the statement for my account all I saw was just some numbers on paper. It did not make me happy at all so in a couple of years I just used it up like any money. I know I could have made it without the money, too."

"So what is important to you?" Elsa said in a very familiar voice.

John hesitated. He thought about what he had used most of his time for during his life. Sex was undeniably an important thing but he was not sure if that was the only important force to wake him up in the morning and plan his day's activities around.

Had he spent all his life just to be able to satisfy his sexual needs? He had been married for over twenty years to the woman that he fell deeply in love with at nineteen. He had put a lot of work into keeping that love alive.

Was all this work of raising the kids, paying a mortgage on a house with money that he earned by hard daily work, sometimes under very unhappy circumstances, was this just forced by sexual need? He knew some friends that had everything in their life but a good sexlife. He could feel their envy when he and his wife showed how much they loved each other still after all these years. Many of their friends were divorced once or more, mostly because of a lingering lust for sharing sex with each other. To talk about sex was very difficult just because of all the grief and indignation it woke up. Very rarely they met couples that could laugh and tell jokes about sex. A good sign of their sexual standard.

"It's all about confidence." John said suddenly. "It is all about confidence in your partner."

"Confidence is important to you?"

"Yes. I think confidence is more important than sex. Because sex without having confidence in my partner is worthless. To get an orgasm I have to release control and I cannot do that if I do not feel sure about my partner. An orgasm is not just an ejaculation. An orgasm affects my entire body and to let the orgasm flow I must totally release control. I really do not know what is coming when I am coming. It is very similar to a laugh."

John was not sure what he was saying but in some way it seemed right to him. He remembered sharing sex with women he did not know very well. Sometimes he had this bad feeling of not experiencing a total orgasm. It was just something that happened between his legs and left him with a bad feeling of unrest. There was nothing wrong with the initial stages of excitement but without a complete end it felt just like a waste of time.

"How many times can you come?" Elsa asked frankly.

"How do you mean?" John was suddenly embarrassed – was she propositioning him or what?

"How many times can you come? My first husband was a scientist and we had lots of fun in that kind of research. I can come however many times I wish. There's no limit."

"Well, I come once, then I fall asleep. To satisfy my wife we have to let her go first a couple of rounds until it's my turn. I have never tried to come more than once. The quality does not depend on the number, I believe."

"My first husband made it up to four on the same erection. But that was when we were young. Once when he came home from his work he was so horny that he did not have time to take off his backpack so we made love with it still on his back. I'll never forget that one. I loved it."

"You really loved him?"

"Oh yes. He was so kind and I can say that I trusted him 100%. He was a good man."

"So what happened to him?"

"He was a nuclear scientist and worked in secret with the national defence system. Once he created a big lake with his experiments. Today, this lake is named after that. I am not really sure about what the local citizens think about his work but there is nothing I can do about that.

"He died of prostate cancer when we had been married for 30 years. The last ten years he had problems falling asleep at night. Every night I had to read books for him to relax so I read all the books I could find.

"After some time I had to read more and more difficult books to ease his mind and I borrowed all the scientific and philosophical books I could find at the library. I studied at the university myself when I was young and the first year at the university was very much about philosophy. I learned a lot during his sickness."

"But that does not sound like you were happy with the situation?"

"Yes, I was happy. He was my husband and I loved him. We could not have sex in the last few years but I was satisfied with what we had before. We had a fantastic life together before he got sick. We went sailing in the Stockholm archipelago. There weren't many people around there at that time and I stood naked in the summer heat at the prow on the boat.

"There was almost no wind and the sea was calm but he was a very good sailor and could use the little wind there was to get to land. The waves on the water were moving so slowly. We made love on the warm cliffs. That was like paradise to me."

John stood up and went to the sink. He had to take a glass of water. As usual he got thirsty when he was drinking distilled drinks and the cognac was strong. Water used to work better than more cognac. His penis was erect in his trousers. He knew he had no way to control that part of his body but did not feel any shame about it. After all it was just a sign of trust and joy in life.

Unfortunately, the clothing industry had not noticed that and there was no place to find comfortable trousers that obeyed these physical and manly circumstances. He felt that this woman had something special but he was not interested in leaving his wife for another woman. Especially not someone who was this old and statistically very close to ending her days on Earth. She was in fact 86 years old. She looked strong anyway, very healthy and well preserved. "Could she make love at all at this age? Would she like to?" He had been there just for a little more than an hour and they were already conversing as if they had known each other for years.

When he sat down again Elsa started to put together the plates and clean up the table. John realized that he was a bit tired after driving around the whole day. The wine and chicken in his stomach took the blood from his brain.

Elsa sat down again. "Do you like playing cards?"
"Yes" John just could not say no.

Elsa opened a little box of playing cards.

"Then I am going to teach you a game that I think you've never heard of: 'Evil of the World'. It is a game using three decks with all the jokers included. Here, take half and help me to shuffle them. When you are finished give us fifteen cards each."

John shuffled the deck of cards and dealt them fifteen cards each and gave the rest of the deck to Elsa. She put the deck together with her half on the table. She showed how the fifteen cards should lie upside down in a stack with the first card turned so it showed its value. Elsa had a 7 which was higher than John's 5 and she started to pick five cards from the deck.

"Here, you start with a joker or an ace." She put down an ace of spades and continued with a 2 of diamonds.

"Every second red and black?"

"Colour does not matter, it is just the numbers that count. You build a suit from the cards in your hand and from your stack of fifteen. There is room for four suits. The suit ends with a queen and then you can take it away and start over again with an ace or joker."

"What about the king?"

"The king is trump and can be used as any number but you cannot put a king upon another king and you cannot use him as ace or joker. Look here, I laid down an ace and a 2 and now I am placing one card in my bank. There are four suits to build on and there are four rows in my bank where I can save cards for later use. It is very useful to put them in the right order. Then I can build up to the suit so I can pick a card from the stack of fifteen."

"So I can pick from three places, my hand, my bank and the stack?"

"Yes, as long as you can build on the suit until the queen. When you cannot lay down any more on the suit then you place one card from your hand onto your bank and then it is my draw. I start with filling up from the deck so I have five cards in my hand again and then I start to build the suit. The goal is to get rid of the stack of fifteen."

"Sounds quite simple to me. Why is it called 'Evil of the World'?"

"Because I can lay down cards to hinder you instead of helping myself. I can use an evil strategy to win. If I, for example, save all the 8 cards, there are twelve of each, and then you find it harder to build. And if you have a 9 on the stack of fifteen and I refuse to lay down an 8 then you get stuck there. Oh, I like it so much because it releases all my aggression. That is one thing that keeps me alive and well! I like it so much to be really angry! Now go on, it's your draw. Take five cards from the deck and if you've got an ace or a joker put it down to start a suit. Then one of the highest in your hand you put in the first row of your bank."

John got neither an ace nor a joker but he had a three of clubs.

"Can I put it there?"

"Yes put it on the 2, and if you have a 4 too then you can take your 5 from the stack of fifteen and turn the next card up."

John had no 4 but he laid down his highest, a Jack, in his bank. Then he had three cards in his hand.

Elsa drew three cards from the deck so she had five cards again. Then she laid down a 4, 5 and 6 from her hand and took the 7 from the stack.

"Ha ha, you see? You helped me! You build on your hand and on your bank so you can lay down many cards at once. I could have laid down just 4 and 5 just to stop you but I want to get rid of all of my cards so I can pick new ones and empty my stack."

The game went on and John tried his best but the cards came in such a bad order that his bank became useless. When he got jokers there was nowhere to put them down because Elsa always had an ace to lay down before him. It was forbidden to lay down king and joker in the bank so he had problems with a half-full hand of bad cards that he couldn't place on the table because of Elsa's skill and strategy. When John laid down two cards Elsa followed up by laying down all the cards from her hand with help from her bank. With no cards left in her hand before laying one on the bank she could fill up again with five new cards from the deck.

Elsa was very happy and beat John three times in a row. John had a hard time keeping up his manners. He could still feel the wine and Cognac and blamed his shortcoming for that.

"There is another reason for playing games" She hummed a melody when she put the cards together looking at John's depressed and hanging head.

"What's that?"

"You're learning to lose. In all games there is one winner and the rest of them are losers. In this card game it is just how the cards are coming. Any idiot can win this game. The worst people I know are those who can't take a loss. Bad losers. Unhappy divorcers, people who have lost in court and can't take it and keep on nagging about it for years, over a lifetime. Or just one moment of experience of having been treated unfairly. I can't help them. Mostly I think that they have been treated right and in fact deserved to lose. But as long as they themselves can't accept that they are wrong in some way they keep on struggling against the world."

"But if one's self-esteem hangs on the case?"

"A person's self-esteem can't be based on one single case. You got to learn how to play the cards of your life. You can't just trust the deal you got. The more a person looks safe in his position the greater is the probability of the opposite. Any king or celebrity can be dethroned if there is no real capacity behind his position."

John felt that he could not take much more and asked Elsa if there was somewhere he could take a little nap before returning home.

"Sure, take my bed, it's ready for you. I have to do the dishes and make some phone calls so I'll be busy for about an hour. The bedroom is behind that bookshelf to the left."

John went to the bedroom and found a wide bed made with pure violet and grey silk linen. He undressed and lay down naked on his back upon the bed. His erection did not seem to go down. "In a couple of hours I will be at home again," he was thinking.

An angel in the room was whispering just before he fell asleep: "Wrong again, John."

3 - Leaving Home

John was woken up by the telephone ringing in the bedroom. Elsa sat at the desk opposite the bed, looking at some papers. She answered the phone:

"Oh hello Mary! So nice to hear from you! Are you back from the trip?"

John remembered a girl named Mary that had given him heartache.

"Aha, West Papua. Where is that, is it Africa or Asia?"

"Straight north of Australia? Aha."

"Oh no! What happened?"

"Did he? All laundry for six months unwashed and left in a heap in the attic!"

"Well, I've said that before; you can't trust a man. But you two have been together for more than twenty-five years?"

"I can hear that you are crying. And your daughter is in Italy with her family?"

"When did you come home?"

"Two hours ago. How are the dogs?"

"Left them to the neighbours, good."

Elsa went silent for a minute while Mary was telling her of the sad situation she had met after arriving home from a research journey to West Papua. She had been studying the songs of the native Papuans. Mary taught music at the College of Eastersand. While she was gone her husband at home had fallen in love with a twenty-years-younger woman and had moved on to her instead.

When Mary came back home, the house was in a total mess as he had just totally stopped taking care of it. All over there was dirt and filthy things. The flowers were dead and the fridge was filled with rotten and mouldy leftovers. It was completely dark green inside. Unpaid bills and lots of unopened letters.

Elsa could hear Mary's despair and anger in her crying. Elsa was breathing heavily while she listened to Mary's story.

"No, sit down Mary. Try to get some heat in the house and stay inside until we arrive."

"Yes, we are coming. Don't worry about the money."

George had had the good taste to drain her bank account to zero as well. No money, no food and too many questions, that's the blues ....

"Now you listen. Aha, you are awake already!" Elsa turned over to John and said in an upset voice:

"Your dear friend Mary that was married to one of your schoolmates has problems and we are going to help her."

"We?" Suddenly it appeared to John that it was that her.

"Yes, she is left in a mess without money and food in a cold house up in the north. Her husband found another woman while she was away."

"Yes I heard something about that." John had a feeling that he was guilty just because he was a man. He could not refuse to help Mary or he would make himself into just another crook. It was true too that George was one of his oldest friends, but since he and Mary had married and moved up north John had not had any contact with them. John's sister was the one in the family that used to keep the social network alive.

"I can't drive any longer so I sold my Saab, but we can take your car. We will drive up to her and help her get rid of the mess. It is just about a five- to six-hour drive. I'll pay for the petrol. Do you know that they took my licence just because they said that my sight was bad? I know that my sight is getting worse but I have learned to compensate by moving my head."

John was not sure what was happening, nor what the consequences would be. "OK. But I had some wine. Maybe we should wait until the morning so I will be sober enough to drive. By the way, how does your brain know if there are things in front of the car or not if you can't see them with your eyes?"

"That's just a matter of confidence. Some people say they believe it when they see it. I say I see it when I believe. I had my first driver's licence in Germany in 1945. I have had experience of driving cars for over sixty years without any accidents.

"Now we are going for a new trip. I hope you are a good driver. Fine!"

Elsa stood up and started to collect things that should be packed for their trip. John went to the bathroom and took care of his hygiene. As it was an apartment house there was unlimited hot soft water. He borrowed Elsa's soap and towels. He was thinking of what he would say to his boss as he was supposed to work the next day too. He would have to check his calendar and make some phone calls to change some meetings. It would be possible to do that in the morning.

He tried to figure out what to say to his wife, too. He borrowed a toothbrush and brushed his teeth. He shaved his chin with a pink women's razor. Naked, he went back to the bedroom and the violet silk.

Later at night he woke up and he could hear Elsa in the dark breathing in his neck. She was warm and totally relaxed. John had a dream that he was flying with his car. He flew over the landscape. He looked around and saw houses and people down there. He was lost in the air. But he could not tell how to land the flying car. He had a sudden feeling that it would end with another crash.

He dreamt that he was lying by the sea where the waves were rolling in to the beach. He woke up again in the dark. Elsa was snoring lightly. John lay on her side with his right knee on her thigh. Perfect warmth. Feet together. Her face rested on his left arm. His other arm over her breast with his hand close to her neck.

Now she was only a biological structure in the dark wrapped in violet silk. Her breath came from deep inside. The sound from her breathing rhythm was an echo from millions of years of evolution. John could feel the warm wind in the hair on the back on his hand. A human with a long, long road behind. Still in good condition. John could feel the heavy weight of his head on the pillow and he did not want to lift it yet. Outside the house he could hear some scattered traffic from below. His thoughts started to wander away again.

"Ho ho! Breakfast is ready!" John was woken by Elsa shouting from the kitchen. For a second John did not remember where he was. Before he opened his eyes he had a feeling of being somewhere else, not at home, not here. His head felt mushy inside but his body was easy and the regular morning erection was there. He stood up and tried to remember where he had put his things. He found his clothes on a chair, under some of hers. John went out to the kitchen. Elsa had made a hearty breakfast. Porridge, eggs and bread. Danish cheese and coffee.

While they were eating Elsa presented the conditions for the rescue of the forsaken Mary. John had only met Mary a few times before when they lived in the same area about twenty-five years ago. She had called once

48

for his help with a broken fence. Even though her cattle were so homebound that they never used their possible freedom, Mary had wanted it fixed immediately, just that warm night in August with a full moon in the sky. He would never forget that night.

"She lives north of Eastersand. It is a five-hour trip if you drive without stops. I have to stop at public conveniences now and then if you know what I mean. I'll also become hungry so we have to stop for lunch somewhere. Oh, I had such a good sleep. Thank you."

"Oh, you're welcome, I had a good sleep too. Usually I have a hard time the first night sleeping at a new place. It seems like I forgot to think about that this time." John began to worry about what he was getting himself into. He was not convinced that what he was doing was the right thing to do. He must remember to call his boss and give him some kind of story about the change to his route.

Elsa took up a big map that she laid over the dishes on the table and they went through the plan. They would take road 70 west, first, and drive south of a big lake and then change to road E45 straight north. When they passed Eastersand they would turn west again and then it was just a half-hour drive to Mary's home.

At eight o'clock John started Elsa's computer and logged in to his workplace at the server in London as if he was really working. He checked the inbox. Answered a few messages, stayed logged in and put the computer to sleep.

Elsa lifted a big pack which contained a full bed, rolled up. She mounted it on a small trolley, and put a cooling bag and her big handbag on it. She fastened it all together with a big rubber band with hooks at the ends.

John got his things together: glasses, keys and his mobile phone. They locked the door and John followed Elsa down to the car. She insisted on taking the trolley herself and did not want John to help her with it.

"But you may be a gentleman and open the doors, please."

The weather was grey and cold. John could smell frost and snow in the air. John put her things in the back of the car. Elsa went back to the apartment to get some more items while John was waiting in the car. He had not put on the winter tyres yet. He had to remember to look out for the temperature dropping and he must have his eyes open for frozen spots on the road. Drive carefully but not too slow. Elsa returned with a little bag.

"Oh I nearly forgot all my medicine and my playing cards."

Elsa was aroused by the prospect of the coming tour and looked bright. She was wearing a grass-green beret, a grey long coat over a red plaid skirt and black stockings. Red leather boots with low heels. She smiled and laughed when she pressed her body into the seat.

"Ah, it's so lovely to be on the road again!" She held her handbag on her knee. John started the engine and drove away. He stopped at the first petrol station he saw after just a few blocks. Elsa got out a credit card so they could fill up the tank.

Elsa was really happy. John saw her smiling and looking at everything outside. Even if it was a grey Friday at the beginning of November.

"I really love to be on the road. You see, I have been a driver since I worked as volunteer in Germany after the Second World War. I had no job and there was so much to do in Germany so I volunteered and cooked for all the poor people and orphans for nearly two years. I had to get a German driver's licence to be able to drive the trucks and cars that we used to deliver the food.

"I made so many friends at that time. Everyone was so kind to me and I fell in love with an English soldier. He just disappeared one day and I never heard from him after that. He was so handsome."

Elsa cried and John could see her tears falling. He took her hand for a while.

"When I returned from Germany I had to get a Danish driver's licence but then I was so poor that I could not afford a car. There were no decent clothes to buy and all I had was my uniform.

"So I took the ferry over to Sweden and was shocked by the difference. Sweden was totally unaffected by the war. The shops were filled with all the things I wanted to buy. There were plenty of jobs as well so I bought a newspaper, called up, and got a job immediately as a housemaid.

"I had no formal education. I was supposed to become a doctor but I could not stand the education in Aarhus. The first year was so boring. It was all about philosophy. I was responsible for the food in a rectory then. I had worked in our kitchen at home since I was a kid so I was confident. But Swedish cooking and Swedish behaviour at the table is not like the Danish. After a while I had to get a Swedish driver's licence, too, so I could use their car for shopping. Then I was the proud owner of three driver's licences. That was in 1948. I have driven many miles since then."

Elsa was happy again. John drove carefully through the landscape and there was not much traffic.

"I met my husband at the rectory. He was there for a visit. His mother was from the area but he was living in Stockholm. After some correspondence we decided that I should take my things and move up to live with him."

"You just fell in love instantly?"

"No, he fell in love with me. I thought he was a nice man but I was dreaming of a tall man with brown eyes. He was short and thin and with blue eyes. He was fifteen years older than me. I was not his first woman. I refused a German and married a divorcé instead. But he was very intelligent and polite. I think it took a year for him to seduce me. That, he did well. A civilized man. And a horny beast. Ha ha!"

John did not know if he should laugh but he saw this woman shine beside him. She was, after all, happy to be in a car on the road.

"I was twenty-five when I moved up to be with him in Stockholm. We married and bought a little house to live in. We did not care much about the garden. Our neighbours hated our garden. They worked in their garden every free hour while we were taking care of ourselves inside the house. Every summer and on the weekends we took our little car for a drive. He knew the whole northern part of Sweden. He was working for the defence ministry so he had maps that showed even the smallest roads. We lived in the car and made love both in it and outside."

"He must have been very happy with his Danish princess," John was thinking. He was thinking of his own story. His wife did not like travelling by car so he could not remember that kind of experience, more than some kissing in the car when they were young.

"I like to be on the road too," John replied. "But not so much for love reasons."

"That was not my intention either. I just loved to travel, maybe I've got nomad blood in my veins."

"I like roads a lot; in fact I am totally fascinated by roads. That was one of the reasons I took the job I have now. The company pays my travel expenses and I have a reasonable excuse for being out on the road." John was thinking back. He remembered when he was a young boy sitting in the back seat, his parents in the front seats, him looking out of the window at the passing landscape.

"I think roads are just fantastic, do you know why?" He looked at Elsa.

"No, I think bridges are fantastic." Elsa had her own opinion.

"Yes. But …. any road is a bridge; the roads are connecting points with each other so we can move between them." John thought he had a rational view.

"That sounds a little bit philosophical to me. I like philosophy better now than when I was young."

"Yes, I think it is like philosophy, but philosophy about reality."

"Have you ever read the book by Jack Kerouac, *On the Road*?"

"Yes I did, but I could not find anything special in that book. I do not like drugs either. I am very suspicious about what drug addicts are saying because they have no reason to think clear and sober, if you understand what I mean. I think that just like it is bad to drive when you are drunk it is also bad to write books if you're affected by drugs. You could cause mental mayhem as books are read by many people who may not see that this is drug-affected fiction.

"My father drove like Sal Paradise all the time. But he did not take drugs. One of his games was to double the speed that was on the signs. If it said maximum speed 50, he drove at 100. We could drive for hours in that way. He laughed when the tyres were screaming from friction. He never crashed. He never got a speeding ticket either.

"But he used to get stuck in the mud now and then. That happened many times. Once, I was very young and we had to walk a long way to get help. My father disappeared and it was only me and my mother on the gravel road. We walked and walked. My feet hurt but I loved to be alone with my mother for hours. I can still remember her voice and the sound of my shoes on the gravel road. I do not remember how we got home but I guess that somebody picked us up."

"My second husband drove like that too. He was a priest so he had God with him he said. But I think that the local people knew when he was driving around and stayed at home."

"I see the modern roads as the biggest wonder in human history. Hundred times bigger than the pyramids of Egypt. You know how much work is put into all these roads all over the world. And they have all been built during the last century! Before we had cars we just did not need so many roads. All goods were transported by boat or train, or by horse and cart." John started to get excited.

"Travelling on these roads is like encountering one of the greatest parts of the history of humanity. Much better than visiting a ten-thousand-year-old ruin. The roads are here, now and today. And it is just a brief moment because I think that these roads are going to fade away just as soon as they were built. Because oil production is going to peak, if you have heard about that[10]. But a lot of road construction cuts straight through the mountains. These scars will last forever on this planet. Thousands of millions of years."

---

10 http://www.imf.org/external/pubs/ft/wp/2012/wp12109.pdf

"What? Oil will peak?"

"Yes, the whole system with cars and trucks running on petrol depends on oil. Cheap oil from the ground. From the beginning the oil companies found so much oil so they thought it to be an infinite resource. Now humanity has built up a structure that needs more and more oil. Some day soon it will be clear that the oil in the ground is limited. Soon it will be clearly understood that there will not be enough oil to feed all these cars, trucks and tractors.

"At that point the countries that still have oil in the ground will start to try to save oil so it will last as long as possible. An army, a military force is completely helpless without oil. There will be immediate oil rationing. That will push up the price of oil so ordinary people can't afford to burn it just for fun Sunday trips to the local amusement park."

"I'll probably be dead before that happens so what do I care? I want to be happy all my life and I like to be on the road, so I do not want to be burdened with some bad conscience for that." Elsa could change her mood very quickly, from happy to sour. The question was whether she was just drifting along with her sensibility or if she had a distance from her emotional self?

"I like to follow the used road banks when I drive. The whole country is full of relics of ancient roads. Over the years I have seen a lot of roads being rebuilt from small and curvy to wider and straighter. If the new road is just beside them I can follow the old one. They are still there as the banks of gravel and sand are heavy to move. There is no money in taking them away. The new road is always straighter so the old banks are curvy and change from the left side to the right side of the road.

"I know roads that are now empty dead tracks beside the new road and I remember when we travelled on the former one. Now it's dead. Some replaced roads are still alive if there are some people living along them. It is like travelling in the past when I can go by an abandoned road like that. Some roads still have the painted lines on them and have the style from the past. Very suggestive."

"I remember when we crossed the whole country and there was no asphalt. Just gravel roads, dusty and bumpy. It took us days to do it. But that was more than sixty years ago. Today that trip is done in about six hours."

"Yes, but now we do not have time to stop and look around. We do not see many people and how they live along the road. Most of the main roads are built to pass outside the cities so you never see them. It is only a question of rational transport."

"Do you think truck drivers are paid to have a view of the landscape? Like a tourist?" She was so pragmatic. "Anyway we should turn left there. We are going to go along the south side of the lake."

"Aren't we supposed to take the shortest way up to Mary?"

"It won't be short if I can't pee. Stop here please."

John pulled over and stopped the car. Elsa crawled out from the car and disappeared into the bushes. They had stopped between two lakes and they were standing on a long island with some bushes on the north side of the road. The lake on the south side was crowded with golden reeds so he couldn't see much of the water. John took his mobile phone and dialled the number of his boss.

"Hello, it's John …."

"Yes. I just wanted to call and tell you that I found another prospect so I am going there today ...."

"Yes everything is fine ...."

"You can look in your inbox for a message about yesterday ...."

"OK, I'll send you a report on Monday. Bye."

John could see Elsa on her way back to the car and hurried to finish the call so his boss would not hear that he was not alone. He took some steps back and forth to ease his legs. He took a deep breath of the autumn air. He was thinking of Mary again. He could feel his testicles moving slowly before he jumped into the warmth of the car again.

"Ready?"

"Yes, let me see you driving again. You're a good driver. You seem to be one with the car. You do not drive too fast and I like it with the radio off. My second husband could not drive without the radio on at top volume. He always preferred sports. I hated it but I could not do anything about it. I had to accept it if I was to go with him."

John checked the mirror and drove out onto the road again. This road was smaller and had less traffic. They were going south. John was thinking about this – why choose a road that goes south when they were going north?

"Why are we going this way when Mary lives north? We are going in the opposite direction!"

"I must have a look at the big lake first. I am so old I do not know if I'll get a chance to see it again. It may be the last trip in my life."

The road was going higher and higher and further west. John could see the lake to the right of the road. It was really a good sight.

"If we went on the north side we wouldn't see anything of the lake. They built the new road to be as short as possible between the cities."

"This road will mean it takes about one or two hours longer to drive up to Mary, I think."

"So what? What is two hours of your life if it is meaningless? I must see this lake again before I die. By the way. On the very first trip sixty years ago when me and my husband were driving up north we took this way. It was so narrow and winding. It was dry and dusty and we had to keep the windows down to get air. It took us one day to go this way around the lake. When we came to the end a bridge was broken so we had to turn back again the next day. On the way back it was raining. This road is so full of memories – aah ...."

"What are you remembering?"

"Guess one time."

John did not want to know more. He started to think about one of his first memories as a kid. He must have been three or four years old. He was sitting in the back of the car and he was trying to figure out what way they were going. He remembered some hedges and houses but he could not put the pictures together. They were going to visit his grandparents, which they later did several times. In the end, he learned the way.

When he was older he used to make-believe that he was going there by himself. He could remember the whole way with all the bends along the road, all the trees and crossings. Later, lying on his bed, he managed to play the route backwards and in both directions. Sometime he imagined that he was walking backwards, seeing all the things along the road from the other side.

"Do you remember all the trips you've made?" John asked her.

"No, that is impossible. I remember when I see the road again. We did several long tours every year over thirty years' time. I have a lot of photos. I took pictures everywhere and made at least one album every year. I should have written my diary too but I was too busy I think."

"But then it would be possible to trace the routes you have moved along since you were born by checking the albums?"

"What for?"

"I do not know really but a person's life is a journey on the Earth isn't it? It starts somewhere and ends at another place. It is absolute and totally real. Anything else seems unsure."

"That doesn't say anything to me. 'Hey, there goes Amy, she's been to Paris!' What's so special with that? Anyone has to be somewhere all the time."

"I did not mean that it should be special. I just think that everyone's journey through his life is different. And just today you and I are going the same way. That's great."

"We are not sitting in the same seat. I see the world from another angle. I was born in another country. I am still a foreigner."

John was amused by her comments. She really was herself and did not just agree with anything he said, but without complaining. It did not fit with his picture of elderly women.

"Hm, you're right about that. I remember once when I was going home from a job. I had moved to another city and the work place was in-between the earlier place and the new city where I lived then. This day when I should have made the turn into the road at home I had to turn east instead of west. That was a deep moment. Suddenly I was driving home but in the opposite direction. I had a hard time adjusting to that."

"Maybe you needed that."

"All the memories we have are placed on the older ones. It is like sand on the bottom of a lake. You see the surface at the bottom and maybe you know something of what is underneath, deeper down.

"Maybe that is how astrology works. You're born at a certain time of the year and all new impressions are placed on the earlier ones. If you were born in the middle of the winter you would see the world as it is getting warmer, with more and more human activity until it returns to your home of the year.

"People born in the summer have another view of the change of the year. That is just an idea. I think that where you are born on the Earth and under what circumstances has much more to say about a person than the day of the year. People born in rich homes have a hard time understanding poor people and vice versa."

"You see the speck in your brother's eye but not the beam that is in your own."

"No, not like that. It is not a question of better or worse. Just that we have different starting points for our perspectives on the world. Our memories come in an irreversible order. That is why I like roads. Living a life is like a road trip through events that are saved into memories. A road of memory making that comes towards you and vanish behind."

"That sounds like a difficult road to drive. I have lived my life and I do not think that I could choose my way all the time. All the times when I get upset because I do not like what is happening. That makes me so angry. I really like to be angry. That is what keeps me alive!"

"But you said you were happy all the time?"

"Yes, I'm happy when I am angry too because that makes me feel alive. I like to fight for my right to make my day. So don't you try to stop me!"

John realized that he may have jumped into something he would not have done if he had known her better. But he could not just dump her by the road. She was a good friend to his sister and making a fuss about of this could cause bigger problems. He also wanted to see Mary again.

"There it is. Would you like to stop here for a minute?" Elsa pointed at a small road to the right.

John slowed down and turned into the road.

"What is this?"

"Would you like a cup of coffee and a sandwich?"

"Here?"

"Yes, I have been here before – there, turn right again."

They were arriving at a small farm. The low houses were grey and buried in a forest of dark green pine trees. Three times higher than the houses. It seemed to be empty. High grass and no car or light anywhere. The green car melted into the picture.

John stopped the engine and went out to have a look.

"This farm must have been abandoned a long time ago."

Elsa was looking for something in the back of the car. She found a big bag that she carried to a broad grey wooden veranda at the front of the house.

"Hey, come on. I've got coffee and bread here. This is a wonderful place to take a rest."

She picked up bread, butter, cheese and coffee from the bag. Hard-boiled eggs in a plastic box. Two plastic cups and two sharp knives. John sat down and took what he wanted. The coffee was hot and smelled very good together with the air from the deep forest and damp withered grass. The houses looked as though they had been abandoned a very long time ago. The forest was closing up to the houses. The soil must have been unused for decades.

"Somebody must be the owner of this place?" John took another piece of bread and smeared butter on it.

"No, this place has been empty since we stopped here sixty years ago. It looks just the same now. The trees are much higher. There was not much forest here at that time. There were huge fields all around. If someone is responsible for this farm he does not give a damn about it. I guess that it is not worth living here.

I would never accept that by myself. It is so apart from everything that living here must have been a very lonely story. I must have good neighbours around me. Today we have cars but people had to walk or ride a long way to meet other people at the time when this farm was alive."

John could hear a raven croak up from a distance. The sky was still grey and he looked around above the trees. John began to think about what the possibilities would be to make a living here.

"A man needs a certain amount of food to survive. Shelter from the cold and predators and so on. This farm must have cost thousands of hours of work to build. The people that built it must have believed that it was worth the effort. All the money and time spent on building the houses and acres from the beginning must have come from a strong belief that it was possible to live here.

"If the soil gave them enough to survive but no more, could they have left the farm just before they got bored or socially starved to madness? What would one need to like a life in a place like this?" John could not think of living a life in this dirt and filth. He did not want to look like a piece of dirt when seeing other people. He liked to afford decent clothes and education. "Decency is as important as food," he thought.

John went to the back of the house to pee. He saw some broken tools, a rusty plough in the high grass. It definitely looked like someone had had a hard time here before giving up. John went to the barn and looked in through a half-open door. Inside he could see more tools, rotten leather straps and woven sacks hanging on a wall, spiderwebs over it all. Dead flies in the window and a strong smell of mould and rubbish.

He returned to the veranda. Elsa's rear in her red skirt was pointing towards him. She had lain down on her coat and fallen asleep. John sat down quietly beside her and waited for her to wake up. He took another cup of coffee. He thought about the farm. It was not too far from other farms. It would not take more than half an hour to walk to the last place he saw along the road. Did that make it too isolated to live here?

There must be several other possible reasons why this farm had been closed down and abandoned. Social or mental disorder? Someone hung himself in the barn? Family tragedy? Or just an economic disaster. Maybe the family could not pay off the mortgages because of a failure of the crops.

He was sure anyway that this place must have had a beginning. As long as the houses were still standing, it was still patiently waiting for the end of the story, or a new beginning. How many stories could be told just about the rise and fall, the family life, of one single farm?

The raven croaked again. Elsa woke up and they put their things together and got into the car. John looked at the clock on the dashboard. They had been out for nearly three hours already. They had driven about a third of the distance. John calculated that with this speed and with stops they would make it in nine instead of five hours.

He put the key into the keyhole and twisted it to the right to connect the circuits between the battery and the electric motor that were attached to the engine so that some of the potential energy in the battery could be transformed into the rotation power that was needed to start the chain reaction of explosions that would transfer the chemical energy in the petrol over to the gearbox.

John turned the car around and put it in first gear. He released the clutch pedal which connected up the rotation power of the engine and set the drive shaft into rotation that was then transmitted to the rear wheels that forced the car to move forward.

John was a bit more into moving faster now. The pleasure trip was over and he wanted it to be done with so he could continue with the reason why he was on this tour. It was not the travelling, as such, but the possibilities that would follow by moving to another place that interested him. Moving and the possibility of getting close to Mary again.

Elsa sat quiet, looking out to the right. John guessed that some of her memories were keeping her busy. John concentrated on the driving and as he had slightly increased the speed he had to pay some more attention to the road.

64

John thought about what they had been speaking of earlier. Now he was driving again. Filling up his life with some more hours of road. Moving forward through the landscape and filling some more miles on the road to his lifelong journey from birth to the eventual grave. He was wondering how many miles he had moved in a car so far.

He remembered when he was a young boy with a bicycle. He really used that bike every day. From his home to school. From school to his mates. Up and down the hills, through forests and along small tracks: those only boys on bicycles could find. He knew every inch of the area where he grew up.

"If I could draw this line on a map it would look like a big nest," John was thinking. "The very start being in the house where I was born and was carried around for the first year. In fact where should it start? At conception between the sperm and the egg? Sometime between conception and birth?" He was not sure what he should call the first moment of being John Smith. "From the development of the first brain cell?"

He tried to compare it with Pirsig's four levels. "Where is the personality based? It is definitely not at the inorganic level as a lump of carbohydrates, calcium and water molecules. What about the biological level?" He had a body that was a huge mass of biological cells. But he knew that he had no control over his biological life, more than to a basic extent. He was able to serve the body with water and food and get rid of waste products. But he knew that it was impossible to control biological functions. "Either you stay healthy, or you get sick and maybe die from something. It is mostly all out of our control."

John decided that his personality was not about his biology. He was just a passenger and in some way the driver of his body. Most of his attention was busy with all he had to do to keep this biology running. His body was calling for food, warmth, air, water, sex and motion. In return he could sometimes get a feeling of pleasure, could feel good. His personality was not how he looked, even if his identification card showed a picture of his face.

"If I had an accident that totally removed my face. I would still be John Smith. I would still be me even without my entire body. But not without my brain. They would have to transplant my brain into another body to change the personality of the body," he was thinking. "The big part of the personality lay in the brain," he decided.

He was wondering again about how much of his personality came from what was going on in his brain. His hunger and his temper, which were feelings that were much of his personality, his characteristic habits as a person. His personality would be more like something about the way he was managing his feelings to fit together with the needs of his body.

"I know I'm different from other people. Everyone is different from one another. That is strange. Most other species on the Earth like birds, mice and insects are very similar representations of a specific biological breed. The young baby's success in life depends on how well it can adapt and imitate its parents. But human younglings, the teenagers, their main purpose seems to be the opposite. For a young man or woman at twenty, the main thing in life seems mostly to NOT behave like their parents to build their own identity. Small elephants are learning the roads that the old mother chief of the herd is showing them."

John's children had no interest in knowing much about where he had been. When he tried to tell them about what he had seen and learned through his life they mostly ran away to make their own mistakes in places in the town where John could hardly go because of his age.

The road ended up at a bigger road and the sign was pointing at road E45 to Mora, a place that he knew they were going to pass. They would be there in about fifteen minutes' drive.

"Yes, we are going there." Elsa seemed to wake up from her dreams. "There is a good Thai restaurant there where we can have some food. I'm hungry. And when I say that I am hungry I mean it. How about you?"

"Sure, I could have a bite." John took the speed up again to a comfortable level. The Volvo was eating road.

"Good. I'll show you which way to go when we enter Mora." John knew that he could have made it simple just by 'Thai' and 'Mora' on his iPad to get perfect road directions but he did not mention that to Elsa.

John continued thinking about the description of his journey in life. He had survived so far and theoretically it would be possible to draw a line from birth until today. But to do that it would have to have been the plan from the beginning and he could not have decided that by himself from birth. A newborn baby cannot do that. When could he himself have made such a decision?

He would have to been old enough to know how to draw on a map. He would have to have had the self-confidence and concentration capabilities to complete it everyday since he started. Other interests may have arisen in-between but he would have to do it every day to complete the drawing. But if he had done that until today, what would be the use of it? John could not see any good motivation for such a project.

His memories were an important part of his life, his personality, what he had learned and what he had done. All that he had seen. All the movies he had watched, books that he had read. All the conscious decisions that he had made, all that he was personally responsible for. That was in some way recorded. But the story was not complete at all. Many things, many decisions he had made, that did not end in success, mistakes and failures, he did not like to be reminded about. His brain served him well in just trying to forget those kinds of memories.

"All the words I remember are the words that I find useful." John was thinking with his mouth. "And all the words that are on the Earth are words that humans find useful. All the words on the Earth that humans use in their language are a collection of pictures that have been built since the first human grunted a sound that had meaning to other humans."

"Yes, and all the cooking recipes there are, are a collection of useful methods to make hungry people into satisfied people."

"I mean that all the words together are like a big cloud of words. A cloud that began somewhere in Africa and is growing and growing outward while its inner deep is diminishing into the oblivion. A slow bang."

"I'll diminish into oblivion if I don't get food soon."

John's head was filled with pictures now. Food. The search for food. The first humans on Earth were interested in food. They moved around to find food. They learned where the oranges and the nuts were growing. By standing upright and walking on two legs they could move fast through the landscape to find fish and meat. They must have had a good sense of orientation. A way to remember and calculate the best ways to find food and water. The best way to escape from enemies and predators.

Of course the brains of the survivors had good orientation capabilities. The first road maps were drawn in these brains. As humans learned to use words they could exchange these pieces of orientation experience into bigger systems that gave the clan an advantage over other clans and species. The tribe that had the best overview of the area got the best pieces of the food.

John saw a picture in his mind of how this map of human evolution had grown from maybe a little valley in South Africa[11]. The pre-historic human beings had spread north of Africa along the coast up to Asia and Europe. For every new find, the map of the surroundings in human minds had grown with new concepts. Every new find of a fruit tree, a new valley with animals to hunt, or a fishing bay, got its own name. Ancient tracks and places were forgotten and new ones were added to the living map. An expropriation of the Earth could not have been done without this orientation capability. People would have got lost without it.

John was thinking about whether there had been some differentiation between men's and women's orientation capabilities. Women more often stayed at home while the men were out searching for new areas to hunt and use to the benefit of themselves and the tribe. On the way out from Africa the memories from

11 http://sv.wikipedia.org/wiki/Fil:Map-of-human-migrations.jpg

the past had been forgotten through the generations as new concepts evolved and replaced the old.

Some memories did survive for various reasons. Dramatic stories like the Big Flood and Atlantis lived on as stories for thousands of years, while information about trees that no longer existed in extinct forests was forgotten because it had no listening value anymore.

When the first humans crossed the Bering Strait and went into what is America today, how much of their past was left in Asia and how much was brought over to the new continent? In that time, long before TV and Internet, John guessed that travelling stories were among the top ten at the gathering by the night fire.

John just realized that he was actually performing one of his own travelling stories just at this moment. He was at the edge of the story all the time. The miles he had done this morning were already behind him. What had happened could not be changed or remade. The past is forever history and done. At its best it could be forgiven and forgotten.

Maps are drawn with roads that are useful to drive. Mistakes are erased or the map will be declared as faulty and disposed of. Modern GPS systems have to be updated so that they are accurate and give the right directions.

Where they were going was in the possible future. They had a goal but John knew that he was free to change his mind and direction anytime. Any choice had its own resulting consequences.

If Elsa nagged too much he could just tell her to leave the car. In-between the past and the future is the permanent state of choosing and evaluating between different possible steps to be taken. For better or worse.

He was hungry. His belly was empty. But much worse was the feeling of the future. It was like hanging him over a bottomless pit. For a second his sight became darkened. He slowed down and prepared to stop the car. Sweat appeared on his neck. His hands became wet and he felt his arms go weak. This was real fear coming. Fear for nothing.

He had to stop just by the road. John left the car and went into the tight bushes nearby, just to get his breath back. He sat down on a fallen tree and closed his eyes. He could hear the wind passing, between the twigs. A flock of small birds flew over his head.

"The Future is coming and it is undetermined." John's thoughts ran around in his head without control. He was sitting in a forest with an old lady in his car waiting for food. Somewhere in the near future he would meet a dear friend, but that was just a mere hint. Most of the future was there as vague outlines. He would follow the road. That was about 99.99% clear unless there was an accident or something. They should eat something and drink. Satisfy their physical needs. They should talk, laugh and just act quite normal and to a great extent predictably. John was not clear about what was most frightening. Was it the predictability of the future or the opposite, the unpredictable tears in the already half-made future web?

He had to control his breath for a while. He realized that every breath was another step into the future. He had been breathing since he was born more than 46 years ago. Every breath since then had been a new one and he would continue breathing until his last. After all, it was no change at all. He had been doing this all the time. The future would always be like this and had always been.

He had always lived by his own decisions as long as he could remember. He wanted to feel free even if he sometimes jumped into the wrong barrel. He liked to make it in his own way. This was his life. His way of living. Even if most of what he was doing was pretty normal and human, he had to have the feeling that there was a way out of the predictable.

The hole in the wall gave him fresh air to breathe. The predictable gave him something to hold on to and the unpredictable made him feel free, unpredictable and growing. Too much predictability or too much that was unpredictable were both very scary. But he was in-between. On safe ground with open fields around. He began to calm down. His heartbeat slowed and the temple sound vanished.

He was thankful of his own decision to just sit down and let his mind flow for a minute. It would have been easy to shake off this feeling just by handing it over to some mighty God acting as a cheap insurance company. Someone to blame and curse if the future went wrong. Any person who felt lost on his way, on land or in life, would be easy prey for someone who liked to make money out of their situation.

John felt assured of himself but he could understand how some people got lost with that feeling he had just had when he stopped. "But what the fuck," he was saying to himself. "That is my job too. I am making my money by guiding business people through the jungle of energy prices and premises. But I am not risking their self-confidence. I am just a guide for a small part of their business." John went back to the car. He was really hungry now. He was cold. He had to take care of his future.

4 - Coal and Petrol

"Why did you stop?" Elsa sounded both angry and a little worried.

John turned up the heat. He did not answer immediately. He was near to saying that he had to do something else but then he just answered "I got so afraid of the future that I had to stop for a while and take a breath."

"If we don't find a restaurant in the very near future then you have reason to be afraid. Drive on to Mora, please." Elsa was very clear about what she felt about the future.

John drove on along the road. The immediate future was very clear. He would follow the road and behave as any other driver would do. Keeping to speed and in the right lane. Stopping at red lights and driving on green in a very civilized manner. Not yelling at people that were in their way and waiting politely for pedestrians that were crossing the road. John was thinking about how much this traffic behaviour affected peoples social routines.

"Traffic behaviour is about the same all around the world. If you act well in it, you will survive. If you do wrong you will be injured, killed or held responsible if someone else is affected badly by your behaviour. Traffic is the perfect social training centre. No other place where it's so easy to separate the bad guys from the good. It starts early in the driving school. The worst guys do not even get a licence to drive. There are also a lot of people who never try to learn how to behave in traffic. But we always have to learn how to behave in the streets and in crowded places like in the kitchen or in the queue to the public loo."

"Welcome to Mora!" Elsa commented on the sign that told them they were entering the city. "We shall see if we can find something to eat here." She sat straight up and looked intently at all the buildings and corners to be sure of the direction.

"There, take a right there." Elsa was now in command for a while. John had nothing against that. He was on the same track. Food. Now. Fast and at a reasonable cost. He drove more slowly so that she should not lose track of the way. "Here it is. 'Mr Wong's Pizza & Sovlaki'."

That was true. It was a mixed Italian and Greek restaurant owned by a thin little man from Thailand with a Chinese name. There were a lot of writings and cards from Thailand on the walls. Beside a moose head John saw a big life-sized statue of Buddha at the entrance with a red and white football scarf from Liverpool FC around his neck. A bouzouki was stuck on the wall of the lavatory.

He could smell the hot grease from the frying pans and several oriental spices. Overall, a tasty impression of fresh food and gentle service. There were a few guests there already, which strengthened confidence in the likelihood of it satisfying their needs. Elsa sat down at a table in the corner and John sat down beside her. Mr Wong came down to them.

"Welcome, welcome, would you like to eat or drink? We have all kinds of drinks and the food is there at the buffet. You can take your own plate and fill up as much as you want."

John ordered a beer and Elsa preferred water. They went to the buffet and looked around at the different dishes. There were no signs but he could see pieces of

74

chicken in tomato sauce. Fried fish and fried lumps of shrimps in dough. All sorts of stir-fried vegetables in different mixes, and naturally, a pan with pizza slices. Boiled potatoes, rice and fried spaghetti. Locally made dried bread. Soft bread made of unused pizza dough. Tzatziki and green salad. Bottles of Tabasco, Rhode Island and Worcester sauces.

John decided to try at least one piece of everything. He filled his plate with all sorts. Even the tzatziki. He realized that there were two kinds of pizza, one covered with mushrooms and Portuguese anchovy, the other with tomato sauce, macaroni and pineapple. John felt the weight of the plate and thought to himself, "Am I going to put all this into my body?"

Elsa took at least as much as John on her plate plus an extra smaller plate for the fresh vegetables. They sat down and poured the drink into their glasses. Elsa's whole face shone and showed John that she wanted to touch glasses. Like they had just won a big battle on the road and now should celebrate the victory.

"Cheers and thanks for such good company!" Elsa held her arm straight and then took a good sip of the water.

"So far so good," John was thinking. He looked at his plate and he liked the sight.

"Why did you take the seat beside me instead of that one on the other side of the table?"

"I used to think that enemies are turned against each other. I like you and want to have the same view as you." John took a pizza slice, the one with the mushrooms and fish by his left hand.

"I like you, too. You are a wonderful man. You remind me of my third man. He would behave completely irrationally and unpredictably. But I always knew what he would speak about before he opened his mouth! I am not really sure about you."

"What did he talk about?"

"Oh, he was always complaining about his former wife. He was a real idiot. Why would he go on about that? That was the reason why I threw him out."

"How long did you stay together?"

"Nearly ten years."

"And he was quarrelling about his former wife all that time?"

"Yes. I could take that but when he started to quarrel about his former wife's mother is when I'd had enough!"

"But how could you stay together so long then?"

"Oh, we had a lot of fun. He was a good man in bed and he had a sailing boat."

"So how do you think that I remind you of him? I don't have any boat."

"The way you are holding the pizza. And there is something else too."

"Like what?"

"I am not sure, but I think that it is your self-confidence. You do not seem to give much attention to conventions or what other people call good manners."

"I thought you would say something about love." John wiped his hands on the napkin and began on the tzatziki and the fried potatoes.

"Ha! What do you know about love young man?"

"Not much I guess, but I think I know how it feels. I have been in love so many times. Mostly with women. I can remember all the women at the day-care place where my kids went when they were little. I and my wife could work and the kids got lot of playmates. I was the one that was dropping off and picking up the kids so I met these wonderful women every day."

John got excited and nearly forgot to eat and tried to avoid talking with his mouth full. He tried to talk slowly with suitable pauses for eating. There was something about talking about love and sex while eating that he liked.

"When I saw how well they took care of my children I just couldn't help falling in love with them all. It was not based on sex, I already had enough of that, it was based on trust. I think I've said it before but sex is based very much on trust for me to come, otherwise it just doesn't work. It is not enough to 'do the right thing', the in-and-out with a woman that looks officially right. But when it feels right, when I know that I can just lose control. It is like falling or something. True confidence in your partner.

"Same with the kids, I had to be sure and relaxed in the feeling that these women took good care of my kids just whatever happened. I liked to imagine them naked, and practising different sorts of sex with them too, of course, but that was just for the fun."

"My last husband couldn't accept my grandchildren. I hated him for that. He accepted all my relatives but not my daughter by my first husband and her two daughters."

"Just like a lion? The lion male used to kill all the small lions when he came into a new group of lions, just to be sure that all the new lions would be his own offspring."

"Watch your mouth! When I am defending my own breed I can be a tiger!"

"Oops, sorry for that, but I meant just literally, as an analogy to the feeling he may have had." John finished his meal.

"Would you like a cup of coffee?" Elsa nodded by way of an answer.

"How do you like it? Black or white?"

"White please, no sugar thanks."

John rose and went away for some hot coffee and a couple of small English biscuits. The food gave him new weight to his body and he could feel his mental forces returning. He could hear how the voices and talk around in the restaurant had taken on another tune since they arrived. It was more of small personal talk and less of loud arguing over jobs and difficulties.

"Sharing food or sharing values, maybe it is in the same file?" He gave Elsa her cup and sat down again. He was a bit excited over the maths that flooded his brain.

"What are you talking about?"

"To be able to cooperate, we have to share values. It is not only about things or sex. We have to have more or less the same values, the same kind of priorities in what we are doing, to be able to cooperate. Feelings of love and understanding tell us that we are on the same track in some way. We had to have, for example, the same food preferences to be able to go the same restaurant."

"That's obvious to me. I knew that this was a good place to eat."

"Yes, but I didn't know. I had to rely on you to be able to follow you in here. I trust you. I love your taste, he he."

"That's an exaggeration. By the way, you took pizza. I did not."

"It does not have to be so exact. But what if I did not like your cooking? The chicken you made yesterday was delicious."

"That's fine, taste is important. The smell at the restaurant, too. I can tell by the smell outside the place

78

if they are serving good food or not. The smell of a man tells me if he is a good man or not."

"Hum, maybe that is why some people smile just to get accepted? A salesman at a shop smiles at you and tries to make you think that he understands your taste. He makes you think that he has good taste too. That makes you like him and trust him because you think that he cares about your preferences.

"A man on the street smiles and says to me 'Hey, nice car!' and that makes me believe that he has the same opinion about cars and then I automatically think that he is a nice person with the same values. I might let him borrow it for a while. Easy way to get your car stolen."

"I would never lend my car to a stranger."

"Neither would I but things like that happen very often. People dressed in decent clothes or some kind of uniform can fool just about anybody. Wearing a uniform or something similar to you can be a way to make you think that we share the same values."

"Everybody is wearing a uniform, so don't kid yourself. Either you are a civilian or not."

"Maybe, but if Mr Wong here were dressed in a swimsuit I don't think you would like to eat at this place."

"I'd like to see that! I like to look at men's bodies!"

"You mean that you would think it was worth more than the 75 kronor we paid for this lunch?"

"I would never pay for that! That would be prostitution!"

"You do not like that he satisfies your need for sexual pleasure but you can accept that he satisfies your need for food? What's the difference?"

"People should be able to handle their sexuality without money involved. There are so many young girls that have had their lives destroyed because of prostitution and drugs."

"But doesn't that depend upon their unbalanced talent for making money? These girls are young and beautiful and sexy but do not know much about how to make money in decent work. With the right sort of education and training these girls would be much better players on the regular market.

"The problem is that their bodies and sexuality grow much faster and mature earlier than their other abilities. You can't just say that the men alone are responsible for this business. I think these girls want money and they want it fast and in an easy way. It is very easy for them to catch a horny man with money."

"The men are responsible for what they do and they should know better."

"In what way do you think Mr Wong's life would be destroyed if besides satisfying your need for food he also offered you the pleasure of the sight of his naked body?"

"But that's different. He is a grown man."

"But you said that you wouldn't pay for it because it was prostitution?"

"I wouldn't do anything that a man wouldn't do."

"But if the fault with buying sex from a young girl is based on her being trapped by being cute but uneducated. If buying sex from her instead of offering her a decent job is a way of keeping her stuck in a shameful position in society. Buying sex from young girls is to abuse the difference between her body and her education instead of correcting it. That wouldn't be the case with Mr Wong?"

"If he couldn't make his living by serving food to people and had to complete his income by dancing naked for his guests, that would be what I call shameful. He should become a better cook instead of a hooker."

"I am satisfied with the food for the price. I think I can have the rest of what I need somewhere else anyway. I think it was a good lunch for the money, wasn't it?"

"I could have done it better and cheaper by myself."

"Really? Here and now?"

"No, not here of course, but at home in my own kitchen."

"Yes, but that's different. You just can't say that something is cheaper if it is not the same delivery. If you have to travel back to your apartment in Livelong then you must add the cost of going there to the price and that would not make it cheaper at all. I think Mr Wong is doing fine by giving us this lunch for just 75 kronor. I can also sit down here for a while and rest my body and I can warm my body, meet other people and use the conveniences.

"That's just what enterprise does. Delivering more value to customers than the price of it. If that was not the case, people would not go there and buy their goods and services."

John felt his brain awakening now. The energy in the food had reached his brain or was it just the sugar in it that gave him a kick? For a moment he saw how all the enterprising activity around the world, every deal, from the beginning of human history, by this mechanism, was built upon mutual benefit. All negotiations were about benefit.

The absolute majority of all deals through human economic evolution were done when both parties in a deal were satisfied with the outcome of the trade. If one of the parties was not satisfied with the price or the barter, then there would not be any deal. Every deal was made from a belief that the trade was better, better than keeping valuable furs or the gold. Thus, every trade made was bettering the status for both parties.

The more trading, the higher the total sum of betterness in the society. That was what all the world economy was about. Bettering the situation for all who were taking part in it. But just because the measuring system was focused on only one side of the system, the money side, people did not see the customer benefits that don't get onto the books. The value to the customer is not counted and why should that be when the only thing we know is that it has a higher value to the buyer than what you can see on the price tag. If not, the buyer should keep his money. If the prospective buyer thinks that his money in his purse is worth more, then he will normally decide not to buy.

"I guess it's time for us to leave." Elsa started moving as a signal to John to rise and help her with the chair.

"I just had a flash in my brain."

"Please don't tell me that you're going to dance naked instead of leaving Mr Wong a tip."

"No, it was about business and economics," John replied while he headed for the door. "I am working with prices on different sorts of energy, you know."

"So what was the flash about then? Are you an epileptic?"

"No. I'll tell you later." They walked out from the restaurant into the grey, half-dark and cold November weather. The path was wet and the wind chilled his neck. They jumped into the car that was cold inside again. Elsa shivered. A man in a tracksuit with a big cap on his head sat in a dark estate car beside them. He was eating something from a tin can.

"Is he living in the car? Look!"

"Hurry up with the heating so I don't di-i-ie from the cold."

"The colder it is in the car the hotter I feel inside my body."

"Please make me hot then," Elsa said with a smile.

"We have been here for less than an hour so I think the engine is still warm. It will only take a couple of minutes to get hot air from the heating system."

John looked back before he drove out on the road again. Small drops of rain dotted the windshield and spread the light that fell on them like tiny optical lenses. John put on the wipers to clear the screen. The beginning of an erection forced him to rearrange his trousers to find a more comfortable position. "Why aren't car seats made like horse saddles?" he thought to himself.

"This car is worn and cheap but it has a good heating system. A lot of the energy from the petrol is transformed into heat so it is nice to drive even when it is cold outside."

"That is one thing that I like with modern cars. When I and my first husband were driving around in the country we had to bring loads of clothing and blankets to keep warm. Sometimes it was hard to find the gearstick inside all the blankets. Sometimes I found something else. Have I told you he was working at Svalbard near the North Pole as a scientist and spent the winter with the polar bears?"

"No I haven't heard that story. It could be a nice one as long as the car is cold inside."

"He had lots of experience from living in a cold climate before, of course, but this was probably the coldest he had experienced. It was in the beginning of

83

the 1930s when a lot of people were seeking jobs because of the economic depression. The Swedish Royal Academy of Science decided to create a scientific mission so that some people could get jobs. The objective didn't seem to be so important. My husband took the mission very seriously from the beginning but later he would experience the real nature of the scientific climate."

"You mean that the result from it was disappointing?"

"Anyway, he and a group of three others were going to study the Northern lights, the aurora borealis at Svalbard. The Academy was helping them with money, a ship and about 30 tons of equipment that was loaded on the ship. They arrived in the summer of 1930 to a disused coal mine. The coal mine was a Swedish settlement called Sveagruvan, lying at the head of Van Mijenfjord.

"They arrived after a long trip over the sea and these young men had no experience of living so far north. They were wearing hats and suits and summer shoes. The temperature was just above freezing point. All their equipment was loaded onto a decrepit landing stage that had been unused for nearly ten years and half crushed by the polar ice. Then the skipper turned the ship and left them to their destiny.

"They had a thoughtful minute when they stood there in the cold polar summer, dressed like city people, watching the ship heading back to civilisation. They walked onto land and searched for the house where they were supposed to live during the year. They found the house buried in snow and searched for a door to enter. The house that they were supposed to spend their time in during the polar winter was filled with snow! There was a mass of ice in the boiler room! Nobody had lived there for years and it had been left as it was with no heating or anybody taking care of it.

"There was a heating system for a coal fire and as a matter of fact there was a lot of coal there, but under the snow. So these poor men had to crush and dig out the ice from the house. This was in the middle of the summer so they had daylight for 24 hours, but it was so cold they had to work and work to keep up their body temperature. They knew that they could not take a rest before the heating was working.

"Finally after about two days and nights they could start a coal fire in the boiler. It did not take long to realise that all the pipes in the system that should carry the heat from the boiler to the radiators were broken by the expanded ice in them. It took them some more days to fix the pipes. They were lucky because they could find spare parts in a workshop close to the mine. When the mine was abandoned all the people just left and did not bring more than they could carry so there were a lot of tools and materials in the shop. But what would have happened otherwise? The ship was planned to pick them up next summer, that was all."

"So they did not have any kind of communication system?"

"They did have a radio so they could listen to what was broadcast at that time but if they wanted to send messages they had to climb over the mountains, a one-day trip if the weather allowed, to a fishing village called Longyearbyen. There was a fur trapper living in one of the small cottages in the mine village too. He had no better heating system and he preferred to stay alone for some reason. He died later after being damaged by the cold. He fell on one of his hunting

85

rounds and was injured and before he could get back to safety half of his head had been frostbitten."

"I think they would have liked to have had mobile phones."

"That wasn't the standard at that time. They had each other and 30 tons of equipment. Much of it was electric equipment like generators and lead batteries. It took them the rest of the short summer to bring all this equipment safely from the stage to the house. They had to do all the work by hand. A brief calculation showed that they needed about 30 tons of coal for the boiler to ensure that they could keep the temperature up during the long winter. The house was built to keep 20 men and they couldn't make it smaller."

"So there was enough coal around?"

"Yes, they just shovelled it up from the ground I think. The mine was closed after it had literally exploded. The mine workers had made a deep pit high up in the mountain above the village, straight in where the coal layer was. All the coal was transported by a small railway down to the landing stage.

"They had a fire inside the mine pit and this fire caused an explosion inside the mountain so all the equipment, train wagons, rails and lots of rocks, and coal of course, were shot out from the pit like from a giant gun. The wagons landed about half a mile from the pit. After that nobody dared to go in there again and the mine was closed. The fire kept on for years as the fur trapper had told them."

"So the fur trapper stayed and he had enough coal to heat his cottage?"

"Guess so."

"And your man fulfilled his mission of studying the aurora?"

"Yes. They stayed until next summer. When he arrived at Stockholm next year and wanted to finish his studies the Academy did not have any money to pay for the working time he needed so all the material and data was stored in boxes in the basement of the Academy. Some years later when a new head of the Academy was appointed the first thing he did was to clean up and all the material was thrown on the rubbish heap. It was quite clear that the whole mission was just a project to give some students one year's rest from unemployment."

"Lucky for him, and for you, that he survived at all." John could feel the hot air blow on his face. The mix of the cold seat at his back and the hot air streaming on his front made him feel even colder for a moment. He leaned forward to get some distance from the cold seat and to let some warmth reach the back of the seat.

John thought about the coal situation on the mission in Svalbard. "What would have happened if they could not have found enough coal to heat the cabin? Or just if it had been too hard to collect it and transport it to the house? Then they would have worked in vain. They did not have to pay anything for it. It was just a question of how much energy they had to use to get the energy from the coal inside the boiler. The net energy from the process was the gain and the work for it was the pain."

"You said you had a flash when we left. What was that?" Elsa held her handbag on her knee.

"I had a view in my mind about the value that comes from all enterprise and business activities. We were talking about the price of the lunch and so on. I was thinking that in all business, in every deal, both are winners. Deals are done between two parties that think that the deal is good for them. The seller thinks he is making some money on the deal and the buyer prefers the thing or the service instead of the money he pays for it. That is his motive to buy. The actual price is somewhere between what it is worth for the seller and what it is worth for the buyer.

"No deals are done if either party does not think that he will be better off after the deal. The seller has his prices and his calculated margins. The buyer buys if he thinks that the thing he is buying is worth more than the money he pays for it. After the deal, the seller is a little richer and the buyer gets something of higher value than before. Therefore, in most deals all around the world, in every affair and purchase, the total sums of values are increased by every case of buying and selling.

"The total wealth of a society and nation, the whole world in fact, the whole wealth of the world is built on all these deals. Therefore it is so important that the rules and laws of trade are followed by all of us. Good rules of trade give a healthy and growing economy. It would be perfect if nothing were consumed, destroyed or thrown away.

"But the funny part of the flash is that I could see that only half of the wealth is counted. Because we can prove the numeric value of the money part that is kept in books. The numbers are reported to the responsible managers of the company, to stockholders and other interested people. But the buyer's part of it, the buyer's benefit, the difference between what the buyer thinks it is worth for him and what he actually pays, that value is never entered into the books."

"It doesn't count because that value is impossible to calculate and I think it is negligible."

"How could it be negligible if that value, the value over and above the actual price, that value is half of the driving force behind all the purchases and trades all over the world? All through the total history of economic evolution?

"The sellers want money and they calculate and set the prices. The buyers do the same thing but from their point of view. If it isn't worth more than the money he trades for it, then he does not buy."

"I still think that the value for the buyer is negligible. They buy because they must buy. That is what Marx meant by the exploitation of the workers. The capitalists took all the value for themselves."

"No, I do not believe in that. It may have been so in isolated communities where the workers got paid in local currency and had to buy all of their food in the local store that was owned by the patron. Then maybe it was like some kind of slavery. But today you can't force people to spend all their money. In fact, at times, finance people at the government accuse people of spending too much and saving too little. Besides, workers have prospered in general. The standard of living is rising all around the world and I think it is because of this, that we all benefit from mutual work and trade."

"So what happens if you call a carpenter to help you and he does a lousy job?"

"If he tries to charge me more than I think it is worth then I get angry, of course."

"Right."

"I do not say that every deal is a fair deal. There will always be cheaters and swindlers around. People who want money but who do not have the talent to do it in a fair way. They do not know how to deliver something of value to the customer.

"Look at these unemployed people, recommended to set up a new enterprise. How they try to find something to sell that nobody else has done before, to be alone in the market and avoid competition. They are forced to find something new to sell to people.

"In the beginning most people could feed themselves from nature. They built their houses themselves. Tools and utensils were made with their own hands. The market for things was not so large at that time. That was just about a hundred years ago. Before the machines and manufacturing industries."

"I made my life by teaching."

"Yes. Your pupils thought that the things you taught, the knowledge they received, was worth more than the money and the time it took to learn. Right?"

"What you have learned once, is useful many times!"

"You got paid and they got knowledge. Both earn on a good deal. And with this perspective on it, it is clear that robbery and theft is totally antisocial. Because in a robbery, the victim gets nothing in return. The victim loses his valuable goods with no compensation. The robber can't see the true value of what he takes because he did not have to trade for it. Both get screwed.

"A thief steals just because he doesn't have enough money to pay for the goods he want. The value of the stolen goods will be much lower than if he had bought it for money. Theft and robbery decrease the total amount of value. If that was taught to all criminals in jail I think they would feel ashamed."

"Shame on all ignorant politicians, too!"

"The prisoners should beg for, call for proper business education instead of feeding pigs and clearing cow shit."

"Wouldn't that increase the number of unemployed?"

"Hm. The more money people can use to buy things, if there are valuable things to buy, the more jobs there will be?"

"And TV channels!"

"Every time you buy, every time you use a note, you are voting for someone's work."

John had to think for a while. The dream of a perfect society in balance was just a dream that he had never believed in. But he liked to think about it as if things just could be a little bit better. There was no reason to realise it if the costs of it were higher of course. Sounded normal to him.

He liked the picture of all the benefits that were created by people working for money, selling crops and tools to each other, where every deal made both parts wealthier. All the value behind profits was a part of the total benefit to the customer – all the value that was transformed into money by the profit the seller made, by selling it at a slightly higher price than the costs he incurred for it, but lower than the value to the customer, to make both parties happy. The profit from getting paid more than the cost of getting it. The total sum of the collected profit of a year's work was the income for a year. Enough to live on for himself and his family through the winter, for example.

Every entrepreneur that wants to make money must be skilled enough for as many as possible of his customers to benefit also. Otherwise they will go to one of his competitors or just stop buying his products. Give and take. Selling power meeting buying power. Not just money exchange but mere exchange of values. A skilled entrepreneur knows what values the customers want to express and see realized. Dreams and hopes of a better life.

Anyone getting rich, by producing something that the market is interested in and wants to buy, is the good guy in this game. Just because his income is a measure of the total sum of customer value he can reveal. The music industry is a good example. By producing millions of records and selling each for a dollar it was easy for artists and record producers to become millionaires.

Record production was a brilliant way to increase value and satisfy the audience. By the technical evolution of record-stamping machines and record players an artist could reach a million-headed audience. In this way he could expropriate the value from millions of peoples musical preferences just by a few songs performed once in the studio. The promotion was achieved through the radio.

Bill Gates and Steve Jobs have done tremendous work by inventing and producing computer systems that people value more highly than the price they have to pay for it. Gates' and Jobs' money is just a small part of the total value of their work. John also thought about Chinese manufacturers of cheap tube socks in bright colours for the global foot market. Any industry manager with a market for his products.

When he considered it more deeply he was thinking that all money in reality, the value behind the coins and bills, must come from this kind of source, the customer value. The value of money does not come from the federal banks. The value comes from the market, the desire and the value accorded by the customers.

Each time a manufacturer signs a contract he has prepared for production of accounted value. The profit margin in the deal comes from the eventual benefit to the customers. This value is printed into the books by the making of invoices where a part of the customer value is transformed into profit. The value of a service or a good is not real before it is sold. When it is sold there is more value than before. Before it is sold the only thing you can be sure of is the costs that are incurred to produce it.

Profit is the result of a deal where a part of the buyer's value is submitted to the economic system. The profit value, the marginal value, does not exist before the deal more than in the seller's hopes. This value first comes into the system when the deal is made and the invoice is written.

The making of invoices and cash receipts, where the new value first comes into the books, represents printing of real value and developing the profit part of the customer value into the reality behind money. Federal banks print money, but enterprise produces the value behind the money.

Manufacturers and entrepreneurs are our modern heroes that give rise to this value by gathering all the customer value into profit. But without a market it would be impossible to gather any value at all. Trying to sell things and services to people without values is just like fishing in the dry desert.

When the artist on stage is granting his audience with "Thanks, thank you, I love you so much, blah blah blah," he is not just thinking about all the real expressed love as affirmation that he is receiving for his work and talent. It is also a decent gesture for all the money he receives, as a part of the story. His part is just a small part of the total ticket fee. Many other people are involved in the organized harvest of public values. These others involved do not get any applause, they're just in it for the money.

From the beginning it was the state that printed coins and bills as an instrument for paying taxes more easily. The state promised that the money they made was worth all the gold in the state, i.e. the gold that the state had already gathered and now was worth the money they used for paying for goods and duties delivered to the state. To gather gold and keep it in a safe place was the first value-making act behind the money.

In trade for goods, the seller got a note that told him that he was the owner of a part of the federal gold reserve. If he got paid in coins it would be real gold to avoid any mistakes. Later the gold was replaced with silver and copper.

Besides that, and even since long before then, every profitable deal increased the sum of value behind money, while bad deals and consumption of goods decreased the sum of value.

Economic value has to be created and destroyed. The value of an apple, wheat or meat is zero and nothing if someone can't eat it. It has to be eaten to be valued properly. Value, represented by money or bartered goods, is created and destroyed. Real economic value and printed money are two separate systems that are meant to correspond.

Value is created and value is destroyed in a permanent process. Notes and coins are not created in the same process as economic values. The value of money is floating around as costs for some people and income for others. When business is going well, profit is created which increases the sum of value. When business is going badly, value is destroyed.

Not all activities in a society can create value. Not all kinds of processes in a company must be profitable. Research, for example, must be a process of using up value without getting any direct value in return. Education of staff and market research also – because they do not sell anything in particular, they do not produce anything invoiceable. Board meetings, security and health programmes, and activities to reinforce competitive strength and position in the market are other value-consuming activities.

There are a lot of activities inside a company that do not directly create value but in the long run it is crucial for the long-term profit and the company's survival.

The case is the same in a nation. Every single citizen cannot pay taxes. Not all citizens can just work and create value for their customers immediately. Children, sick people, old people and politicians must have the right to consume value.

To some extent we are free and to some extent we are not. We can choose our political standpoint, how hard we will work and where we want to live. We definitely want to make our own choices about what we think is important, what we value. We want to be free to decide what we want to buy and when we want to do it. But we cannot choose our sex, our age or tribal heredity. We cannot choose parents or sexual preferences, nor when we will be hit by accidents or catch diseases.

Business people and working people are performing valuable services and selling valuable goods to customers. Entrepreneurs create value directly, part of it coming into account and the rest coming to the customer. Sellers write bills and cash in the money.

People in a managing position like that of politicians can't write invoices for their daily work; they get a salary to be able to perform their role. The court can't send bills to the public for trials because no one can tell what it is worth to get something that is an equal right for all.

Same with the police, health care etc. Scientists, teachers, artists and researchers. All these that are working with what we cannot choose, where there is no real market for buying and selling, where we are not free. You know that there is a cost for it but you can never tell what it gives you. These public services should be free and at no cost. Freedom to choose to be cured or not but paid for by public society. People working in public services are people that are using up value created by the enterprising side of the society. But they create value in the long run for the society and our culture. Our way to do it. That is what taxes are for. A considerable share of the sales income in a company is used for long-term value production.

A people without values makes a dead market. A good market is built of desire and services that create real value when they meet. The trick is how to place taxes so they will not hamper the value-creating activities. Value-Added Taxes, VAT, are a good example because they are a taxation that is placed directly on the production of customer value, at least in theory. The politicians must be able to balance the creation of value with the destruction of value so it will fit the amount of printed money. It must be a hell of a job to be a national accountant. No wonder there are so many financial crises at times.

Today, states do not have gold enough to ensure the value of all the printed money. Instead the states take loans, sell government bonds, with the coming year's tax income as security.

Modern financial advisors know that there are an unlimited number of fiscal years coming in the future.

96

Therefore there is no limit on how many years of tax income a state can use as security for new loans. State deficits can grow without limit as long as the state can pay the rent. Mortgages are made by taking new loans.

Printing new money and bringing it to the market in an attempt to support the market that will buy new products is the modern method of boosting the economy. The problem arises when people believe in the value of this money.

How can you guarantee that people will pay taxes in the future? National economists do not appear to be aware of the real value of the benefits from production and merchandise. If the people of a nation go into a real depression and do not value services and goods. Then the production of real value will diminish into oblivion without anyone understanding what is happening. Money will be worth less because of diminishing underlying value.

When people have a little too much money, they tend to overvalue goods and services. Prices rise too high and too much profit money is created. The profit accumulates and exceeds the customer value, that way causing inflation, devaluation of the currency.

We say the times 'are good' when people have faith and believe in the future. Good times are the best climate for economic growth as customer value is high and the margins for the seller to get a higher price are better. The difference between the cost of production and the value to the customer is greater. The medium price is higher. More money is coming into the books and the created profit has something to rely on. The gross profit is supported by customer value instead of future tax prognostics. There is a big difference in money based on faith in the security behind government bonds and money that is based on the customer value on the market.

John turned to Elsa.

"Every time you buy something from somebody, you are giving that person a job for a moment. But if you do not value what he has done, then the money he earns is not worth anything. It is all based on our own values. What we prefer to have or what we prefer to be done. Our belief, our confidence, gives the value of money and meaning to the one who does the work."

"I don't really follow. Do you mean that the money in my purse is not worth anything?"

"It is not worth anything until you buy something with it. When you buy you are trading your money for something that is worth more to you. If you buy something that is nearly worthless to you, then the money must have been worth less than the value of that shit you just bought. Price is not as important as the value of what you get."

"I would never do that!"

"That is just what I mean. You wait until you see something that you believe in, something of value to you, higher value than the price you have to pay, the money in your purse. Then you are ready to buy. Even if you know that the seller has not paid as much for it as you do. You can accept paying him his share for what he has done to make it possible for you to get it just there. Right? You know that the fisherman has to collect a decent amount each day to keep on standing there and offer you herrings every day."

"Aha, I see, yes it is all based on my confidence, how I value the lunch. But that is very vague and imprecise isn't it?"

"That is no problem. People are different and have different taste. The profit the seller makes is just a kind of security margin for if there is a customer value or not. If he puts the price too high, he will not sell to more than a few. If he puts the price too low, he will sell it all with just a small profit and maybe stop selling it. It is important to be able to catch enough from the customer value. That will affect the customers who would like to buy more over time."

"That may be the explanation why that restaurant has closed." Elsa pointed at a small restaurant by the road. "I think their speciality was serving waffles to tourists, but there aren't many tourists driving this way this season."

"No, I think the only profitable business along a road is a petrol station."

"And motels."

"Not too many and not too shabby either." John was thinking on some occasions when he had to rent a room on his trips. Some of the places were really bad.

"Have you heard about the value of oil and petrol, the real value of petrol?"

"What is that? I thought you could read the signs at the pumps."

"No, that is the price to buy it. The amount of money you have to trade for it. Petrol contains energy. What you buy is energy. You trade your money for an amount of energy."

"What do you know about energy?"

"That is my job. Oh, I do not really know so much about energy chemically or physically. I work with the energy markets, the prices in the gas, oil, and electricity market for example. Water, sewage and central heating, central cooling."

"My man was a nuclear scientist you know. I spent 30 years of my life with him. I learned a lot from him and maybe he learned something from me. So what about the value, the real value you mentioned?"

"Well, the money you can get by hard work, this money is what you spend on petrol. If you did not have petrol, what would you do then?"

"I would walk."

"If we walked then it would take us days to come this far. And to bring all the things we have in the car it would be really hard work. We would have to be very confident about the value of such a walk."

"I understand. The love of Mary would have to be strong as hell!"

"So, for just the money that I can get in two hours' work, I can pay the petrol needed for transporting us, the car and the things in it a certain distance that would take us many hours to do without the petrol. It is possible to calculate this physically: the amount of energy in one glass of petrol is about what is needed to move the car one mile and that costs about one Swedish kronor. But if you hire people to move the car by hand it will cost a fortune. It takes one man 27 hours of labour to generate the equivalent amount of energy to what is contained in the glass filled with petrol."

"That cannot be true."

"Yes it is. One glass of petrol is about 2 thousand watt-hours and one strong man can generate up to 75 watt energy[12]. 2 thousand divided by 75 is about 27. He has to be in very good condition to work as hard as that in 27 hours. To move the car one mile by hand."

"It would be done with the same speed."

12 Pimentel & Pimentel; "Food, energy, and society"

"No and that is another problem, it would take him 27 hours! If you would like to have it done by 27 men, they may be able to do it in one hour, which is also too low a speed. That is at the speed of one mile per hour. The problem is when they are finished; they want to be paid for the work. Twenty-seven men working for one hour. Is it worth it?"

"Twenty-seven times 200 is, hmm, 5400 kronor or about one thousand dollars."

"And that is the value of one and only one single glass of petrol at the speed of one mile per hour! The price per barrel would be absolutely hilarious. Six glasses per litre is 5 thousand dollar per litre. One barrel is 159 litres times 5 thousand is, uuuh, almost one million dollars. The value of petrol should be compared to the energy of human labour worth about one million dollars per barrel instead of today's one hundred!"

"What about the 27 men, do they walk home again or do they need a cab?"

"Ha ha, don't bother about that, it was just an example. This would never happen in reality. But, if oil and petrol energy were priced from its labour energy value in the industry and for heating, then this value could be real and considerable. Remember before the oil age, at that time winches and small machines were dragged by horses and slaves. Without the oil we would still be there. In 1890 one kWh of electricity cost about two hours' pay. That would be 300 kronor per kWh today."

"We would have had more steam engines."

"Right, but that is still the same energy mathematics. Man can't generate very much energy by himself. Just imagine all the work in the fields, ploughing seeding and harvesting, if it had to be done manually."

"The world would have been cleaner."

"Maybe, or maybe not, it depends on how much coal we would use then. It takes energy to clean up too."

John took a look at the petrol gauge. They had been driving for about four hours now and less than half the tank of petrol had been burnt.

"How far is it left to Mary's?"

"I think it is about two hours' drive from here. Depends if we make any more stops. If I have to pee you must stop immediately because I cannot piss in a bottle like truck drivers do."

"Sure, just honk the horn, lady. I am not finished yet."

"What? Are you peeing in a bottle?"

"No, about the petrol price, the real value. If we think about this value of petrol, oil, kerosene and stuff, all the oil that has been pumped from the wells, sold and burned in engines and boilers – the total amount of the energy value from this oil that is delivered to us, the real value for the customers, above the price we had paid for it – it is easy to make a rough estimate.

"We are using 33 billion barrels of oil per year[13]. In the last century consumption has risen from about zero to 33 billion barrels per year. The average is around the half of 33 times 100 years which is, half of 33 and two zeros, 1.6 thousand billion barrels times the value of one barrel from the customers view, one million dollars. That will be 1.6 billion billion dollars of customer value brought to the world economy by oil. An absolutely fantastic value! More than 100 thousand times the US gross domestic product. More than what

13 International Energy Agency; Oil market report

is produced and invoiced for in the US for 100 thousand years! In one single century!

"The US national debt and the GDP are about 15 thousand billion dollars and some people think that is a big sum. Wow, the value of the oil is just like an economic Big Bang delivered to humanity during the last century! And only the average of 50, from zero to 100, dollars per barrel of this real value has been invoiced for and taken into account. Fifty of a million is just one half dollar out of each 10 thousand dollars of working energy value booked, accounted and brought into the GDP. What economic ignorance!"

"You should be very happy then to be driving this car."

"I am, and I enjoy your company."

"Thanks."

5 - What is a Waste of Time

"Do you mean that the oil saves time?" Elsa asked after a while.

"Time?"

"Yes? If you say that it would take this or that time for us if we didn't have petrol in the tank. Then it should have taken us much more time. You say 27 hours to move the car one mile."

"That is at the speed of one mile per hour. We are moving at 50 mph so you have to multiply it by 50 which is ... oh gosh, 1350 times better!"

"Jeesus. Are you sure about that? How can you calculate that fast?"

"That's easy, I do it in steps, 20 times 50 is 1000 and 7 times 50 is 350. That is 1350 together."

"Oh."

"I like to be sure of my calculations so I do it in small and nice steps. It takes one man 27 hours to move the car one mile. Two men can do the same work in half of the time which is 13.5 hours. 27 men can move the car one mile in one hour. At the speed of one mile per hour. To move the car at double the speed it takes 54 men to do it. Then the mile will be done in half an hour, only 30 minutes. 270 men can move the car at 10 miles per hour and to move it one mile will then take six minutes. Doubled again, 340 men can, at least in theory, move the car at 20 mph and the mile will take three minutes. The power of 1350 men is enough to move the car at 50 mph and the mile will be done in 1.2 minute."

"Are you sure about that?"

"Well, if we didn't have petrol and wanted to move the car at this speed, yes. The petrol saves our time 1350 times better."

"Time is money."

"No that is not correct, saved time is money!" John's head rushed again.

There it was! Time was the value behind it all!

He could feel how his eyes were moved to tears by the excitement. He had to slow down for a while to keep control over the driving without losing his focus. There was not much traffic on the road but faster cars came up from behind and there were heavy trucks on the road meeting now and then. John wanted to keep up to speed and avoid time-consuming stops.

"How do you mean?" Elsa had a hard time following John's intensive thoughts.

"I mean that values are collected all around by all business deals and organized economic activities. It is all about time, saved time! Saving time means creating value for people and that is the ultimate basis for the economy. Economy means literally, 'Resource management', and the ultimate resource is time!"

"Time is a resource, and economy is about resources?"

"Yes, economy is about managing resources. Time is the ultimate resource. It isn't the time itself that is the money. Time is **not** money! Time is a resource but the value behind the money is the **saved** time!"

"It might be interesting but could you please explain that again? What is it that is so fantastic?" John was not sure if she was interested or just liked to keep the conversation going.

"First, it takes time to do things. Let us take an example. Humans need food to survive. It takes time to get that food."

"Yes."

"Now presume that we find a tool that makes it easier to harvest. Less time is used to find the same amount of food, right?"

"Or you will get more food and be fatter."

"OK, but this is the thing – the tool makes it easier to harvest. It can be a stick that makes it easier to dig for roots in the ground. Instead of taking eight hours to find food enough for the day you can do it in six hours with the stick. You save two hours per working day with the tool. The value of the tool for you, what you can pay or trade to get this tool, is what you can get in the time that is saved by the tool. If for example you can find 16 carrots per day without the tool and 20 with the tool, then the tool is worth up to four carrots per day, OK?"

"But if you have agreed to pay four carrots per day for the tool and only find 18 then it's a bad deal isn't it?"

"Yes, or even when finding 20 per day it is not a good deal because then all the value of the tool goes to the toolmaker. Then it's no better for you with or without the tool."

"You can make a stick on your own. Then you don't have to pay anything!"

"It would still be more worth to me, the more carrots per day I could find! But what if it is a more complicated tool that I couldn't make but had to buy? A fair deal is 50/50 – to equally share the value, which is two carrots per day. Then it is worth the same for both. If you are without the tool you can get 16 carrots per day. If you buy and use the tool you earn four more

106

carrots per day and the toolmaker gets two per day as payment for the tool."

"But you said that it was worth time. And who buys a tool with a daily payment? He must be able to use it more than once, I think."

"Yes, because the real benefit with a better tool is that you get more done in the same period of time. A better tool doesn't mean that you need more carrots.

"A tool will normally last for a period of time. Let us say 200 days of use. If you pay 400 carrots for a tool that lasts for 200 days then the price is two carrots per day of use. The toolmaker understand this and knows that the tool is worth the sum of the daily use of it."

"Both have to understand that to make a fair deal."

"Instead of working the whole day, say eight hours, and getting 16 carrots in that time, you can work less if you have the tool. If the tool makes you more effective so that you can get 20 carrots in eight hours, then you can stop already at 18. That work gives you the 16 you need for the day and also the surplus to pay the toolmaker his two carrots per day. After the 18th carrot you have got some time left over. The tools move the moment when you are finished with your work about one hour earlier. The future is coming closer. The tool is a time compressor. Tools are time-compressors."

"If you have got the skill to use it. Yes!"

"That is why I think the duration of a tool is important. The tool that saves time can also be a method such as information that makes it easier to find food in shorter time.

"Information is intellectual tools. Intellectual tools can be distinguishing names, calculating methods, information about how and when to do things. Intellectual methods do not wear out like tools and machines. They can be out of time. A new invention

107

lasts forever or as long as it is saving time. It doesn't cost much to produce and distribute. The value of new knowledge can be absolutely priceless!"

"It can be easy to find but hard to learn. I know. I have been teaching all my life. Knowledge and skill don't come easily to people. Knowledge is perishable."

"Skill is as good as tools. But skills last longer than tools. The value of the tool and the skill to use it is compressed future! Working with tools, using skill and knowledge, organising labour is compressing the time it takes to get things done. It makes you able to choose what to do with the time that is saved. Saved time is compressed future time. With the time saved you are free to do something else when you have acquired what you planned!

"This must be the ultimate source of freedom! Saved time! Everything that can help us do more in less time is giving us free time. Value is what you want to have, what you want to be realized, multiplied by the time it takes to get it. If someone can help you achieve it in a shorter time by using some tool or information, then this tool or information is worth about the half of the saved time for both of you.

"Take, for example, a boat or a net that can increase the amount of fish you get from the sea. You can choose to finish when you have enough fish for the day or spend the same amount of time as earlier and get more fish. With a bigger catch you can feed more people, that's right. That surplus catch has about the same value as the time you saved by using the boat. But for the other people the extra fish are worth more because they can stay at home and do something else."

"But we aren't fishing now, we are on a rescue trip to Mary."

"Yes, by using the car and burning petrol in the engine, we can be there in a few hours. She would probably have been old and forgotten our names before we could get there if we tried to walk. The car costs a lot of money to buy and maintain, but the general benefit from the petrol makes it worth it because the car still saves a lot of time for us. Like a bridge or a boat that lets us pass over a river faster than before. A nation with bad roads and a lousy traffic system loses in competition with another nation with highways. The time taken for transport between the industry locations, homes and markets is saved by the smoother traffic.

"Oil and petrol is very important for GDP. Very big money in that! That is why I like shopping centres where I can drive at 50 mph straight to the door and have free parking. Instead of sneaking around in old city blocks planned for traffic by horse and cart. Like in the streets of the Chaplin film *City Lights*."

"Oh yes, I remember that film. Charlie Chaplin was a very handsome man at that time."

John could feel a hot stream of fresh blood running up in his neck and around in his head. This was very exciting. Saved time was the key to the solution to many questions that he had been asking himself for a long time.

"When I think about how humanity evolved, the absolute first tribe in Africa, the first human that rose and stood upright on its feet so he could see better – standing upright hc could get more information about the surroundings in a shorter time and that gave him a time-saving advantage over his competitors. He and his tribe could orientate themselves better in the surroundings by sharing his find of time-saving information. The information was used to gather a picture of the surroundings with names of places and roads to use. Maps became better and better. Sharing valuable information with his tribe made it even more valuable as the information could save time for more individuals in the group. Holding a rock in the hand, making spears and tools, finding new and better words, all were means for saving time.

"And the fire! With the power to make fire, the tribe had more light time per day, they had shelter from predators, they could cook meat better and get more energy out of it. They got time to reflect on their experiences and share information. Today's television and the Internet must be what fire was for the first human tribes.

"Inventions are about saving time. If it does not save time or give more during the same amount of time then it is has no value, it is worthless. The use of time and how to save time by finding better methods is the ultimate source of economy. The use of our brains, our thinking and our memory. I guess that every word and concept must be of the same kind. If a name of something makes it easier to live then it is worth remembering. With a general concept, a name of a valley, for example, then there is less time for confusion about what valley we are talking about and the hunt or search will take less time."

"Yes, where are we?"

"On the road, on our way to Mary. Excuse me, I'm not really sure at the moment but we have been driving for about one hour. It takes about two hours' driving from Mora to Sveg so we should be somewhere in the middle, then. It's just forest and bushes here and I do not remember the names of the small villages here. What was the name of the last place we passed?"

"I saw the sign but I didn't care. I was listening to you, but I think you're right, we have about one hour left to Sveg. There is a nice place to have a cup of coffee there."

"Ha, that was a wonderful way of saving time. Instead of troubling yourself with the name you just ignored it."

John continued thinking about saved time. Saved time is vulnerable to revaluation. People change their minds and interests. Prices vary. Trends and fashion come and go. John recalled Pirsig's four levels of evolution. From the inorganic, through the organic and the social up to the intellectual level. The higher the level, the more vulnerable it is to revaluation. Value might be very steady for precious metals, real estate and housing; for organic stuff like grain, food and coffee, it might be more flexible. Social commodities like clothing, entertainment and travel vary even more. Intellectual concepts like political ideas and information business are the most valuable and also the most vulnerable for revaluation.

John suspected that time must be the lowest common denominator for evolution at these four levels. Time has something in common with gravitation and the space between particles inside atomic structures. Like stable waves and particles in self-oscillation. Declaring what angles the electrons will have to each other in molecules.

Saved time is definitely the case for the organic processes. The ability to gain enough power to survive in competition with other species is a result of how well an organism can use its time to nourish itself. At the social level an organized group of any kind has to use its time perfectly to survive the competition between groups and tribes. Save time and use it in the right way.

Warfare is very much about timing; use the forces in the right place and at the right time. Enterprises too. Time in and time out. Sports are maybe a way to exercise cooperation in time to be a winner? Football is a religious rite. The goalkeeper stretches his hands and he looks into the future.

But how does time comes into the intellectual level? Music is definitely a matter of timing as organized sound. Without time music would be totally chaotic and meaningless. Without value.

John had rationality in mind as the most correct idea would consume the minimal time to execute. When it came to engineering and constructions, the best time-saving ideas would win naturally. The best economic theories that saved the most time and money and caused the minimum of crises and losses would be the winner. Laws and fundamental truths are eternal and timeless.

They had been going for another hour on the road since they left in the morning. They would make another stop at Sveg and from there it was about two hours left to Mary's. Hours, time; John was thinking about what time was, the nature of time. The only thing he was sure about so far was that time was running, changing, no stop, no pause. It is possible to hold your own process for a while but time will continue. As usual. Nothing new, but for John this view was totally new. He felt like his consciousness had fallen off from the time flow and he was watching it from outside in the dark nothingness.

From this point everything around was black and empty. The only thing that existed was the passing perpetual wave of time. The now was filled with life, colours and sounds. The engine hummed, the wheels rolled and the car was moving through the landscape of forests, valleys and creeks. The dark and silent trees pointing up in the sky, unable to move by their own force, doomed to a life in one place and one place only all through their life cycle. "Firs, pines, birches and alder, all different species that have evolved since the beginning of life on Earth, from the first bacteria to mould and algae. Every species had its origin in mutations into new forms of behaviour and structure that gave it a better chance to compete on the ground. Those who had the best strategy survived."

John was thinking that there had to be an element of luck in it, too. But the general goal was to be better, to save energy, find better ways of defending its origin. Those who did it best, who gained the most energy in time, those who were best at saving time were the winners. The time that was released gave them time-space to expand and evolve.

Mutations, the inner occasional errors that gave rise to new combinations of DNA, were no conscious activity. "Mutations are more like accidents in the reproduction of the process information inside a species. But there is no way that species at that stage can be regarded as conscious. Not all people are quite stupid, they are just unlucky when they think."

John liked this. He had good thoughts while he drove the car. Elsa had fallen asleep. Still holding her handbag on her knee. Mouth open. "Was she dying now?" No, she was breathing deeply. John looked at the meters, 50 mph, lots of petrol left, temperature OK. No strange sound or smell from the machinery. Outside he could see signs of falling temperature, smoke on the water, but the road was dry and there was no risk of ice yet.

The conditions that made evolution possible via mutations must have been in place from the beginning. Mutations happen, but there was no guarantee that a new mutated form of life would survive the competition. John could see that the trees around him had made it through evolution. They were winners so far. Well done. John gave them a respectful second. Mutations, a very slow process of trial and error.

Unconscious creation, a long row of problem-solving experiments, where the fittest would survive and the unfit die. So many hits and so many more mistakes. The time it took biological nature to reach so far as to hold trees and flowers was long, very long, many millions of years. Those who believe in a conscious creator, a God, must believe in a very mighty figure. Those who say that they understand or know such a conscious God must have very big brains and big mouths to speak for Him on order to convince John about their reliability.

The geological processes took billions of years. The biological made it faster, in millions of years. John saw in his mind how every level of evolution was superior to the former by being faster and more efficient in saving time. Social strategies evolve in thousands of years. A social culture, a society, appears and changes in centuries and wins over those who can't save enough energy and time.

John remembered a movie, *The Last Samurai*[14]. Japan was really a meeting place between different social strategies. The disciplined men with swords and loyalty lost the last battle against the modern soldiers

14 http://en.wikipedia.org/wiki/The_Last_Samurai

with the more effective machine guns, more beats, shots per minute. Mary had just returned from West Papua where a similar fight was on.

What about mental strategies, ideas? How fast will a new idea about economic or environmental issues be adopted and a winning strategy? A new pop group can be famous in a week. Financial crashes can spread over the world in one night. John thought that humanity had a problem with its fast mind. Human conscious thinking and evolution might be too fast for its biological and social levels. Every new intellectual mutation, conscious mutation? Every new mental breed could spread and dominate in a much shorter time than mutated social and biological strategies. Less saved time was needed to find a new intellectual solution than a biological one.

Instead of changing our own biology to fit into the world, we are changing the surroundings to fit our biology. "If the shoes do not fit, change the shoe and not the feet"; that was something John remembered from reading Wilhelm Reich's *The Sexual Revolution*. Reich was fighting for a better human form of sexuality. John thought that the man maybe missed the fact that social and intellectual strategies are superior to biological strategies.

Humans who know how to control their sexuality will win over those who do not. Social sexual strategies that make things better and more comfortable for their members will win in the competition if they make society stronger in the overall competition about time. Reich's hope was that people would be healthier and better workers if they were sexually satisfied. Sexual frustration was causing a lot of strange behaviours in the Victorian culture of the 19th century.

Reich had learned from Sigmund Freud that most people's problems at that time were caused by unsatisfied sexual needs. A culture where sexual life was too much controlled by the social system began to be a problem in competition between nations. For example, "Fewer people decide to move to a place where the chances of getting laid are worse."

John had had some funny experiences from visiting other countries. He was definitely not a person who could say that he had his sexuality under control. But he tried to follow the social rules and to be an ordinary honest man. Sex was something that he could not control and so far he had been lucky with that. His biology had its own opinion about when and where to get alive. An orgasm was always something new to him. It was never like something he had experienced earlier.

Reich had a theory that there was some kind of universal material radiation that came in from space which we receive at the moment when we can't hold back the inner forces of sex, when we come. Reich called this kind of radiated material Orgon and that is why it is called Orgasm.

John remembered a girl he met who said that she liked the ones that came from inside best. If she was forcing herself to come it was not nearly as good as the ones that just arrived by letting it come "by itself, from inside", by losing control. John had had the same experience and that was maybe why he just let sexual events happen by themselves. There was no use in trying hard to make it happen.

"Have sex, or do sex?" John was thinking about sex as an event with both a passive and an active side. Something between two people. People with trust and confidence in each other, enough to lose control. It must be real and couldn't be something artificial.

Just like trying to laugh in situations that are not funny but socially it is the right thing to do. No one can be fooled by these false laughs. John was confident about Elsa. "She is no false laughing or smiling person. She must be a real bitch sometimes," he was thinking. As she told him about her former husbands it was with no idea of trying to do something improper.

John liked that. He was confident about her. If Elsa smiled it would be a real smile. He could not imagine making love and losing his control with a person he was not confident with. "A waste of time," he was thinking.

"Stop!" Elsa shouted. "I must pee!"

John slowed down, pulled over and turned into a small road. It led into another road that went parallel to the main road. He stopped and let Elsa leave the car. John could see that this was a part of the former road. He went out of the car to take a closer look at the place and stretch his legs. He could see her buttocks shine in the bush.

The main road was straightened and rebuilt and moved just a few yards west. Probably to avoid some sharp bend here. John could follow the road where it vanished into the bushes. He could see how this road was more narrow than the new road. It was probably the first road since the beginning. It seemed to follow the natural surroundings.

At the beginning of the automobile age, roads were built for transport with nothing heavier than horse and cart. The roads later had to be reinforced and widened to be able to carry the new kind of vehicles. Since the Stone Age, transport through the country had been achieved by walking or by help from some animal and primitive carts. These roads for walking and riding were cleared by hand and followed the easiest way through the landscape.

John remembered his grandfather who said that in his time there were no roads at all between the farms where he lived; "We just drove over the fields."

"As speed was low on old horse tracks there was no reason to avoid sharp bends. These roads were as curvy as the land and law like written characters in the landscape between forests and fields. Any one travelling along the road was 'reading' this characteristic letter of the country. Quite similar to reading a primitive mantra," John was thinking. That was what it must have been like to go along a well-known road. When he was following a road that he knew well he could feel how he was prepared for what was coming in the end, a shopping mall or another city.

Learning a road was easy for John. He could imagine going on roads he knew in both directions. He knew some points on it and could follow every bend, mostly. "It's much like music," he was thinking. "It takes a while to learn a piece and then, when you are listening, you are travelling along its lefts and rights to the end and if something different appears, it is very easy to notice."

Straightening a road was well motivated of course, as it shortens the travelling time for everyone going along the road. Fewer accidents and a higher average speed. The ultimate ideal must be exact straight roads between cities and waypoints. But the maximum time-saving from building a road must be made at the very first time it was built because at that time the win was total. From a state where it was impossible to pass, to a travel time of about, say, one hour to cross a forest. That difference is priceless.

Every vehicle that uses the road is saving an unlimited time as it was impossible to go there before the road was built. Next time the road is redone and, maybe, travelling time is decreased to 50 minutes, 10 minutes are saved for every traveller, increasing the average national yield of saved time.

"In the end when the road is completely straight there is no possibility of making the way shorter. At that moment other ways of saving time had to be used if it was to become better. Wider road, safer lanes to allow higher speed? But who was paying for that? Someone must be the one that pays?" John had to think this over again some day.

Reaching a maximum of efficiency like that was interesting. From zero efficiency to 100%, to one. Was that what happened when evolution went over from inorganic to organic? When nearly 100% of all mass was balanced into elements and molecules, the next step starts? Is the human brain about nearly 100% perfect for the next step, the evolution after the intellectual level? What will start when human understanding of "it all" is nearly 100%?

Elsa came back from the bushes. She looked fine, her face was red and she smiled.

"That was a close call. I thought I should die! I was dreaming that I was swimming around in a stream and suddenly I felt like I was drowning!"

"No problem for me, I liked stopping just here, it gave me some good thinking and some new problems."

"Like what?" Elsa jumped into the car.

"Roads are made to save time for people."

"Of course they are."

"Yes, but whose time is saved?"

"Without a road we'd have to walk naturally."

"Yes, we would be back at the Stone Age. The Stone Age kept all the values we have revealed by the rationalisation of our way of life since then. Without primitive civilisations there would be no value in being modern. Without the possibility of walking there would be no value in riding a bike."

"Ahh, people walked when I was young too. The German soldiers that left Norway at the end of the war had to walk through the whole of Denmark to come home to Germany."

John drove out on the main road again. He had to concentrate his mind for a while to turn in the right direction.

"I like bridges, I love bridges, they are so beautiful!" Elsa said after a while.

"Yes, those who are building bridges must see that it is worth the money for it. Bridges are very expensive projects I think. What makes you think they are beautiful?"

"I don't know, I just like bridges. I remember when I was a girl and we were going to Copenhagen and we had to go over the Sound by boat. Now there are bridges over all straits in Denmark."

"So that is the difference? You know the difference and then you can put a value on the bridge?"

"I don't put a value on the bridge, I just like them. The look, the power, the effort and engineering skill behind the construction. It is a majestic feeling every time we pass over a big bridge, like a stairway to heaven. Looking down is like flying. But you can be right about the difference of being without the bridge. I feel safe with a bridge in place instead of going on an unsteady ferry."

"Experiencing a value must be experiencing a difference I think. We can't know the value of a modern society if there aren't people living in older civilisations. Like the Papuans."

"They are poor. There are poor people everywhere in any society."

"Yes, but poor and inefficient are not the same thing. The people in Papua seem to be very healthy and efficient. They just do it their own way. Our biological constitution is designed for that kind of life. We are the modern people that have changed our methods for collecting food and build our own shelters in a faster and more effective way. But we still have the same kind of biological processes."

"You said that saving time made us free to be intellectual."

"Hm, yes. Why did I say that?"

"You said that the invention of the fire gave humanity more daytime and time to contemplate around the fire. Saving time to think things over."

"Yes, that is a little bit weird. I can drive my car as I do now and think that I am driving my car. Sort of looking at myself from outside my car. I am aware of myself sitting in the car and driving."

"Don't forget to keep your hands on the wheel."

"I can also think that I am watching myself while I am looking at myself driving. I am aware about that I am aware of myself and what I am doing."

"Don't get lost!"

"It is like having a mind mirror! A madhouse of mind mirrors!"

John laughed at this crazy perspective. It was clear for him that the difference compared to an unconscious animal, the difference in conscious animals, is that humans have some kind of mirror in their brain. A picture of themselves.

"We are looking at ourselves by mirroring the outside inside our brain. Our brain is producing pictures of the outside. Concepts are pieces of the pictures of what we sense from outside. If we put the pieces together in the right way we'll get the situation right and can come up with a plan for the next step. Those who can't put the concepts together in the right order will fail."

If John's picture of how the car behaved through the trip was right, then he would be able to drive and they would arrive at Mary's place in a couple of hours. But he did not need more than one mirror to understand his purpose, the other mirrors were not adding much information. It could be useful with an extra mirror in the bathroom to see how his neck was looking sometimes, maybe, but everytime he tried to trim the hairs on the neck his hand would not follow his intent. Something happened with the perspective with an extra mirror.

"We can't fail now, that will affect Mary!"

"Don't worry. I know what I am doing, in fact I am broadening my understanding of what I am doing by doing it and looking at myself in my mind at the same time."

"You are driving, isn't that enough to understand?"

"Yes, I have learned the skill of driving. I know how to drive and I am so trained to that so I do not have to think about every little step. That leaves my conscious mind free to reflect over what I am doing. If I were not that skilled then my conscious mind would be totally absorbed by the task of keeping the car on the road. It's all about margins. Spare capacity. That is what makes it so hard to drive when conditions are rough, like snow, darkness and bad roads. This is easy driving. If I slowed down it would be even easier to drive. I could keep my eyes on you more and use more of my brain capacity to keep you happy."

"I am happy enough if you drive safe and not too slow, please. Don't waste your time on me. I know you are a good driver, I can feel that. You seem to be one piece with the car, almost."

"Yes, I have been driving this car as much as six times around the whole Earth. And this is not my first car. I think that I have been driving around for nearly 30 years now. That must be over 20 times around the planet."

"Just to come to this place, huh?" Elsa did not pay much attention to what John had achieved by driving around all these years. Driving had become a big part of his life. To travel around to places and to meet people, leave materials and fetch things. A lot of driving was done to search for information. A lot of driving was for shopping, filling up at petrol stations, visiting restaurants and to get the car a tune-up or have it repaired.

John began to think over all the money he had paid for this driving. All the petrol, mortgages on new cars, insurances and tyres. He knew that the monthly costs for the car were often higher than what he spent on his house and the food for his family.

Some days ago he heard about Irv Gordon[15] who had driven his Volvo P1800 nearly 3 million miles. And that without wrecking the car in a crash. "That man must have had a good portion of luck," John was thinking.

---

15 http://en.wikipedia.org/wiki/Irv_Gordon

John had had some serious accidents through the years. He had not been seriously injured but the cars were more or less written off. He knew that he could not trust the road or other drivers 100%. "Accidents happen, there is no such thing as 100% safety in technical terms. That, is one thing you cannot choose," John was thinking.

"Well I guess I could have made it different."
"Too late to change that, young man."
"I could have saved a lot of time if I'd known better."
"It took you that time to understand!"
"I could have saved a lot of time with better planning in my life. If it was not because of the time we are living in today with cheap petrol and cars I maybe would have been walking around in the same place or riding around on a horse. That would not have been so many laps around the Earth."
"How do you know that it would have been better? There is no possibility of living twice."
"Hm, I guess you're right. But it would be different if I had not learned to drive."

John did not regret what he had done – some small moments perhaps. Elsa was right that learning takes time. Without mistakes he would not have learned much. Maybe he could have used his daily time more efficiently by thinking over what he had done from one day to another.

But to learn that also takes time, years, lives. All of what a human culture understands is experiences collected from mistakes and successes. All that humanity knows about cooking, for example, has evolved that way. Knowledge about edible vegetables, hunting techniques and how to preserve food. Loads of knowledge refined through generations.

Time is used to learn, learn and learn, practising and getting better. Just like all words, languages, technical skills. All human knowledge evolved by someone spending time on it, reflections and systematic analysis being spent on it. Human knowledge is the sum of millions of humans' individual efforts. Common knowledge is shared and altered, mixed into new blends. Not many have much knowledge that is based on their own experience. The absolute majority of every individual's part of the total knowledge comes from parents and other teachers.

Human intellectual evolution is growing out from the public reserves of saved time. The sum of all individual efforts together. Word for word, idea for idea, step for step in mathematical or other special expertise. Without time to reflect, no evolution.

The value of words in a language is created by using time to think it over. But a language is dead if it just exists in writing but no one is able to use it. Knowledge has to be preserved, heard and practised. Over and over again. An aeroplane is worthless if no one knows how to fly it. An enterprise is doomed if no one knows how to manage it. The value of a screwdriver is dependent on the skill of the mechanics (and whether there is something that has to be screwed).

John began to realise how saved time was used up at the other end. If you had some time to reflect then you had time to keep a distance from the reality. No panic, saved time means time to study and contemplate the situation and take the right decision for the next step. Saved time means freedom to think. Freedom to do just whatever you want away from physical restraints. You can daydream about flying to the moon but gravity will make it hard to do it for real.

"Art and mutations are just a big waste of time."

"What?" Elsa had not heard John's last thoughts.

"That was a joke, but I am serious. Saved time is used for evolution. Biological evolution is triggered by mutations that could take advantage of the time saved by their predecessors. The saved energy, is used to build the mutants' new existence on the so-called lower stages of evolution."

"I thought mutated species just were better at competing."

"Yes but it is clearer if you look at it with a million-year-scale perspective. It is quite obvious if we look at this natural experimenting, these randomized mistakes in the reproductive process. In the end it is producing new forms of life. We can see that this trial-and-error process is using up a lot of time for the underlying species that is affected by the competition from the mutants. United mutations are the thinking of the biological level. It is a very slow kind of problem solving that leads to better and stronger life forms. The time needed for this evolution is delivered by the pre-existing species. When a superior lifeform is taking over, it sort of kills its mother, feeding the next generation with her.

"I said that art was a waste of time. I was thinking about the role of art in human society. There are a lot of people that are just not able to work as normal persons from eight to five. Their brains are already mutated and their task, their object is to come up with things that are different.

"Like Einstein, Gandhi, Steve Jobs or the great Stephen Hawking. Without the use of these different persons evolution would go more slowly and life on Earth would halt, don't you think?

"I would say that Art and mutations are just a big and very important use of time, not a waste of time. I think that those busy enterprising people who are busy with saving time have a hard time seeing how different persons are using up the time they have saved so hard. But it has to be done."

"Parents have to take care of their children. Kids can't work, they are using their parents' spare energy to grow. Children's growth is definitely not a waste of time."

"Yes, you can give them all the support and time you have, but you can't go into their brains. There is always one or more of them doing something different from what their parents expected. That must be a strong urge for freedom, to make your own life. Brain researchers know that no brain is similar to anyone else's. We are all different from birth. Regardless of parental guidance and expectations."

"Yes, my mother was a religious fanatic and she spent all the time she had on me to make me into a pure fundamental Christian. But I refused since I was six and experienced that God was not real. There was no way for her to convince me. I learned a lot about what was written in the Bible but I do not believe in God.

"I do have respect for some Christians. I have indeed lived together with a priest for ten years even though we were not married. The higher churchmen and especially their wives had a hard time with me. I argued with the bishop, he let me sit on the first row in the cathedral when my man was in the centre of the attention for some occasion. The women wanted to close me out. We were living in sin, they said."

"Ha, you're a nice mutation! I like your style, baby. That bishop knew something about how to forgive, perhaps by his own experience."

"My daughter left me when she was sixteen, or maybe I threw her out. We couldn't cooperate. But it works better now. STOP!"

"What is it, we stopped just a few minutes ago?" John slowed down anyway.

"It is a nice place to take a rest here. We've got some coffee left in the thermos and there are more eggs and bread."

"I thought we would find some café in Sveg?"

"No, that takes both time and money, there, turn right there." Elsa pointed at a small parking lot beside a wild river.

John parked the car. Elsa went out and searched the back seat for the bag with the coffee. A big information sign told them that they were at the Bear Falls. A small wooden table with benches next to it stood by the riverside. Elsa went there to make it presentable.

John had to pee this time. He looked around for a nice place to do it and chose a wide pier of rocks and stones that stretched out beside the river. The rocks were big and lay steady so it was easy to walk out on them. He had to place his feet carefully to avoid slipping and falling into the river. The stream flowed just under him and he let his urine fall out on the surface of the running water. He was looking at the stream running from left to right. He nearly lost his balance for a second by looking at the movement. "My stream is crossing another stream," John was thinking to himself. Some sudden drops made rings on the water. Rings that grew and crossed each other while they followed the stream.

The sound of the river was fresh and it was a nice change from the sounds inside the car. Elsa sat with a cup and a sandwich already in her hands when John returned to the table. They had their coffee without talking. The rest from the car and the fresh air and the nature at the place caught their attention. The sound from the running water made it hard to speak gently.

"It's nice here!"

John had to speak loudly to Elsa to tell her that he enjoyed her piloting talent.

"Mmm." Elsa hid her face in the cup and John saw that she was smiling at her own thoughts.

John finished his coffee fast before it got cold. The air was nice to breathe.

6 - Thermodynamics

A fire. John was looking at some pieces of coal lying in a circle of small rocks. It would have been nice with a fire in the fireplace beside the table. He missed the heat radiation and the smell of tar and smoke from a live fire. The sound of the fire would drown in the sound from the stream. It takes time to make up a fire. Collect wood, tear it into pieces and put together a small heap of tiny twigs that could start a small glow hot enough to make thicker pieces of wood catch fire.

A fire runs on energy of its own that is consumed by new cold pieces of wood. It is only the energy not consumed by the cold wood that is radiated out to those who sit around it. Most of the radiated energy is lost as the energy goes out from the fire in all directions. Only the energy that happens to run towards your body is warming.

"A fire. It would be nice with a fire to get some heat." John shivered.

"We do not have time to make a fire. We will be warm in the car again. I like to get some fresh air and the smell of the forest. Can you feel that we are far north now?"

"I can't say that we are more north now from the smell of old trees and the dirt by the stream; but it's different, yes."

"We are close to the sea, too. The sea is just about five hour's drive from here, straight west. If the wind comes from the west you can smell the sea even here."

They put the things together and jumped into the car again. John was cold. He had no coat on over his jacket.

He did not like to wear too much when driving. In the back seat he had a thick coat, thick gloves and an ugly cap of wool. It was quite practical when he had to leave the car in bad weather.

When they were up on the road again John continued thinking about the waste of energy by the fire.

"Funny that energy is impossible to destroy but still it is so hard to keep under control. It is such a waste all the time. When we sit here in the car and want to get some energy from the petrol that is burnt in the engine in order to be heated, most of it just runs away. We can't just heat ourselves with it, we have to heat the whole car to get some of it to us."

"You don't know much about energy do you?"

"Well, I know a lot about energy pricing and the difference in practice between different sorts of energies. Like how oil and coal interact in the market and why the electric energy plants and companies are dominating the market situation."

"That's not energy, that is business. Have you ever heard about exergy?"

"That sounds like an Italian company in the energy business?"

"No! Exergy is the practical work performed by energy, when energy is changed from one qualitative level to another. Exergy is what drives the world, time, and everything. I listened to you when you were speaking about time and how saved time is transformed into values and money. You did not mention anything about the change of energy states that is what makes the time run at all. It is called the second law of thermodynamics."

"What is the first?"

"The first law of thermodynamics says that energy cannot be created, nor destroyed. There is also a third

131

law. Some people do not believe in these laws because they think it is interfering with their religion."

"How can you know so much about that?"

"My first husband was a nuclear scientist I told you. He taught me a lot. We used to talk about just about anything that he worked with. I was very interested. I read most of the books he read in his work. The transformation of energy is the basic engine for time to exist. Exergy is needed for any change to take place and time is crucial for the changes to appear in the right order. He was very very keen on calculations regarding big bombs and explosive power."

"I liked to make my own firecrackers when I was a boy. Maybe he felt like a boy with the biggest firecrackers in town?"

"Please do not underestimate his effort. His work was very important for national security."

"To keep safe against other boys with big firecrackers you mean?"

"Stop that nagging, he is dead and can't defend himself. Let him rest in peace, please."

"There are a lot of people like him running around today playing with big guns and bombs to keep the peace in place. What if they are more into the fun of big bangs than the peace?"

"My man was very gentle. We never fought or argued. He was very polite and understanding."

"Yes, he was just a scientist in the nuclear defence system. He was not the one who planned war and defence strategies and placed the orders. Einstein made the nuclear bombs understandable but you can't blame him for the bombing of Japan 1945."

"He was very friendly, I loved him."

"Sure. No question about that. But anyway, that was interesting about exergy. You mean that the happening, the event when energy is changed from one state to another, like in the engine of this car for example. The energy that is changed and causing work and rotation, heat and sound, you call that exergy. Why not just energy?"

"Because energy per se cannot be created or destroyed. The total mass of energy in the universe is constant, it is only changing form and location. The universe is seen as a complete system, all included, even a God if there is one. If there is something outside the universe then it is not the whole system. So all the energy in the system is there and nothing is added or subtracted from it. That mean that the laws of thermodynamics are also included in the system."

"I would call them conditions, not laws. Laws are written by politicians."

"The first law of thermodynamics says that energy cannot be destroyed. It can only be transformed into various forms. The second says that the quality or the usefulness of the energy is always decreasing. Every change takes some exergy to happen. There is no such thing as a perfect exchange. There is always a loss of some exergy. Over time more and more of the exergy is lost into oblivion.

"That is called entropy. In the end there will be no exergy, only entropy left in the universe. In the universe we have an amount of energy that is the same from the Big Bang to the end of time. But it changes its quality from exergy to entropy.

"We have billions of stars and clouds of energy all around in the universe and they are all sending their energy out. They are all losing exergy while the energy is going out into the space. The sun is heating up other colder planets like the Earth, Jupiter and Mars. For several billion years the exergy on other planets is raised by the received radiation from the stars.

"The net exergy on a planet depends on how much is received and how much of it is lost to space again. At the end of time all stars and planets have lost their exergy and the whole universe is just a grey mass of equal temperature all around. Everything goes from high temperature differences and order to low temperature and disorder."

"You are really talking big business now. I've long had the feeling that all things, every change, is driven by the force of the Big Bang. The Big Bang created all the stars and gas clouds that condensed into rocks and planets and after that everything tries to come back to the ground. Just like a toy propeller turns when you blow on it … But according to you, there are two aspects of energy: its indestructible Mass, and its changeable Quality. That sounds like two separate worlds?"

"Sort of that, yes. My man was working a lot with how different nuclear particles where acting in time. He was an expert on how the pressure wave expanded. Very small pieces of time. In some way it is like what happens in the big reality, when things are rotating and pendulating. It is just smaller values but similar maths behind it."

"Mathematical conditions must be the same everywhere, mustn't they? I mean 1+2=3 and so on?"

"Yes mathematical conditions are the same but small parts of energy, electrons and neutrons, are affected by magnetic forces and electric load in a way that big chunks like us are not."

"I have heard that the gravitation force is too weak to hold hydrogen down on Earth. Lots of hydrogen and helium gas is leaking out in space while rocks and stones are dragged down to Earth by the same force." John was not sure about exactly what gases were leaving the Earth but he felt that it did not matter. They were just talking about principal differences in nature.

"That is also why a small fly can bump into a window without getting hurt but if we run into a window at the same speed we get hurt. Small and big things differ. The weight/speed ratio is different."

"Hey! I have seen that! If I drive slower than 35 mph the flies and insects aren't crushed against the windscreen. In the summer when the car is clean and there are millions of insects and bugs in the air I prefer to drive slow just to avoid a dirty screen."

"That is one thing I like about November. No mosquitoes."

"They'll be back."

They passed Sveg without stopping. They were lucky and had green lights at the only junction with traffic light. John thought they should turn right but Elsa said that it was closer if they continued straight north over a mountain massive instead of rounding it. She wanted to see the skyline. John stepped on the pedal and the car accelerated along the road.

A stop of about half an hour makes the way longer in time equal to 25 miles. John tried to calculate how long it would take to arrive at Mary's. It would soon begin to get darker and he wished to drive as little as possible in the dark. There was just a little more than 100 miles left so if he stepped on it, they would do it in two hours.

Elsa sat quiet and looked out of the window. John was thinking his own thoughts to himself. It seemed obvious that energy, or exergy and time were connected to each other.

"Nothing happens without a change in the energy quality. A change of something just had to happen in the right order. No, order was not the right word. A lot of things that are happening are accidents and faults, fails and mistakes, crashes and stupid abnormal processes. Right order can't be the true word for it. Most of the world is abnormal," John was thinking.

"Or, just that everything is working through normality. From the extreme differences to the grey mess of boring indifference. But if the Big Bang made things happen by its force that came from one place, aimed out from the place where it started, how could things keep on happening in the opposite direction?"

John remembered a book he borrowed at the library, written by Stephen Hawking – *the Universe in a Nutshell*. He read it for his sons on a rainy day. John wanted to show them a picture of the universe because they had asked for it. In the book there were a lot of beautiful pictures of stars and planets. Time was illustrated as a big cone with a rounded base. Naturally, one of the boys asked what was outside the universe. John could not accept that illustration but the boys liked the book. "There must be something outside that cone for it to be complete," he was thinking.

He was thinking about energy and exergy again. He saw for himself in his mind an explosion and when it was over there was a huge cloud of scattered energy in the air and then it all started to behave by itself. "How come? The gravitation between particles building clouds of gas and material condensed into planets. Stars were born where nuclear reactions started when the critical mass was reached. The heat radiation from the sun is following the second law of thermodynamics and thus heating the Earth on its way, out in space.

That way the exergy on Earth must be increasing. But time on Earth, is that driven by the burning of energy?

"Oil is saved energy from the sun. The sun made the biological processes possible that resulted in thick layers of old dead biological material. This material was later pressed down into the ground, building layers of oil and coal under the rock. A process that took millions of years. Oil has a lot of energy, exergy, and can be used or misused in many ways. Until someone finds an idea to use the oil in a better way.

"Is that against or following the second law of thermodynamics? It takes energy to put something in order. It takes more energy to build a house than it takes to tear it down? The amount of energy is constant and time is driven by the change of energy from more useful to useless.

"No, time goes on even if there is no process running. That is what makes waiting so boring. Time goes on even when nothing is happening. More than enough time to experience how boring it can be to wait for a bus or for a friend to come."

John drove the car on the straight road north through the forest. Most of the trees along the road were pines and about the same size. Thousands of pines. The sky was grey and very few other cars were on the road. The only interesting thing was that they were slowly closing in on Mary. Poor Mary without food or money. He hoped that it would be worth the effort of going there.

His brain went on. "If you have something, or miss something, that is something real. Energy or money, time or space, it's all real. The amount of energy, the exergy, is about 'is' or 'not is' and can be measured as mass, weight, power. You see it when it is in action.

You can feel the weight of a brick, thrown in your neck and the impression it makes." It puzzled him.

He had to ask Elsa again. "Is there any law of thermodynamics that says whether two amounts of energy, or exergy, can be in the same place at the same time?"

"How do you mean?"

"As I said, can two lumps of energy sort of melt together to become one, like light and be separated later?"

"Well, rays of light can cross each other without interfering. But I do not think that the mass of two atoms or nuclear particles can be at the exact same location. There are attracting and repelling nuclear forces that keep them apart. They are doing a lot of research using particle accelerators where particles collide with each other. I do not think that would work if particles of energy could be in the same place. There would be no collision if they could be in the same place."

"I was thinking that if that is the case, then we can define space. Because there must be space and room so all these particles can have a place."

"That is no definition, that is a postulation. Thermodynamics can't be defined anyway because we are using energy and mass itself to measure it. You can't measure a potato with potatoes."

"But if there is a universe, with lumps of energy in it, then there must be a space in-between that shows that there is something around it? We are two different people and there is a short distance between us. It would not be fun if we were the same person sitting in the same seat. Still with two perspectives on the driving."

"I wouldn't find it amusing if you were like me."

138

"So there is energy, exergy. And there is space between. If there were no space between, there would only be one and only one lump of energy in the universe."

"So you think the Big Bang was just a creation of space amongst the energy in it as the energy can't be destroyed according to the first law?"

"Maybe. I like to talk with you. You are different from me in many ways but you make me think in new ways. I like to be surprised by you."

"I like to be your passenger. You are a good driver. I feel comfortable with you. You remind me of many many miles of travelling with my former men. But you are too young, lad. You are 40 years younger than me. I do not want to be accused of child molesting so there will be no sex!"

"I maybe have another view on sex. I think sharing thoughts and feelings is as good as sexual intercourse. There are other kinds of orgasms than just from traditional sexual exercises. The orgasm comes from inside, from deep inside, from your inner secret places that you do not know. If you want it to happen when you are together with someone else you must feel very sure about the other. Same with listening to someone else. I am confident, I can relax and listen to you."

"I feel comfortable with you. I rely on you. You would not be so safe from me if I were younger! I might have had many orgasms in your company!"

John was lost for words for a moment. He could feel another erection growing at these words. He looked at Elsa and saw her as a living woman. More alive than he had seen most of the women he had met before. She really was well aware of herself and what she felt about being a human being. He wished that she had been in his own age for a moment. With the experience of an

139

86-year-old. She really knew how to speak freely without being rude.

"I think we should keep it on a decent level. You are a wonderful woman, Elsa, but I think I am too young for you. I am fully satisfied with talking to you. You're really giving me head!"

"No, it is me that is too old. My body is too weak for sex. It could be dangerous to me. We can talk about sex but there is no use in doing it for real. Besides, I have had my portion already."

John took her hand and smiled. Her hand was warm and soft.

"If sex is so much more than just intercourse then maybe there is still some more to do. Travelling together is fine too, isn't it?"

"Sex is better."

"Yes."

7 - At the Top, and Down Again

John held Elsa's hand and kept the car on the road by holding his left hand on the wheel. It began to get darker. The light from the car was reflected on the traffic signs. They passed a big dark lake and a decayed farm with unused fields and a littered yard. Broken fences, dirty cars and rusty tractors were spread around. Trees growing close to the walls. He could see one single lighted window in the grey house. No other signs of life.

John tried to imagine what kind of life there was inside the house. Maybe the person who lived there was the last one in a long chain of farmers who had made their living out of these fields for centuries. No young successors taking up the tradition. No one that could be satisfied with working hard in the dirt for just food and shelter.

Farm living deserves a social structure, at least two strong young people that can share the work and its outcome. Someone to talk to and to rely on when times are hard. Someone to share the small glimpses of happiness and joy with. Loneliness can be very destructive. John knew that so well.

He felt much better driving around with Elsa beside him. The radio could not satisfy his need for someone to listen to. Elsa was alive and she could give an answer on anything that came up in his mind. Their relationship was unique and no one else's business so they could speak freely about just about anything. John began to think about values and time-saving again. He was curious about where the saved time came from. "Whose time is saved?"

"If the people at that place knew that there was fish in the lake but they couldn't catch them, what would the value of the fish be?"

"I don't understand? What fish?"

"Say, the people in that farm we just passed, if they knew that there were fish in the lake that they could eat if they just knew how to catch them. One day they found a method of catching a fish. That would be a great day, yes?"

"I grew up at the seashore. We had lots of fish all the time."

"Exactly. That is what I mean. If fish is nearly impossible to catch, then catching a fish has an enormous value. But if you have access to it all the time, then it has no value, because it takes no time to get one."

"Easy come, easy go. Billions spent on travelling to the moon." Elsa looked around to see if the moon was up.

"But what I was thinking about was this: if we invent better ways to catch fish, to get things done, when we are improving our ways to do things faster and better, when we are saving time and compressing the future so it comes closer to us, what happens is that we are depreciating the value of the fish.

"Say the only apple tree in the area is growing on the other side of a deep canyon and nearly impossible to reach. One day someone builds a bridge over the canyon so you can pick all the apples in one hour. At that time the apples are not so expensive any longer. The value of the apples are decreased by the bridge.

"No wonder people do not care so much about the environment any longer. We are so good at finding

142

what we need from nature today with all our machines so the value of the products from nature is almost nothing. Still, everything we eat is grown from the dirt in some way."

"So why are you trying to find an answer to this? Isn't it better to keep your own questions unanswered? To preserve their value."

"I just can't stop my brain from thinking and making up fantastic dreams. The unknown is worrying and it teases me to try to find what's in there. Like this road. I always want to look at what it is like behind the next bend."

"What are you looking for?"

"I really do not know that. I think I've got some kind of hunger for something new all the time. Like I want to complete my picture of the world or something. Everything I see is added to what I've seen before. What I like most is the moments when I see something that is fantastic. If I look carefully there is mostly something that I think is fantastic."

"How do you know that it is fantastic?"

"I don't know that. It is a feeling I get. It is a feeling that comes to me when I look at things. I can't find it consciously. It comes to me when I look and sort of forget what I am looking for."

"Sounds similar to what you said about sex. You release your self-control and let the response to the picture come to you from inside. From your deep insides."

"Ah, right! Eye orgasms!"

"Hey, take it easy now! Both hands on the wheel, please!"

"But I like it, I really do. Every time it is something new." John was drumming with his hands on the wheel.

"So you mean that this is different from the fishing. The value of every new fantastic find is the same because it is something new you see. If it was the same thing you found everytime when you were looking then the value should fall. You would be bored and blasé. But you do not get bored by your sight orgasms?"

"No, I don't think so."

"So you mean that to feel rich, to have the feeling of living a rich life, you should not strive to get more and more of material things because that lowers the value of each one. But instead you should try to not learn how to get more of it and that way keep the fascination high of how hard it is to catch the first fish?"

"Yes, that maybe keeps me happy but it does not please the producers of fishing rods. Sellers of bait and tackle do what they can to convince me to work hard so I can buy their things."

"What if you're hungry and need fish to eat?"

"Then I can buy fish from some fisherman. He's maybe bored about his job but that is a problem of his own."

"So how do you manage to get the money you need to buy the fish?"

"I do something boring just to make my living."

"Saving others' time but not yours?"

"Sort of, yes."

"So in some way you must get bored to make a living?"

"It must be possible to have a pleasant job."

"Is your job pleasant?"

"No, it is very lonely but it is easy money. I am only in it for the money. It is so easy for me to do because I have the right training, education and maybe some talent too. It is not hard for me to do but that also

144

makes it boring. Sometimes I get the feeling that they pay me to not have to do the work by themselves.

"But one nice thing about it is that it is based on reality, real meetings with real people. Despite telephone, Internet and mail. My work is still based upon live meetings. The people I meet and that I have to deal with, I meet them alive. There is so much in the interaction between me and our customers that can't be sent over a thin line of copper."

"I would not like to be at the other end of a copper line from you. I like to travel around in a car and watch the world. By the way how's the road? We are going to climb over a high pass soon. It can be tough if the road is frozen. Are there snow tyres on the car?"

"No, but the tyres are quite good so I think we can make it if the snow isn't too slippy. I'll drive slowly."

"I think you should try to keep the speed up."

"OK."

John could see that there was a thin layer of snow beside the road. It made it less dark to drive, but to drift away from the road, in this wild forest with nearly almost no people and no traffic, was not what he longed for.

"We will pass the Who Valley soon."

"Why 'Who' and not 'What'?"

"The name 'Who' has nothing to do with an unknown person I think. Names on places are usually ancient and have forgotten stories."

"Names are agreements. For every word we use, we must agree about its meaning to be able to understand each other. Every disagreement over the words we use causes a conflict. It can be the beginning of a new language, or a pun. It can be conscious or unconscious and sometimes it's just funny."

" — My dog has no nose. — So how does it smell? — Awful!"[16]

"That was a cheap one, wasn't it?"

"You asked for it. I saw Hitler say it on TV."

"But it is hard when people think they are using the same meaning for some words even if they are not. What is good for people and the economy, for example. Some people believe in violence to force people to behave and act in a certain way while other people believe in human sense and morality to make people behave in a civilized way. They both think they are good, but they keep a different definition of what the word 'good' means."

"I think you are a good driver and a good man." Elsa smiled as they arrived at the beginning of a long uphill stretch.

" — Oh please beat me! said the masochist. — No! Said the sadist." John leaned forward against the wheel to get a better look at the road while he pressed the accelerator to keep the speed up.

"How long is this uphill section?" The road did not look icy yet. It may have been gritted but he could not be sure. It was all black and looked wet as if the temperature was still above freezing point.

"A few miles only."

"A few miles? That is long! How high are we going?"

"I am not sure but we are going high up and then we are going down again on the other side. You are a good driver. I think you can do it."

John began to realise why there were no other vehicles on this road now. Every other driver must had chosen the longer road around the massive incline.

16 http://www.montypython.net/scripts/funniest.php

Only idiots and potential suicide candidates chose this route on days like this. Longer but quicker in the end as trucks used to get stuck on the slopes when the road was covered by snow. John had seen it many times.

"We have to do something if it is icy in the upper parts. I do not want to get stuck."

The rear wheels slipped. There were spots of ice on the asphalt. A sudden drift nearly forced them off the road. John began to think over the situation. He had no chains to put on. He had a blanket that he could cut into strips and wrap around the tyres. That would help but would not last for long. How would he fasten it to the wheel? Iron thread! He used to keep a long piece of iron thread in the boot under the spare wheel. Iron thread had helped him many times on the road. John pulled over and stopped in a small parking lot along the road.

"I thought you were going to keep the speed up for the hill?"

"I'm going to put something on the rear wheels to help." John opened the boot and found the big roll of thick iron thread. He picked up cutting nippers from the little toolbox. He worked fast with cold fingers and drew the thread through the holes in the wheel. He made a knot on every turn in case one circuit should break. He did not want to have a nest of iron thread rolling around.

Elsa went out to the forest for a minute and looked from a distance at his work. He had thread enough to place eight rounds on both the rear wheels. He went into the car and loosened the parking brake to roll slowly backwards a few feet, turning the wheel. Then he could reach the parts of the wheel that were against the road before. He could fill the gaps up with thread, and now they had a very temporary snowchain on the

147

rear wheel. John expected the thread to last a few miles until they reached the bottom on the other side. He had to drive carefully not to wear out the thread too early.

They set off again and they could hear a new rattling sound from the wheels. John took it very easy with the clutch to change gear. He thought that the way down would be the hardest because there he would not have as much weight on the rear wheels and there would not be much power to brake. As he assumed, the road began to turn white and frozen. The slope kept on up, straight up. No return.

"I have to take it very easy downhill." John was thinking about the exergy again.

"According to thermodynamics, we are now exchanging exergy from the petrol into height exergy."

"It is gravitation that draws us down again."

"I do not care who or what is drawing us, I want to come down safe." It seemed like the threads helped them up. He felt like the rear wheels get a better grip. If he stepped on the accelerator they certainly would, but he had to take it easy with the threads. He wanted them to last.

"Hey, now I think I get it. The weight of the car is one thing. Where it is or what speed and temperature it has is something different!"

"Naturally!"

"I mean that – what you said about the laws of the thermodynamic. The basic energy in the car is the steel and the rubber, plastic and glass. The atoms are mass and energy, but that is energy that just is. Stuck in some sort of stable eternal form. Atoms are as old as the universe right?"

"No. Atoms are quite solid but it is the neutrons and the protons that are the oldest. But for us that is no direct problem. Unless we aren't exposed to nuclear radiation."

"Well, that is the mass, the weight of the car, independent of where we are. And then I understand that the exergy is the useful part. The amount of petrol that can be burnt. The speed of the car if it hits something. The height over the sea which can change this trip into sleighing down the hill. They higher we climb the further we fall. I'd like to take a breath at the top if we get there."

"Ahh! Isn't it beautiful? I love to look at the mountains!"

John did not answer. He had all his concentration on keeping the car running and keeping the pace up. A big skiing centre with lifts and restaurants, hotels and bus parking showed up. It looked empty. No people. The lifts stood still and there were no cars or buses in the parking area. Dark windows. The dead look gave John bad feelings.

The slope ended and John found a place to park by the side of the road. They were at the top now. John went out to look for the threads on the tyres. They seemed like they would last for a few more miles. They were bent backward and stretched taut to the pattern. He went into the car and the warmth again. Elsa poured some coffee in a cup that she handed to him.

"Are you nervous about going down?" She looked at John.

"No, but we have to take it easy. It will take us some time. If it is too slippy I think I can drive with the right wheel at the side of the road where there's gravel. There isn't any snow so the gravel will be enough to stop if we need to. But I have to drive slowly to keep the car on the road if we only have a brake effect on one side of the car."

"So now you aren't the best friend of exergy?"

"Well, it'll at least be cheap to go down! It takes no petrol." John tried to figure out how long it would take to come down. He had not checked the mileage before the slope started. But it felt like it took about 10 minutes to drive, the time to put on the iron thread excluded. If the speed was around 30 mph it must be about five miles up. If the slope ended at the same level on the other side it would be about five miles down. "A lot of things can happen in shorter distances," John was thinking.

"But where do they come from? These conditions that determine that it is exergy or energy? Is that just a slump or is it written somewhere?"

"Do you believe in God?"

"No. I've never believed in that idea. That some grey-bearded old man is sitting on a cloud and running the world holding a huge steering wheel. Listening to each and every person's personal wishes and prayers. That may be natural for people who are used to following an authority, like a father or a local boss that sets the rules and regulations."

"Scientists sometimes believe in a God, as a summary of the rest of what they do not yet have a full understanding of. Like the conditions behind the laws of the nature."

"These laws are the same all the time, aren't they?"

"Yes, otherwise they would just be temporary forces. Scientific research is to find what is forever. What is eternal and timeless."

"There must be some kind of mighty force behind it all but I'm sure that mighty force is no kind of thinking individuality. The conditions for it all, the natural laws and all, have to be the same from the beginning to the end. It doesn't work if some thinker behind it suddenly decides to change the rules of the game. It would be ridiculous if some prayer would suddenly manage to change the universal prerequisites. No, the rules must be firm and set from the beginning. But how can there be time and something that is timeless simultaneously? Which came first?"

"That must be the timeless."

"But if there is something that is unbiased by time, then it must also be before time?"

"Hard to say that. Most scientists believe that the creation of both time and the conditions for time coincide. Before time there was nothing."

"But you said that the law of thermodynamics postulated that energy could not be destroyed or created. If there is a beginning of time then the energy in the universe must have been created."

"That is because from the start of the time, the distance to this point is infinite. It doesn't matter how far you look back, what kind of magnifying glass or method you use to look for the start, the beginning will always be too far away."

"But what about the Big Bang then? That event must have happened sometime?"

"I have heard a lot of numbers for that and I think that the Big Bang is supposed to have occurred about 13 billion years ago. A lot of measuring of how galaxies in the space are moving is the key to solving the problem. It is possible to measure how galaxies are moving away from each other. At the Big Bang, all matter must have been located at one single point."

"Another theory to be justified. What if the matter came from two locations and the Big Bang was just a big hit, a big collision? Maybe we are just a big experiment in a giant particle accelerator?"

"Well, well, who knows? More coffee?"

"No thanks. I have to take us down safe and sound. But I am still confused about these conditions behind the laws of thermodynamics. The first is about mass, the energy that can't be created or destroyed. Only moved or transformed into other kinds of energy. And two pieces of energy can't be at the same location or they will collide or react in some way.

"That means that energy and mass is kind of a hard real stuff, the hard reality. And then as two pieces of energy can't be at the same place simultaneously, we can be sure that there must be a room, a space between them. That means that there must be some kind of relation with a measurable distance between pieces of energy. These relations must be placed under conditions, timeless conditions, that tell how pieces of energy are related to each other. Is there a law of thermodynamic for that too?"

"There is one, one that is called the law number zero of thermodynamics, which, as you say, postulates that a temperature at one place is also the same temperature at another place if the thermometer is showing the same digit. Maybe you can call that evidence for spaceless conditions. Same rules everywhere."

"Then you said that the quality of the energy, which is the exergy, the quality is changing. The same mass, or energy can have different qualities?"

"Yes, the amount of energy is not the same as the quality."

"So then the timeless conditions for energy must consist of more than one single set of conditions. Sets that are independent of each other. Different and independent sets for amount, time, space and quality for example. That sounds huge."

"I have never thought about it in that way. It sounds rather complicated."

"I thought we had enough problems already. But in one way this is no problem, because this is something that has always been and will always be, right? The answer to that mystery doesn't help us on our way down."

"You'd better pray. The wind comes from behind, from the sea. If that wind is warmer than the air beyond the top there will be more snow on the way down."

"If there is more snow then the iron threads will last better. Let's go before it is too dark. But I have an idea how to better our odds."

"What's that?"

"We need as much weight as possible on the rear wheels to get maximum brake power. If you lie down in the back of the car we will get better balance of the weight."

"It is fine for me if you say so. But I want to have the seat belts on in case we are going to end up in the ditch."

"There are no seat belts in the boot, but I have some ratchet tie-downs that could do."

John and Elsa got out of the car. He opened the back door and moved the luggage around to make space. Elsa crawled into the car from the back and lay down on the floor with the end of the bedroll under her head. John put a blanket around her and tied her up with the two ties. He fastened the hooks at four steel loops in the corners of the boot and stretched the mechanism tight enough to hold her in place but without

153

suffocating her. John double-checked the ties and closed the door carefully.

He examined the iron threads on the tyres again and tested the snow on the road with his shoe to see if it was hard, sticky or soapy. It was a thin layer of snow, about half an inch, and there was some ice under it. If the snow wasn't frozen to the ice it would be very slippy on the way down as that would make two different layers between the tyres and the asphalt.

"I better take it very slow," John was thinking. "If this takes 10 minutes more it is better than not making it at all."

"Are you ready for a ride?" John shouted to Elsa.

"If you take it too easy I will fall asleep!" she answered from the back.

"I'll do my best. Here we go!"

John started the engine and drove slowly out onto the road. The slope down began rather gently and he let the second gear run with no gas so the idling engine would resist any attempt to accelerate the car. John kept his eyes on the speedo-meter and held the right wheel near the side to be able to brake in the gravel. The ride was gentle and very quiet as the snow layer became thicker and it was soft. John felt it was like driving on a white carpet.

After a while he began to get bored of the low speed and applied his foot easily on the accelerator and let the car roll little faster at about 20 mph. The road was wide. There was a slight bend to the left far down and there was no oncoming traffic. John put on the cassette player with a tape that played Georg Frideric Handel's *Water music*. Nice and relaxing. John felt that he had full control and was convinced that in 20 minutes they would be down at the bottom of the valley.

After the bend to the left he could see that the slope became straighter but bolder, much bolder, and he pushed the brakes carefully to slow down the car a bit. The rear wheels locked immediately and caused the car to drift a little. Elsa shouted in the back. John's pulse rose and he had to try to find some gravel at the side to get a better hold for the wheels.

As he closed in to the side he felt that the softer material slowed down only the right side of the car which drew the car to the right. This nearly made him drive off the road and into the deep ditch so he had to quickly abandon that idea. He had to come back into the middle of the road and try to keep the car rolling in the right direction.

The engine rolled faster now without any gas and he couldn't gear down. The slope down was bending slightly left. He saw that this was only the beginning of a long trip down. No oncoming traffic, but if this went on he wouldn't be able to stop the car. Twenty-five mph. A little too fast; the engine was roaring on second gear and the rear wheels began to slide again. He geared up to the third to have some grip left. It was impossible to keep the speed down. John released the gear after some seconds and now he was powerless against the rising speed. The engine went down to idling and it all became very silent except for the music.

"If I am going to hell it will be to music," John thought while he watched the oncoming road run under the car.

After the next slight bend he could see that the road went straight down and far away it went up again! Just as high as where they came from. The road was all white and he realized that the next problem would be to get up the next slope again. He put it in the fifth gear

155

and pressed on the accelerator. The car gathered speed and they ran down the hill at 70 mph. He was amazed at the mix of the silent road and the music. He could see a long white cloud of snow behind him in the mirrors. Like he was driving a space-ship in another world.

No sound from Elsa. There were no time to stop and let her sign some kind of paper that told how she had let herself be tied up by her own free will. He had to step on the accelerator to give the car enough speed to climb up again. Now there was even more snow and the road up again wasn't as straight as it was on the way down. The car drifted but John could feel that the threads on the rear tyres did their duty. Elsa's role in the process was reduced to just physical weight but very important. The more he accelerated the easier it was to drift and control the direction.

At the end of the slope up again he felt that he had enough speed and geared down again to see what it was like after the top. But it was not the top. It was just a short flat stretch and after that a new slope upwards. John had to step on the accelerator again to try to get more speed to be able to reach the top of the next one.

He could see the headlights from something coming down towards him. When closer he saw that it was a truck with a wide snowplough mounted at the front. John could see the snow squirt high to the left side. He kept to speed like he was doing a chicken race. He concentrated his sight at a point slightly to the right of the snowplough where he could possibly pass.

"oooOOWHAMPpppssshh...."

Elsa shouted loudly in the back. Lucky for John that she was tied down like a turkey and could not move. They passed the snowplough which left a wide cleared track behind. John held over to the clean left side of the
156

road and took a breath. His mouth was dry and his tongue got stuck. Now it was easy to get to the top of the hill.

At the top he could see some lights far away. The road was still icy but clear of snow on the left side so he slowed down and let the car run down in third gear with no press on the accelerator. This time it went all the way down and he could keep the speed low until the last bit where the slope became steeper again. John saw that the road bent very sharply in the far end. The road was cleared of snow but icy, and now he had no other chance than stepping on the brakes to try to find some contact. But using the brakes made him unable to steer. He had to rely on the rear wheels that were clutched to the roaring engine.

The rear wheels couldn't hold longer and the car was slipping down faster and faster. The dark road with the bend ran against them. But naturally there was a happy ending to this little ride. The ice had melted in the last 100 yards. The tyres screamed like a landing aeroplane and the engine roared before John realized what was happening. He released the clutch and used the brakes, which worked on the front wheels also, to slow down and enter the bend carefully.

They were down again. The bend ended with a crossing and he turned north. Far away he could see the big misty lake with its islands. They had only about one hour left to drive to Mary's. John pulled over and stopped the car. He got out on shaking legs. He opened the back door to see how Elsa was doing. He loosened the ratchets and helped her to crawl out from the boot.

"Oh, oh oh, I thought I should die! What was that crashing sound? I made me so-o scared!"

"We met a snowplough. Lucky for us. I don't think we should have made it otherwise. This last slope was tough. I would have had a hard time explaining if I'd crashed with an old lady tied up in the boot."

"I would kill you if you did!" Elsa took some steps to stretch out her limbs. She looked happy, like she had enjoyed the ride.

"One hour left to Mary's. Do you think you can make it?"

"Ha, sure! I have done worse trips than this. I remember a trip when I was young and the driver was sick in his stomach and he had to sit on a bowl while driving. Phew, that smell!

"Come, let's go again. I can't wait to see the lake and the bridges."

"It's beginning to get dark so maybe there isn't so much to see."

"There are always lights on the bridges. Watching the city from a distance at night is so beautiful."

"I have to check the tyres first." John picked up the thread nipper and cut away the rest of the threads. Most of them were already broken and could cause damage to the car if they were left on the wheel. He wound all the pieces together in a nest and put them back under the boot floor beside the spare wheel and closed it.

Back again in the seat behind the wheel, John realized that his arms were shaking. The rush down against the bend was repeating in his mind and he felt that he had to have a break. He had been driving since the morning and this wasn't the everyday way of driving around. His brain was filled up with both thoughts and pictures.

"What about a pause if we can find some café or something along the road?"

158

"I've still got some coffee in the thermos. And some bread and an egg. If they aren't smashed." Elsa picked up her bag from the floor.

"OK, that sounds fine to me. I think I need some rest too but I can take a nap in the seat for a few minutes to reset my sight. These last miles have been hilarious."

"I can take a nap too. It wasn't too comfortable for me, either. I was preparing to die!"

"Me too!" John laughed, he began to laugh loudly for a while.

"Yes, that was a real ride! I would rather like to see that on TV! I am really happy that we made it. You said that I was at one with the car and that is right. I was totally absorbed by the machine and how it behaved on the slope. I had no other feelings than how the machinery was involved in the situation. I had no time to be scared, but now I am shaking all over."

"I think I would be happy to not see anything." Elsa picked up the coffee thermos and poured a cup for John. He took the last egg and a piece of bread with nothing on it. The coffee was half-cold and he drank it in one go.

Elsa went back to get a blanket and put it over them in the front seat. John showed her how to adjust the backrest of the seat so it was more comfortable and possible to lie down. John did the same with his seat and leaned back under the thick blanket. He took off his shoes, loosened his belt and closed his eyes. He wanted to be mentally prepared to meet Mary but first he must clear his brain from the last few puzzling hours. He began imagining the trip backwards from where they were now. He could see the trip from outside and the car was going backwards in his mind, as he recalled every memory of the trip in reverse order. He enjoyed the picture of a snowplough moving backwards. Collecting the snow from the ditch and placing it on the road in a smooth layer. When he got back to the restaurant at Mora he fell asleep.

8 - Big Fish and Big-Box Money

John awakened slowly to the sound of a car passing by. A light beam turned around over his face. He kept his eyes closed and listened to the sounds around him. Elsa was snoring beside him under the blanket. He could feel her hand on his lap and his trousers were open. A grand erection tickled him. He was warm and his whole body was relaxed. Outside the wool it was cold. His feet were warm but outside the blanket and touched the cold floor.

John wanted to stay in this perfect state of rest and ease as long as possible. His brain was cleared and washed. His body was in a perfect state of rest as long as he did not try to move. There was nothing to disturb his biological process. Socially there was peace at the moment and his brain was idling. He was listening to his own breath and he could feel his heart pumping slowly, like waves rolling inside his limbs. The blanket was itching his bare penis but if he just stayed still it was comfortable enough. He knew that it would come to an end sooner or later. There was no opportunity for intercourse yet and he preferred to let biology stay subordinate to the social forces.

Elsa was still in a deep sleep. John listened to her breath. She snored rather loudly now and then. In-between she was very quiet, so quiet that he wondered if she was breathing at all. He took her hand. It was warm. He moved his fingers slowly and felt her soft skin.

He tried to imagine what this hand had been into through time – work, love and pain. Hands are involved in almost everything in human life. Her hand

161

had been cooking food for people around her for more than seven decades. She had used it to eat every day since she learned how to feed herself. Holding water to drink. Brushing her teeth and combing her hair. Dressing and undressing again. Washing her skin. It had caressed lovers and struck against bad behaviour. It was a means for social expression that had been involved in life for so many years. It had held the steering wheel of many cars, thousands of miles around the world. And it felt kind to hold. John had begun to like her. He had no clear picture of what it meant. He could feel some kind of pleasure by just holding her hand under the blanket in the dark.

Maybe he had a bad conscience about the risk he took earlier in the ride down the mountain. He didn't want to see her hurt. He felt that she had something to do with his own life. Maybe he was a bit grateful to her wide open mind that provoked his own thinking, but not as a disruption, more like some kind of gentle support for his curiosity and his wildest questions about life and all.

John's experience was that a narrow-minded person wouldn't catch on at all. Elsa's mind was open for anything new. John felt assured that he could ask her just anything without making her upset. "I've never felt so free in my mind before," he was thinking. "Her nuclear scientist husband must have been a very lucky man."

John began thinking about what he meant by freedom and free will. He knew that free will was nothing absolute, more like something possible. Like some kind of room for choice. An area where the future reality is not yet definite or determined. "To the extent that we are able to predict the future by repeating a
162

process, like baking bread, to that extent we are conducting free will under circumstances that are known. But when we have to accept our own shortcomings before the unpredictable, to that extent we are bound to accept the causality of the undefined reality. In that case we are experiencing a part of the future that is determined by something that is not determined.

"Freedom is just like a hole in the fence of established boundaries. No dogma is complete, there is always a way out somewhere. The task is just to find the tear in it. It must be a very suffocating feeling to not have access to that hole."

"Do I feel free now?" he asked himself. "Yes, my biological process is idling. I have nothing that hinders me more than the gravitation against the chair and the blanket upon me. I have thousands of opportunities. Some bad and some better. Elsa is my friend and we share the same goal at the moment. But outside the car it is cold. That is bad in the long run because the heat inside will leak out. No heat is brought in beyond the burning of exergy in our bodies at the moment. In a while we will get hungry again and we have to refill our magazine of calories."

John still did not want to open his eyes. He started to hum a simple melody. He hummed a waltz he learned by heart when he was a boy It was a waltz about yearning for love in the blue faraway forests. He did not remember the words. But the melody was enough to understand it.

Elsa stopped snoring and became quiet. John went on humming and took up the melody again and again. It went more easily for every time round so he began to enjoy it himself, too. He wished that he knew the words, too, so he could strengthen the expression even more. John was sure that Elsa had awoken and was listening. It was nice to do something for her pleasure to pay her back for the company in some way.

Elsa took a deep breath. John opened his eyes and could see a star in the sky in the east.

"Oh, I had such a nice dream. I was awakened by your song. I felt like I was still dreaming when I heard your humming. I was dreaming that I was lying on a bed, floating in a boat on the Nile river. There was a naked handsome man at the rudder singing ancient songs to please the Gods."

"I envy you for that. I had a nice sleep, too. But I do not remember any dreams, I just feel very relaxed and reset. Thanks for the company." John was still holding her hand.

"What time is it?"

"Three-forty. We have been sleeping for half an hour."

"We really needed that. It feels like hours since we went down that hill. But now it is beginning to get dark. I think we should go on again. Mary is waiting for us."

Elsa rose up and put away the blanket, adjusted the back rest to sit up again and stuffed the blanket into the back seat. John put his shoes on again and corrected his clothing. He went out to stretch his body and crossed over the road to pee on a tree. The air was misty and cold and he was shivering a bit. "Time to warm up the car again," he was thinking.

They went away again along the road. Now they kept silent as if they were trying to preserve the magic from the boat on the Nile. John drove slowly, the road was free from snow. Houses and farms along the road showed some small lights. The world around was dusky and full of secrets.

After a while they saw some yellow lights on the horizon. They decided that it must be the lights of Eastersand. But they were on the wrong side of the big lake.

"How do we get over to the east side? Are we going around the whole lake?"

"There are bridges between the islands so this is the shortest way there, but not the fastest. Years ago there were ferries."

The first long bridge took them over to an island with a high mountain in the centre. There was no ice on the lake. The water was warmer than the air so the water was covered by slowly rising mist. It looked like thin figures were making a parade along the surface. The road on the island followed the border north. It was narrow and curvy. High brown knotty tree trunks at both sides, close to the road, making a picture of an ancient alley of mysterious creatures. John drove silently and devotionally alongside the lake. Elsa seemed to enjoy this part of the journey.

A few miles later they arrived at another bridge. This one was bigger and had lights on both sides like a starship that had landed on the water by the island and was tied to the shore.

"Oh, I love bridges. They are so beautiful. It is such a miracle that mankind can create such beautiful bridges."

John had a hard time seeing any beauty in a bridge. "It is just a mechanic construction decorated with electric lights like an amusement park," he was thinking. But he kept that to himself so as not to hurt her feelings and positive mood. John had built timber bridges himself. Not big but strong enough to carry tractors and cars on his parents farm. "Beauty must be something that is alive," he was thinking. "But maybe that has to do with how different women and men may look at the world."

They came up on the next bridge. Elsa had her sight fixed on the city at the other side of the lake. At a distance the city looked like a big machine. "A construction made to maximise the making of money," John was thinking. "It is lit up so people can use all hours of the day and night to move around and meet other people and conduct their business, share work and find information. The shorter the distance the better the economy as the time used for every moment is minimized."

"Do you know that there is a rumour, a saga, that there is a huge monster in this lake?"

John looked around from the bridge as though he thought he could find a monster right there and then. "There is no clear evidence for that, I think?"

"No, naturally, but they sell boat trips to curious people and tourists that hope to see the monster. There is also a big reward for any evidence for the monster."

"Financial positivism: Anything that can be sold or bought is real! Just like sending the first man to the moon or finding the Higgs boson particle[17] at CERN. Anything that makes people curious can be bought and sold, to a very, very high cost just because it is so impossible and time-consuming to find it.

"I was thinking about what I realized before about the fishermen. The better the equipment they have, the lower the value of the fish. Eventually no one likes to fish anymore and the fish will be close to extinction just

---

17 http://en.wikipedia.org/wiki/Higgs_boson_particle

because of their lowered value. In the end the fish will be caught in masses and served as food for chickens or fur farmers."

"Isn't that a very depressing view?"

"Yes, but what if it is true? We would be better dreaming about giant mystery finds than wasting millions of the last ones on the rubbish heap because they were so easy to pick at the end of the harvesting technique. I think it would be better if life was full of fascinating mysteries than crowded with cheapness and junk. You know that I have thought about that many times, especially when I meet entrepreneurs all over the country. What they all are making profit on is producing things more and more cheaply.

"Competition is the key to and the cause of that phenomenon. To be able to make money on your own and survive the competition you have to find something that you can deliver to your customers at a lower cost than your competitors. One must choose the appropriate Competitive Strategy[18].

"The market, the buyers are always looking for the cheapest buy. They do not always want the best quality but more often the cheapest. Because the price, the amount of money you pay, is easier to evaluate compared to the quality of the thing you buy. Great effort is put into how to produce things cheaply. Cheapness is killing the skill and mastercraft, how to make good things that will last. All the marketing with words like 'Quality, Best Buy, Guarantee etc.' is to hide the very fact that it is nothing else but cheap."

John continued: "McDonald's, for example are making billions of dollars by producing cheap food that you cannot make better by yourself. All the

---

18 M E Porter; "Competitive Strategy"

burgers they deliver, the money they receive for the burgers, is won from competitors that produce more expensive but better food. Instead of growing skill and expertise in the customers in how to cook tasty and healthy food we have a decreasing and depleted food culture.

"People spend billions on building decent-looking kitchens with luxury machines but they do not know how to use them. Carpenters are losing their skilled mastercraft and jobs because the market, the buyers, ordinary, decent normal people, prefer cardboard boxes for wardrobes and cupboards from IKEA. The buyers prefer to give their money to manufacturers of cheap doors made of pressed chipboard instead of doors of real genuine wood that last for centuries. Houses blow away as sticks and straw in the first hurricane like the little pig's house. Who's to blame, the customer or those who market the trash? Well, those who makes most money from it should have the strongest urge to act responsibly.

"Think about all the fantastic cars that were made in the fifties. They were beautiful and robust. If you knocked on a fender the steel would ring like a church bell. These cars needed no safety belts. They were modern at that time and could have been technically refined in another way from today's small over-electrified tin cans. The skill to make them is dead. The workers don't get paid for that skill anymore and the knowledge is dying.

"Japanese samurai warriors stood firm in their tradition and competence. They wanted wars to be decided by noble fighting with sword and spear so that the victory should go to the best men. But most of them were killed by modern machine guns in a few battles in the 19th century.

"Most conflicts can be solved by negotiations and discussion. If people have a different opinion, which is the natural state, then it is a question of how to make different opinions meet. It should be a rhetorical and pedagogical matter, not a matter of violence.

"Any bad social manners by a person are learned and controlled by his evaluating system, not much by his biological instinct. If you want him to act differently you must look at his values. To change a person's values you will do better by using pedagogical methods than pure force or red tape.

Terrorists have tried to change the normative values for centuries by placing strategic bombs in public places. How many of the victims and their relatives have turned their values towards being more positive to the terrorist view? Not so many as expected. That is my guess. Fundamentalists would be much more dangerous to the post-Victorian society if they cut their hair and learn to breakdance, sway their hips and dress like Lady Gaga!"

Elsa listened with half an ear while she looked at the lit city on the right-hand side of the bridge.

"Here, you should take a right here so we can reach the next bridge."

"Another bridge?"

"Yes, we have come to the other island now and we must go into the city to buy some food for Mary. Don't forget our mission."

John had to look to both sides to come into the right lane on the bridge which led straight into the heart of the city. It was easy to find the way to a shopping centre. John just had to follow the signs. He found a multistorey car park and drove into it. He had to ascend two floors to find an empty lot. The shopping centre was planned so it was possible to drive straight in and do all the shopping you needed and drive away again without being outdoors.

They went into the centre by a red door and took the elevator down to the base. Elsa grabbed a trolley and rolled it into a grocery store. She first headed for the greens and vegetables and filled the trolley with potatoes, carrots, cucumber, onion and cauliflower. She found kohlrabi, parsnips and black roots, garlic and tomatoes. The trolley was already half-full.

Elsa ran on again, she had a tremendous speed in the shop and John had a hard time following her. She picked from the shelves bread, grains, flour, butter, milk and honey. She found two big boxes of wine, one red and one white, and some beer. At the fish counter she ordered salmon, herring and crabmeat. At the meat counter she ordered pork and beef, bacon and different types of sausage in tiny little paper parcels.

Elsa knew Mary well after living and working with her for extended periods so she knew her preferences well. She was in charge for this part of the mission and John just had to follow her. He spent most of the time looking around, listening to the sounds in the store. He smelled plastics, sweat and print colour from the packaging.

There were all kinds of synthetic and real sounds. People arguing and mumbling. Crash and squeak sounds from the trolleys. An elderly man calling home on the mobile phone to ask about some brand of taco chips. A young woman asking the staff where to find the hair shampoo. Kids crying and kids running around playing hide and seek. Small loudspeakers in the ceiling above the shelves that was supposed to stimulate the customers' buying instincts, like the sound of sea at the fish section. He heard a mooing cow at the milk cooler. Sounds from exotic birds at the vegetables.

There were advertising monitors at the ends of the shelves showing some phony presentation of a new kind of scouring pads. From floor to ceiling a million things to buy. All equipped with fluorescent tags that said "Cheap! Buy now! Opportunity! Sale! Big Deal!" It was so much information coming from all directions. For a moment John forgot to keep an eye on Elsa so he lost her.

John turned back. He started to look around but could not see here anywhere. He began to walk towards the checkout to see if she were standing there in one of the queues. She was not there either. He went to the entrance again and followed the path they had taken from the start. It was hard work concentrating on looking for Elsa in this crowd and in the storm of information of things to buy.

John remembered that Elsa was so funny-looking as she hung over the trolley and looked down at the floor when she moved around in the store. He was looking for a grey figure with a green beret and a red skirt. His eyes was collecting information. His brain tried to sort out from all these pictures something that matched the search criteria. No match. He made another lap and tried to find a place with a general overview of the store but it was more like a labyrinth.

John made another attempt. This time he went from the checkouts and backwards against the stream of customers and trolleys. He looked systematically from left to right until a red-checked rear popped up into his visual field. He found Elsa with her head deep down in a freezer looking for ice cream.

"I am looking for the dark chocolate cream spiced with extra-hot red chilli."

"I lost you for a while."

"Really? I've been here all the time."

"Here at the freezer?"

"No, here in the supermarket of course. I am almost ready now."

The trolley was filled and they went to the checkout. They helped each other to place all the goods on the conveyor belt so the cashier could put the numbers into the register. Elsa showed her credit card and signed for the purchase with her code of four digits. John was standing at the other end. He put the shopping in paper bags and put the bags back in the trolley so they could take them to the car. Elsa bought some tulips in a plastic twist and placed them on the top of the goods.

Back at the car again, they put the bags on the floor of the back seat of the car so they would not fall over. John went back with the trolley and picked up the coin deposit for it. He was a bit dizzy in his head from all the disturbance at the shop but he felt refreshed in his legs from the walking. He planned to take a longer walk after they arrived at Mary's. It was not far away now.

They took the same bridge again back to the island called Freysland. They followed the road west. Passed an airforce base, went down to a new bridge and up again. The skyline turned yellow and looked like it had caught fire when the sun on its way down managed to shine in under the clouds.

"Now we're back on track. Next stop will be Mary's house." Elsa declared with a ceremonial voice.

"I'm really looking forward to that," John answered. He was hungry again. He checked the petrol level. They still had a lot of petrol to use. At the top of the hill they saw a huge area of building projects scattered with strong lights. John's first thought was that it had something to do with the airforce base. Then he saw that it was the building of a new shopping centre. This was not so far from the next main crossing of two roads. The one that went east-west and the road going north from the city. A perfect place for a shopping centre to serve customers coming by car.

The buildings were wide and high. Shiny white and with the facades arranged in a half-circle like a giant stadium or theatre. On the facades there were places for advertising and giant signs for the different brand names. The entrances were fanciful constructions, higher than the rest of the building, all to make a ceremonial impression at the entrance to the shopping centre.

"Look, Elsa, these big-box stores are the modern churches!"

"I do not see any church there!"

"Yes, these are the modern churches because people today believe more in Price than in God. Instead of going to church and trying to be a better Christian they spend more money and effort believing in that they are making their lives better by finding bargains and cheapness. This religion is the consumerism, the belief in fair and low prices."

"You said you do not believe in God yourself so why do you complain?"

"Because I think that this is even worse. Christians and Muslims try to be better humans, most religious teachings is a kind of school that makes people behave better socially. But consumerism is only driven by economics. Economics is the crucial part of greatest importance behind most political and entrepreneurial decisions. Any decision that is not economically defendable is a weak and bad decision. Consumerism is the major contributor to the GDP. If people buy things then the people get jobs and they will pay taxes to the government and enterprises will gain profit. Religious devotion does not contribute much to welfare."

"Aha, yes I understand. So instead of promoting churches and religious worship the local government is, rather, promoting shopping centres and bank loans. The more people buy, the more jobs and the more profits. But most government people talk a lot of their faith and how much they believe in their God."

"That's just a marketing facade. Every president must show moral values that correspond to the voters' belief. The voters maybe do not know that their real faith is placed in money, price and being rich." John sounded a bit upset. Elsa wondered what he had been through.

John continued, "We don't need things. We need fresh water, life energy and minerals. We need shelter from natures' threats. We need biological stimuli like the taste and smell from natural foodstuffs. We need a social atmosphere with good friends and meaningful work. Labour doesn't always have to be paid for by private customers. A public need that is satisfied by being a lifeguard, litter-picking or ringing the church bells is just as good. Instead of selling crap to customers you can do something that is decided on by the local council. When they decide to build public schools they buy. They pay with the taxpayers' money. We need free access to information and the right to free speech and opinion."

"Don't we have that already through the commercial system that satisfies everyone's personal taste of what he wants to buy?"

"If the purpose is to fulfil a good life it is OK. If it all is about getting rich, being a celebrity without any other content than a fat bank account, then the purpose of the commercial system is a tragedy. I think it's all about confidence. If you believe that the meaning of life is getting a lot of money, then it is OK for you.

"But those who know that there is a difference between inorganic, organic, social and intellectual values; those who know how to distinguish these levels; those who know that, they will think different, their values are different."

"So what's wrong with being rich?"

"Being rich is just having control of a large amount of money. That doesn't mean that you are happy. Being rich is a measurable way to easily define a person's celebrity in a society. Being rich by your own capabilities means that you are good at taking sound decisions on economic issues. The whole civilisation of today is built on people making sound economic decisions.

"In every question to the board there are a number of alternative choices. To evaluate them you need independent variables. The calculations must be measurable with a common system. The dominating variable is the economic profit, the outcome from each of the alternatives. The yield from every possible choice. You don't build an enterprise, a shopping centre or a nuclear plant just because someone wants it to be there. There is too much money involved for that. There must be an economic reason behind the decision. Decisions are taken because the members of the board think that it will give more money back than the costs for it. There is money to get from it, profit and return on investments, employment and tax income, Gross Domestic Product and economic growth."

"That sounds very natural to me."

"Yes it does, in an economic sense it is absolutely true. Our time should be named the time of Economism as economic sense is dominating our rational mind in big business as in small business. Worship of God is no longer the main issue. Religious faith and piety has lost its power.

"Since the middle of the 19th century it is money that has commanded our life. Celebrity is mainly possessed by the persons that have got rich by their own power. They have the highest reputation in the society as we think that they know best what decisions to make in any question. We no longer ask the bishop, the imam or the pope for the right answer, but the president of the big self-made company."

"I don't have so much money. I have to look for things that are cheap."

"You are just a slave under your mind then. You can be smarter and choose how to use your money and compare the price with the real value to you. The better you know the value to you, the better deals you make. The price is only the seller's view of it. He cares less about your view, as long as he gets his money. The value of it to you should be higher than the price. The value is what you get. The price is the money you trade away for it. You should concentrate on the value you get from the buy, not what you give away. Petrol is cheap. Very cheap."

"Yes sir! I am very happy to do this trip!"

"There is too much attention paid to the price I think. But the men in charge cannot take decisions upon the alternative values. They don't believe in values that are not measurable. They are dependent on price as the lowest common denominator. They must rely on price, that the price behind every single number in the calculation is right. Without the premise of a true price it is impossible to make an economic decision. Faith in Price has replaced God."

"Uuh, you are scaring me!"

"Not to mention how they feel when they have to take decisions that cost money. Like taxes, charity or cultural issues. Taxes are paid to and managed by politicians that have gained power without the urge of being economically smart. These people might be clever on other kinds of values but numbers and business decisions aren't their strongest suits. That is probably why they choose to make their career in some other arena than in the commercial world."

"One point to the Tea Party"

"Such a thing is quite scary for the men of big business. I think that Faith in Price and the low confidence in political power is the reason why men of power want to be rich, just because they know deep inside that the value of money is so insecure."

"I think you are jealous."

"No, I feel rich enough. I have enough money to buy what I need and to keep me sheltered from physical threats like cold, drought and rain etc. I also have a lot of friends in my neighbourhood to rely on in economic crises. A normal person today has money enough to maintain a decent living. But you can't eat money and money can't buy you love. It's all too much."

"Rich people love money. That's why they build these enterprises."

"I think exaggerated need for money in the future will be regarded as a mental dysfunction caused by mistrust in society. Loads of money can't cure you from disease. It must be possible to define celebrity by other means than money. Billie Holiday was poor, Elvis was rich."

"Elvis was rich and lonely but he was not mentally diseased. But you think that he would have been happier if he had been living with a couple of good friends instead of the money?"

"Maybe, but the dream of getting rich is an important force to make people think up new ideas that can give a lot of money to the inventor. The dream of being a billionaire just by some smart solution, a hit song or a new design. But as usual, easy-made money is easy gone. People who have worked hard for their money put another value on money than people who just inherited money or got it by chance or luck."

"So what should the rich people do. Call a shrink?"

"I wish that they understood that the value behind all money is saved time. And it is not the rich people's time that is saved and has built their economic fatness, but their customers time.

If the customers suddenly change their mind about what is worth spending time on, then the value behind the money vanishes into oblivion and cannot be restored. Things like that happen all the time and we get financial crises and no one understands what's going on. The subprimers abandoned their houses too easily. That's what I think."

"What about poor people?"

"Some people are poor in money but have a rich social life. They have plenty of friends and earn deep respect from their social surroundings. Those people are more remembered at the grave than rich lonely freaks. It is a big shame when people have to die or suffer from diseases that are easily cured just for the sake of a few dollars per day. The cost of an extra summer house for a professional golf player could pay for the education for a lot of children.

"Bill Gates is doing a lot of work in that way. He seems to have got it. But if he had lowered the price of his computer programs instead, he would have less money but would get rich enough on the skill he had already. Now with all his millions of dollars to give away he has to learn how to choose between a lot of different charity foundations. He must learn and understand medicine and human health processes. That is very different from being a skilled computer programmer and business leader. Not all of the charity projects are the best for humanity, I think."

"But what if that is what Bill Gates wanted to be from the beginning? He used his business talent to end up as a donor. If that was his dream?"

"That would be different, I agree.

"There is another reason for building these shopping centres."

"And what is that?"

"The consumers want to buy things at the lowest price. Competition is all about finding a way to sell at a lower price than the competitors. The purpose of marketing is to make the buyer believe that he is seeing the lowest price of products with the same quality. Everyone knows that the quality is not equal, but cares more about the price.

"The monumental building, the temple-looking entrance, big advertising instead of an altarpiece, the total disorder inside with the massive exposure to buyable goods and the sharp coloured pricetags are the modern sacraments that make us believe that it is cheap. Instead of going to the church or the library, you go shopping and think you are performing a good deed for yourself."

"But if it has the lowest price, how can you say that we are fooled? Numbers are real and objective aren't they?"

"There is another pricetag in the dark. The cost of getting it at home. I have already told you about the petrol price. The car is the ultimate solution for distribution of the goods for the last part of the transport chain to the consumers home. We pay for our own delivery. And that is not cheap. How many hours do people work each day to be able to have and use a car? You must add that time to the cost for the food and the goods you consume."

"Hey, we turn right here!" Elsa pointed at a sign at the road.

John took the turn and continued after some thought.

"I think that it would be better if we had a more conscious political discussion; where the difference between printed money and saved time was generally understood, the difference between biological and social prerequisites, freedom regarding choice. Where it was commonly understood that no one is able to choose his age, sex, colour of the skin or religious origin. You can't say that it is a crime to be born in a certain year, for example. No one chooses his parents. No one chooses to be sick, no one chooses what disease he catches. To be cured must be a certain civilian and human right, paid for by taxes that are collected from the common reserve of saved time. My sister is my worst enemy in business but I will be the first to help when she is in trouble.

"People are different, you can't blame any person for being different because he is a human, right? But you have to follow the common rules of the society because that is something anyone can, and must, choose. Driving on the right side for example. It would be totally stupid if someone claims that he has the right to be different in that respect. What you can choose and what you can't choose is forever separated. We have our biology and we have our social reality. We can't control our biological processes more than up to a limit."

"So why don't you work politically?"

"To gain the voters' confidence. To be a reliable representative in a party you have to use your elbows. The way up is crowded with strong competitors. In every election you will be opposed, discredited, rhetorically trapped and scrutinized for every single step you have taken before. The way up to the top is very tough. It is supported by the silent majority that should be proud of themselves everytime they succeed in picking a good representative. But it is windy at the top.

"I think that when you've reached the top you are so contaminated by the fight that there is not much space left for being a nice guy any longer. Obama appeared to be a nice guy but he has to be very tough to keep his reputation and reliability. Not to mention Bill Clinton. Do you remember him playing the saxophone on stage after he was elected? He failed just because a woman loved him a little too much. Had that been in Zambia he would have married her too."

"So you've abdicated from the throne already?"

"Sort of yes. But I miss Miss Lewinsky. I think she was cute."

"But you are already married."

"I could always move to Zambia and convert to Islam. In the name of love."

"Far out! I do not think you could afford that!"

They passed through another village and over a small bridge. The road was curvy and John had to take it easy on the bends as the road was unknown to him. Cars meeting them were signalled by their light that was reflected in the phone wires hanging in the poles along the road. There was more snow here and the road was dotted with small twinkling stars of ice. They followed a long ice-free misty lake. After a while Elsa pointed at some postboxes on a stand at the left-hand side.

"There it is, turn left there, between the birches."

It was an alley of birches. The temperature must have been below freezing point and very little wind for some time. The birches were covered by a thick layer of long ice crystals. John turned left and followed the magic alley down to a big white mansion house with two white annexes. All the windows were painted in the same green colour. Elsa pointed at the left annex and John parked the car in front of the dark green door. Some window were lit but no movement was seen inside the house. John went out and knocked at the door. He could hear a dog growl behind the door and his neck hairs rose instinctively.

"No, that's no use! You are only making the dogs upset. She is not at home yet! Her car is not here. The door is open anyway so we'll just put our things inside and wait for her." Elsa was already carrying one of the bags from the shop.

She opened the door and three dogs ran out barking on the ground. One big grey wolf-like and two smaller ones. One of them ran right up to the car and urinated on the tyres. They barked all the time. The big grey one disappeared in the dark behind the house.

182

"Shit! The dogs have got loose! How do we catch them?"

"We don't have to catch them, they'll come back soon. I know these dogs. But beware of the cat!"

John went into the kitchen with two bags in his hands. On the kitchen table lay the biggest cat he had seen in his life. The tabby-coloured cat stared at him with giant eyes and made no attempt to move. He placed the bags carefully on the floor and went back out to the car. After a couple of trips all their things were inside the door and John could hang his coat on a hanger inside the door.

He took off his shoes and looked into the kitchen. The cat was still lying on the table like a little pasha. No sign of respect for the superiority of the human breed. A dog was barking outside the door. John opened it and all three dogs ran in and took their places in the house. The big grey dog jumped up onto a bed in a room off the kitchen. One of the smaller ones, a grey long-haired Chinese-type dog crawled under the table and continued to growl. The other small one, a white whippet type, went into the corner and began eating from a steel bowl filled with dried dog biscuits.

The kitchen was huge. Modern equipment, cupboards from the sixties and a wood stove. The house was made of stone with two-foot-thick walls and small windows. The cupboard doors were painted brown and white. The walls were covered with blue patterned wallpaper. A big table of genuine wood and some antique chairs. A wooden sofa at the table by the wall. A stack of newspapers and post, a radio. A wonderful blue glass creation functioned as a lamp over the table.

Elsa opened the cupboards and the fridge to check their status. Mary must have been cleaning them well because the fridge looked like new. The fridge and the freezer were completely empty. Elsa started to fill it up with the things from the bags.

"I'll take care of this till Mary arrives. You can take a rest in the living room."

"Thanks, that's what I need I think."

John went across the house and into another room at the other side. It was bigger than the kitchen and there were windows in all three directions. Small hanging lamps were on in the windows. A scent of musk and tobacco met him. The room had a fireplace, two soft sofas and a piano, stereo equipment, CDs, vinyl records. A lot of red, yellow and dark green oriental wooden tribal masks and other things hung on the walls, funny instruments, some spears, a bow and a big shield that looked African.

Mary taught music so John was not surprised to find a lot of other musical instruments around the room. A Fender Telecaster with amplifier, a trumpet, an acoustic guitar. Sheet music high and low. Spread all over the floor in a corner. John put on the stereo and pressed play. Soft music by someone called Michael Franks; "Tiger in the Rain," filled the room.

John read the titles and looked at the picture on the cover. He sank down on a sofa and pulled a blanket over him. His eyes were playing the backwards game again and everything tried to back away from him. After a while with closed eyes he realized that it was time to find the toilet so he got up. In the aisle between the room and the kitchen he found a promising door.

It was a long bathroom with all the necessary convenient installations. He found a lot of magazines, a Chinese method of massaging your eyes, a pair of
184

scissors and postcards from all over the world. A copy of *National Geographic* hung on a string and when John read it he could see some pictures taken by Mary in it. "Well done," he was thinking. "Hope she got a good reputation from it." They were of birds in the Amazon.

He decided to take a shower to get rid of all the dust from the trip. The shower was a narrow transparent plastic construction placed in the corner of the room. When he closed the cubicle doors he felt like he was placed into some primitive washing machine. He let the hot water flood over him. The heat in his neck gave him goosebumps at the beginning. The sound was terrible and the shower cubicle was not installed steadily so every time John changed his weight from one foot to another the cubicle tilted with a loud bang. That made it even more complicated to keep his balance while he attended to his back and feet.

John found some shampoo and mysteriously shaped bottles and tried everything. Anything that made him smell better was OK. He found a towel on a hook, dried himself standing in the cubicle to keep the floor outside free from dripping water. He put his socks and underwear in the basin with hot water and poured some soap over it. He worked them by hand a little so they would be cleaner. John found a used but sharp razor and shaved his face. There was a bottle of after shave lotion too. He rinsed his clothing in fresh water, wrung out the water and hung them to dry on the shower wall.

On a hook hung a bath robe of a material that must be pure thick satin. John took it down and weighed it in his hands. It was heavy as a clerical amice. It was deep blue with depictions of thin white flowers and small cottages. A huge yellow and red dragon on the back. For some reason the dragon was pointing down

185

on the back. John saw that the material in the robe was cut in one piece over the shoulders. To keep the pattern the right way up on the front it had to be upside down on the back. John decided to borrow it until his clothes were dry again.

The house was warm enough to wear just a kimono. He guessed that it must have central heating and that the heating central was situated in the mansion with buried hot water pipes leading to the annexes. "But Mary said that the house was cold when she returned from West Papua? Did the landlord turn off the heating because George didn't pay the rent?"

John went back to the room, folded his suit gently and hung it on a chair by the guitar amplifier. He lay down on the sofa again. Now he was prepared to meet Mary. He could hear Elsa working on something in the kitchen. Something fell with a crash and bad curses filled the house for a moment.

9 - The Kimono and the Stranger

John tried to relax on the sofa. It was comfortable but too much around him was new and unfamiliar. After all, the house was new to him and he hadn't seen Mary for decades. "What if she should seem like as an absolute stranger? Maybe she doesn't recognize me?"

The music was still playing when Elsa shouted "Ho ho, dinner is ready!"

John went out in the kitchen. Elsa had been working hard and the tasty smell from a big pot on the stove filled the air. On the table was bread, butter, salad and wine. Candles and fancy wrinkled serviettes.

"Hey, what a restaurant!"

"Hey, what a nice outfit! Did you wear that under your suit? You look like superman or something!"

"I found it in the bathroom." John turned around on his toes with his arms stretched out like a model at a show. "I had to clean up my own clothes a little. Heard anything from Mary?"

"No. But I know her. She'll come when she comes. It is always like this when I am here. She used to be very busy out on her job. She teaches several hundred pupils at the school. Taking care of the parents takes as much as time as the kids. Every mother wants her little Caruso or Carusina to stand in the first line of the choir at Christmas. She has to start up all that work after her absence."

"I've heard about Caruso, but Carusina?"

"Ah, if it is a girl or a boy it is the same. All artist names sounds like a brand of chocolate to me."

"So what are we going to do? Sit down and wait for her or are we going to eat now without her, in her own house? That feels strange?"

"We will eat now. The food is ready and I am starving after today. It doesn't hurt if we begin without her. We will be in a better shape to take care of her when she arrives. Hungry people can be dangerous. Please." Elsa brought the dish to the table. It was made of vegetables, cream and meat. It smelled wonderful.

Elsa and John sat down. John sat on the sofa against the wall. The little hairy dog was sleeping on the floor beside him, slightly snoring. John decided that the dog wouldn't bite his feet. They started the dinner with bread and salad. Elsa poured red wine into their glasses and raised her to make a toast.

"A toast for the host!"

"Schkall und bonn voyage!" John raised his glass and clinked it to Elsa's. John had no higher education in etiquette but he wanted to show that he was pleased with the situation.

They were both hungry and ate silently and concentratedly. John tried to slow down and looked around again in the kitchen. He looked at Elsa and found her even more beautiful now. He could see a nice girl with a long journey through life on Earth behind her. Elsa's face changed colour from very pale to peach. She took a deep breath after eating a portion of the dish. She took more wine and stretched her back.

"Ahh," she said.

"Yes, that was good. I like your cooking."

"I have been cooking since I was twelve. There was no other way to survive than learning from the beginning. My mother sent me and my little brother outside to fetch a chicken and then we had to kill it and

188

pluck it. It was still warm when I held it so my brother could take off the feathers. It was hard in the beginning but as soon as it was plucked and the guts were removed, our father helped us the first time, when the body was rinsed and cleared, then I remember I saw food and after that it was easy."

"You had no canned foods at that time?"

"No, everything was freshly made I think. No, we had dried and salted fish and we had salted dry and smoked meat. Once a week a fish salesman passed by with his horse and his cart. Eggs were canned in their own shell, seeds like wheat and corn last for long time in their hull. We made our own flour in a hand-driven mill when we were going to make bread. Dried apples, cheese, potatoes and carrots in sand-beds in the cold cellar. We had a lot of food at home."

John raised his glass of wine again. "Compliments to the cock!"

"Thank you!" Elsa replied.

John finished his wine and poured water in his glass. He wanted to be sober when Mary arrived. He presumed that he would be driving the next day too. Elsa took another glass of wine and took some more of the dish. John did the same and they began eating silently again. Time went on slowly, he heard that there was fire in the woodstove, the candles were burning peacefully and their hunger was slowly exchanged into satiation. Outside the snow was falling and John could see the lights from cars passing on the main road.

"It is a nice and peaceful house to live in." John tried to start up the conversation again. "A house to take care of your personal needs in. A house to eat and sleep in, in-between working hours."

"For women a house usually is a place of work, a place to take care of children and their men. Cleaning and washing, the fire must burn all the time to keep cold away in the winter. No peace or time to rest as long as you're awake."

"That's another view."

"And if you want to feel free from that housework, you must work somewhere else and get money to pay someone else to do it. I am not sure if it is worth it. But just to get out to another place, to meet other people at work, maybe is worth the pain. I wouldn't like to be chained to my stove at home. Men that think that women's place is in the kitchen should remember, that's where the knives are kept!"

"How about the other people in this place. I suppose there are more people living here?"

"Yes, there is an old couple in the mansion that owns the farm. In the other annex is a young family that does the farm work. He leases all the acres. They have a business connection but they are not familiar with each other. None of the landowners children wanted to take over the farm. They moved to the city and took well-paid white-collar jobs and prefer to live in an apartment. There is not much money to be made in farming today."

"I never longed for that either. But at the time when George and I were boys we worked on farms to make easy money, digging for beets and driving tractors. We took care of the cattle on a big farm for some time. That was fun, we got money and we felt responsible for something real. We were still in school at that time and had to get up very early in the morning to feed the calves and clean up their boxes.

"When we arrived at school we would smell of cowshit but we felt like grown-ups and just laughed at

190

those who couldn't stand the smell. We got strong from the hard work, too, and no one dared to pick a fight with us. It was harder with the girls because some of them really hated us and spread lies behind our backs. Like we were potential rapists in the dark."

"Young girls can be cruel."

"Sure, but we couldn't take them all on anyway so we didn't bother. There were girls that lived on cattle farms too and they had no problem with our appearance. George had an older sister that had a daughter that was born the same year as me and George, so she was in our class too. She was nice, I liked her."

"They should see you now. Clean and shaved, in an absolutely wonderful dress. You'd look like a Chinese emperor if you had black hair."

"Thank you. Western clothing isn't always too comfortable. It is a pity that it is not conventional to wear things like this today."

"That may change in the future. It all depends on whose interests are in charge. A tailor asked Louis Armstrong if he wanted his trousers to be wider at left or right for his penis. 'Let it swing!' he answered. I'd vote for men wearing kimonos." Elsa smiled with peering eyes.

"If enough women preferred men wearing satin kimonos with bare legs I think it would change." John looked at himself and touched his arms. Loosened the belt a bit as the food needed more space. He wasn't sure about he would wear something like this in public or if it would be convenient in his job.

"But who is in charge of the dress code in business? The owner of the company or the chairman? Who decides what is convenient in business meetings? I wear a suit and tie just to make an impression of reliability. After all, a suit and tie is an English horse-riding outfit from the 19th century. How does that create a confident impact at a board meeting? People are very sensitive to clothing codes, but is it a sign of intellectual quality? If you are looking for a doctor you don't want him to be dressed like a pimp."

"You certainly don't look like a doctor in that dress! But I like it. Shall we play while we are waiting for Mary? I'll put the pot on the stove so it keeps the heat." Elsa rose and picked up the deck of cards while John cleared the table to make space.

They began playing the game 'Evil of the World' again. Elsa was quiet and concentrated. John tried to make some small talk but she didn't seem interested in a conversation while playing. They played game after game in silence. The dogs were sleeping. The cat came into the kitchen, ate some dog biscuits, lapped some water and disappeared again. The little hairy dog moved close to John's feet, which warmed both his feet and the dog. John was wondering if they should call Mary on her mobile phone but Elsa said that she was probably busy with some night course and would be late.

John lost every game and once he lost by having only kings and jokers in his hand which left him unable to continue. Elsa called it 'check-mated'. Elsa was so successful. John realized that she had a better overall strategy. She tried to get rid of the cards in her hand as often as possible because that gave her more new cards from the deck. John learned a little by studying her way of playing. She asked if he was playing dumb just to let her win but John denied that. He assured her that he was trying his best.

"I don't like to win if you aren't trying your best."

"You just wait, you feckin' bitch!" John replied. He blushed and felt a bit ashamed because he had lost his temper for a second.

"Ha ha! That is why this game is called 'Evil of the World'. It entices the worst out of people. After a couple of games you will be a nicer and better person! I really love this game!"

"You mean that it doesn't make me a bad person if I swear at you?"

"No, not at all you little beast! It is just a game. Getting angry and feeling anger towards the counterpart in a game is like therapy to me. I love to get angry! That is what makes me feel alive. In fact I began to get angry at you because I thought you weren't trying your best. I thought you were afraid of beating me in case I wouldn't like to play anymore."

"I began to get angry because you are winning all the games."

"Good! Just remember that it is only a game. I am not afraid to lose. That means that I will learn and have to try better."

"I promise that I will try my best in the future…"

WHAM! The outer door was opened and closed. A stranger in a big white fur coat, a big white knitted cap and high leather boots ran into the house and into the living room. Both John and Elsa stood up to see what was happening. John went to the door, just as the stranger came back with one of the spears in his right hand. John backed fast into the kitchen again. Elsa screamed. All the dogs were now awake and began barking and jumping around on the kitchen floor.

"What are you doing here? I'll kill you!" The stranger roared loudly and threw the spear at John. John ran backwards and tripped over the big dog. He fell on his back with his arms outstretched and his chin to his chest. He saw the spear fly over his face while he fell to the floor. The spear got stuck in the lower cupboard door under the sink.

The big grey dog roared and caught his left arm in his mouth. The small hairy one attacked John from under the table and took a bite of the robe very close to his noble parts. Elsa took a piece of firewood and hit the big dog on the head so it would let go of John's arm. It didn't work. The stranger ran back into the living room again and returned with another spear and held it in both hands. Now he advanced, roaring wildly, towards John with the spear in his hands, aiming the point at John's bare throat.

"Mary! Mary! Stop! It's John!" Elsa shouted, and grabbed the spear from the side and wrenched it out of her hands.

Mary dropped her chin and stood breathing with her mouth and eyes wide open for a while, staring at John as he law on the floor with the growling dogs holding him down to the floor. The white dog was barking and running around while Elsa looked at Mary to be sure that it was her and not a stranger inside the massive clothing. Mary bowed down and began to laugh hysterically. Loud and long. She had to take deep breaths between the attacks.

"Ha ha ha haha, ha ha ha! heee,

"I thought it was George! heee,

"Ha ha ha ha ha! heee,

"Oh my God, heee,

"Is that John? Ha ha ha hah ha hh, Yiiahh! heee,

"Ha ha ha ha ha! heee.

"Oh my, oh my! You look so stupid in that robe, heee,

"I gave him, heee,

194

"he never used it because, heee,

"he didn't like it. Ha ha ha ha ha haa-a---a--a! heee,

"Right at him! Oh I saw you from outside, heee,

"oh what a shock! I thought George had returned, heee,

"and had put on the robe, to sort of please me, heee, to take him back!

"Oh I got so angry! Ahhh!

"And you! Hey Roy! Let go! Let go."

Mary shouted at the dog. The big dog released John's arm and crawled back half a yard, still pointing at John. He wasn't badly hurt but the dog had strong jaws and his teeth had made two rows of deep painful red marks in the flesh.

"Go to bed!!" Mary pointed with her arm and ordered him back to the bed in the room inside the kitchen. "Wow wow wow!" The white one kept on barking,

"Silence! Silence!" The white dog stopped barking but the small grey one still held a piece of the robe in his mouth growling.

"Ha haha hahha hha!" Mary turned hysterical again and sat down on the floor, laughing and crying at the same time. Elsa laughed too, still holding the spear. John sat on the floor applying some massage to his arm.

"Ha ha ha ha ha, Oh shit! I peed in my pants!

"Ha ha ha! You look so stupid there on the floor. Excuse me.

"Ho Ho! I must go to the loo." Mary ran away, kicked off her boots, threw the coat and the cap on the floor.

"I think she was glad to see me."

John rose and tried to force the little dog to release his grip on the robe. He had to put a piece of meat into

195

his nose to loosen it. John straightened his attire and moved back to the sofa. Elsa drew out from the cupboard the other spear that had made a big hole in it. She took the spears to the living room so they were out of sight. She returned and began to shiver from the episode so she had to drink a big glass of water.

Mary returned after a minute with a towel around the lower part of her body. She cracked up again. She had to laugh for several minutes more to be able to breathe and talk. She walked around and every time she looked at John she started laughing again. But every time it was more and more relaxed.

"Oh, ha ha haha! This was a big surprise! Oh, you are so welcome! Both of you. I am so happy!"

"But you knew that we would come! You called!" Elsa looked sharply at Mary.

"Oh, I forgot that. I was on my way back from work today. I was absorbed in how angry I was at George. Then the car broke down just a mile from here. Didn't you notice it? No, anyway, I put on the warm clothes I had in the car and began to walk. I was so down that I went up in the forest to a summer museum for tourists. I wanted to think it all over, maybe even just commit suicide if I couldn't continue after this mess.

"I guess I had been sitting there in a tepee for three or four hours, maybe more, when I decided to walk back. I was thinking of my daughter and her newborn baby daughter, and also I was hungry. But I think I was so depressed that I forgot that you were coming. She cracked up again. "Ha ha ha ha! What a turn-up of a day! And that figure you brought here Elsa! I can hardly believe that it's you Johnny! Nice to see you, it was a while ago."

"Nice to see you too, I am glad you're alive!"

"We brought some things from the grocery. We filled your fridge for you and I've cooked some food for you too. Please sit down Mary and take some stew from the pot."

"Oh thanks! I see that there is wine too! Wonderful!" She sat down at the edge of the table. John poured wine into her glass and she drank it all up in one. John filled the glass again while Elsa sat down with her.

"Now you will eat and then you can tell me the story of what happened with George." Elsa served her from the pot and completed it with bread and salad.

Mary ate with a good appetite while Elsa gave Mary a brief review of their trip during the day. She told Mary that John had driven with summer tyres over the mountain pass but she didn't mention that she had been tied up in the trunk. Mary took nearly all the food that was left. Elsa could see that she probably hadn't been eating too much in the past few days.

Mary began to relax and she talked more slowly. John took another glass of wine to recover from the shock. He realized that had been saved from getting killed with the spear by the big dog. The hair on his neck rose when he thought about it again.

Mary told Elsa the story about her and George again. John hadn't met him since George and Mary had moved north over 20 years ago. He remembered that George had suspected John of cheating with Mary. Even if it wasn't true John couldn't do anything to make him believe it and that was the end of their friendship. John guessed that it had more to do with Georges relationship with Mary. That George was desperately seeking a cause of interference from outside. Something out of his own control so he could have someone else to blame apart from himself.

Of course, John had deep emotions about Mary but he wanted to keep them from being expressed and realized just because of George being his best friends. But who knows, maybe George could feel John's emotions inside and became jealous as George didn't share the same intensity. Love maybe makes its best impression at a distance.

At that time John did only watch Mary, and no expectations or duties lay on his shoulders. He could just taste her sweetness and admire her appearance from a distance. George had to deal with all her sides, close into his own skin, day and night, at full and dark moon, all the year around. Now he had left the building and lived together with a twenty-years-younger woman. John wasn't jealous of George anymore. "That difference in her experience and expectations of life has its price, it will suck hard. Either George is very brave or he is just stupid," John was thinking.

"I had to throw out the fridge and spent my last money on a new one. Then I had a new fridge but no money to buy food to put into it. I must work a full month to get any salary. Oh, that made me so sorry that I could die! And I've got no petrol in the car, that is why it stopped on me."

"I'll give you the money you need. I think John will help you, too. Right?" John nodded to Elsa and Mary that it was OK. He didn't know if he had any money but that would be a problem for later. John and accounting had never been best friends even since he had got his degree. He thought that he would like it better if he studied accounting but all it did was cost him a fortune and give him more reasons to hate it.

"I have a spare tank in the car with a gallon of petrol. Maybe that's enough to drive the car home and get to the petrol station tomorrow."

"We can pick it up in the morning when we go back." Elsa was the most practical person of the three at the moment. She put away the things on the table after the meal, even the wine. Elsa then attended to the dishes. Mary sat well fed and pleased on the chair and shone brightly at John.

"You look well after all these years!"

"You too. But you nearly killed me!"

"I was really mad. I am sorry."

"No problem, I'll forgive you anything. If you had been successful with the throw and killed me you should know that I think it feels better to be killed by someone you love than by some one you hate." John didn't know where that came from but it felt right to say.

"Do you still love me?"

"Of course." John swallowed.

"Great. That's good. I like you too. But I am not letting you move in here at once just because. I am a decent woman, grandmother and all."

"I have got no plans like that. I just wanted to see you again." John's genitals began to move again, free under his robe.

"He's coming with me!" Elsa shouted from the sink.

"Ah, it's so wonderful that you came here just now. The last week has been a real disaster. It began with a meeting with the guerilla on Papua. I was asked to deliver weapons – 'How many guns can you bring us?' – That scared me to death. Maybe that question was just a mistake and was meant for somebody else."

199

Mary went to the electric stove and put on the fan. She lit a cigarette and began blowing the smoke into the void.

"I can't smoke indoors because of the landlord. Anyway, I wasn't there to help the guerilla. I was there to record ancient tribal music. But I had to get help from the guerilla to find the way into the mountains to meet the tribal people there.

"So I fled. I interrupted my stay and ran to the shore. I tripped and hurt my ankle. I managed to get help to find a boat and a flight back to Singapore and then back home again. Just to fall down into this mess. I don't think I could have lasted much longer."

"But your daughter? Isn't there anyone else around?" John thought about the other people living at the farm.

"Yes, I think so but coming home from a six-month stay on the other side of the planet with no communication during that time is as strange as landing from a plane in the middle of the jungle. Everything is a green mess and you have nothing to refer to from the beginning, nothing more than your own body. I came home and my home was a mess, it was empty, full of shit and dirty laundry, no man, no dogs, no food or money. I guess he drove my car until the tank was nearly empty too. Oh, I hate that fucking creep!"

"Don't think about that now. Now it is time to play cards!" Elsa sat down and spread the cards.

"Sure OK, ha ha ha! I'd love to." Mary laughed again and accepted the invitation, glad to think about something other than her mess at the moment. Mary knew the game already. She stubbed out the cigarette and sat down at the table. The big cat ran up onto the sofa and sat staring at John.

200

It was more complicated to play the game with three. John was beginning to get used to the games strategic possibilities and won the first round. Mary and Elsa were the more experienced so he lost most of the time. Elsa and Mary were swearing high and loud, and laughing loudly in-between. John was accused of being a fink and a cheat but he returned all the worst he could summon at the ladies who gently smiled back at him.

"He's beginning to learn." Elsa said to Mary.

"Yes. I think that we can make good use of him." Mary answered while she adjusted the towel around her body.

10 - On the Bridge and in the Towel

"Tea anyone?" Elsa stood up and poured water in a pan.

John and Mary said yes.

"Are you the host in Mary's kitchen?" John asked.

"She is used to it." Mary answered. "She has lived here so many times over the years. She has been my rescuer on many occasions when times were tough."

"I saved George too, when you were away for months in South America!"

"Maybe you should have been here on this trip, too? Maybe it is your fault that he ran away with that slut. If you had been here it would not have happened." Mary sounded accusing.

"Pah! He is a grown man. He should be able to take care and act responsibly and not let his prick decide."

Mary looked worried again as she was reminded of George. The end of a twenty-five-year-old relationship is a big change. Unwanted changes in a person's social surrounding are the heaviest burdens to take on and carry. She searched her mind for something easier to deal with. She turned to John.

"You left me too. At the bridge."

"What?"

"The first time that Elsa and I stayed together. We were engaged in a rural heritage project. Showing tourists how life could be at an old farm. We lived at the Hammermill, do you remember? The mill at the small creek up in the forest."

"Oh, yes. I will never forget that."

"Really? My kids were small, Ranny was just a small baby in a cradle. George was away fishing and hunting bears in Alaska. He was to be there for three months, the whole summer! Elsa was the one I needed then. I would never have made it without you Elsa! I am so thankful for all your help!"

"That was the first time. We could have manage much better without Mr Lindberg, the local priest. He was fooling around causing a lot of work and trouble for us all the time. It was all his idea from the beginning to the end. A totally stupid project. Who can run a farm and take care of a lot of visitors at the same time? And we had to take care of Mr Lindberg too. He just stood there with his big white hair like a helpless saint, waiting for us to make coffee while you had to take care of a small baby."

"You left me then." Mary looked at John again.

"No, it was you. You chose to stay. I couldn't." John had a dark memory of that night.

"I called you because the fence was broken and the sheep had to be shut in. I was afraid of the wolves. You came and helped me. You had a big shiny red car filled with tools and things. You were so healthy, natural and wild. You were an expert with your tools and your iron thread. I remember how I was watching your hands. You worked so fast and concentratedly and were able to talk to me at the same time. I was really longing for a friend. Nothing against Elsa, but someone to talk to, my own age."

"There were a lot of black flies at that place. They breed well in streams like that. I had to work fast to avoid their bites. My face was all covered. It felt like a hot massive soft beard."

"Yes, we had a big bottle of mosquito oil to help both us and the cattle. We nearly had to brush our teeth in it." Elsa sat down at the table with a teapot, honey and three mugs.

"I fell in love with you at that night. You made me feel real again. You were different but kind and you were listening to my heart. You liked me too, didn't you?"

John became a bit embarrassed in front of Elsa and looked at her but she smiled in a friendly way at him so he decided to be honest.

"Yes, I knew you a bit before but, you know, I was living alone at that time. I had my own place that I tried to farm and that was hard labour all day. It was easy as I had no one to consider my plans or schedules with. But I was lonely. I think that I was working so hard to stave off my loneliness. I was longing for a woman to share my days and nights with. I was an easy catch for any woman who could cook and take care of a man. I received many suggestions but no one to my taste. I already knew what I wanted.

You were married already to George, one of my best friends since we were boys. You were taboo, forbidden fruit. I wasn't to fall in love with you. Until I touched you by accident. I'll never forget your little touch back to me by your fingertip on my shoulder. I was … it made me …"

"I was so touched by you that I could hardly speak."

"You were beautiful. You smelled of milk and honey."

"We stood at the bridge with the water running under our feet. It felt like I was flying. I wanted to hug you."

"I had the tools in both my hands. I would have to drop them to hold you, but I couldn't. They could have fallen into the stream through the holes in the bridge. You were hot and red in your face."

"You smelled wonderful, smoke, Earth and wood."

"You had mosquito oil all over your body. I had none. My head and hands were covered by itchy gnats. My whole face was rocking. I couldn't stay at the bridge any longer. I had to go. I asked you to follow me."

"But I wanted to stay, on the bridge, the running water under me, and I – I – I don't know why really."

"You stayed because you had a little baby to take care of and you had to take care of your reputation." Elsa cracked the illusion with a strong voice. "Ah, you are still so young and sensible."

"But I think it was the most romantic moment in my life. I will never forget that feeling you gave me, Johnny. You made me so sorry when you left." Mary had tears in her eyes and John was convinced that she was honest.

"Romantic moments are not real. Romance, love, passion, life and the erotic are not things or moments, nor subjects, they are events." Elsa was in charge again. "All events result from the clash between the casual state and the general conditions."

John and Mary looked at Elsa. John thought that Elsa was maybe expressing jealousy of Mary. Mary felt a sting of sorrow about her age from Elsa. Elsa kept on with a milder voice.

"Love is not a thing, not a noun but a verb. The erotic is something that happens between people who like each other. But it has to be watered, soiled and it needs sunshine. If you two keep away from each other there will be no such event."

"But she was married to George!" John tried to sound moral but Elsa and Mary could hear that he was sorry about that.

"Yes I was married to George, but at that moment I was in love with someone else, Johnny. Please forgive me but I couldn't stop my heart beating."

"I drove home and I was so angry. I knew I could have stayed. I went out on the field in the night and dug a long worthless dry ditch just to try to break down my anger. It was only me and the birds in the morning. I worked so hard that I fell asleep by the ditch and slept all through the next day until evening. Later on I decided to sell the farm and move south. That is why we never met again."

"Isn't that beautiful then that you two can sit here and look into each others eyes once again. Love is an event, don't you ever forget that. There is no end, love continues." Elsa sounded so wise and motherly.

"Lucky for you that I believe you, bitch." John answered her with a gleam in his eye.

Mary took John's hand. "Yes. Elsa is right, love continues. I am so pleased to see you here Johnny. You make my heart warm again."

"You should be glad that you missed with the spear earlier. Better see if he's got an erection again." Elsa blinked at Mary.

John leaned forward.

John poured some more tea in his cup and turned to Mary.

"That reminds me of a funny situation that happened to me just after that. I must tell you this. I moved south to a new area. I bought a little house close to Charlestown and looked for job. I didn't know anybody there and I felt more lonely there than at home.

"One day I saw a sign at the local shop. It was a new gym group starting, arranged by a local organization.

Everyone in the area was welcome. It was at the football stadium at a time when there was no other training. Just before noon, but I thought it was a good idea to meet other local people. I wanted to find new friends, maybe some way of finding a job too. I had a lot of money saved from selling the farm but I wanted to take part in something practical and new. I bought some jogging clothes and shoes and walked there on the right day. In the dressing room I realized that there were only women there so I backed out and thought I made a mistake.

"Hey, where are you going?" a big lady in a pink training suit shouted at me.

"Oh, I'm sorry but I made a mistake. Where is the men's dressing room?"

"This is the mens dressing room. You seem to be the only man yet however. Welcome to our new local exercise club! All the others happen to be girls. But come in. It is open to all. I am sure there are some more boys coming. Hi. I'm Maude. Please, take a hook and help yourself."

"I hesitated for a while but rather than hiding like a scared rat in a toilet and keeping on being alone I followed the advice and took a hook in the corner close to the exit, changed my clothes but kept my underwear on. I could see that many of the women were naked for a short second and I could see their private parts and all. They laughed at me and I felt lonelier again, but Maud, who appeared to be the exercise leader, told them that this was open to all and no one should be laughed at.

"She wanted the group to be equal and as big as possible. It had something to do with the fact that it was supported by the public services for increasing health or something. The intention was that it should be a meeting point between people of all sorts. But at that time of the day the only people that were free to do something like that, the only kind of people that could take part at that time of the day were free housewives. And me.

"Anyway we ran out into the football arena. Maud in her bright pink dress had a whistle and some handwritten signboards with easy exercises that we went through. I tried to do my best and it felt nice to work out with my body. I like to get sweaty and to test my body the best I can. It feels heavy in the beginning but after a while I can feel that my muscles are responding better, both in terms of strength and timing.

"Most of the women were weak and inexperienced in gym training so they failed and laughed at each other all the time. I took the exercises seriously but their jiggling and laughing made me jealous. I wanted to laugh, too. That made me feel alone again. You can't talk to people and do gym exercises simultaneously. I began to be bored again and saw no meaning in it. I could have done my training at home.

"Now comes the fun part of the story. When it was over all of us went back in a long line to the dressing room. I was exhausted by my efforts and sweaty and I had to take off my wet clothes and needed a shower. I had to undress and show my body in the room with all the naked women. You know that I never have been able to control my bodily functions. I've always felt different because of that.

"George was the same so we were friends. We used to talk about how impossible it was to control it. We had erections now and then but that was never a big problem between us two. But we never saw any other men with erections, including our own fathers. We

208

were used to the studs and the bulls in the fields that showed their penises with no shame and felt more like them. Even male dogs would show their erections freely.

"But now, in this dressing room, I had to take a shower and there was no way to hide my pride. This was a public arrangement and I was declared welcome. I saw that the women didn't hide themselves very much so I walked from my corner across the whole dressing room to the shower with my dick pointing at the stars in heaven. All the women suddenly became quiet at first, and then some began to laugh scornfully at me, some gave low whistles, others were clapping their hands. Then I heard Maude's angry voice: "Don't you have any shame, young man?"

"I stopped and answered loudly and slowly, expressing each word clearly so everyone could hear: 'Listen ladies! I can sense the smell of a lubricated woman for miles! I know that there must be at least a dozen of you in this room right now with a rattling tickling little baby snake between your legs, so why should I be the only one to be ashamed?' It was totally quiet. They were listening. I heard no answer but some giggling and grumbling.

"I took my shower and there were no more comments. But I didn't have the guts to go there again. I didn't see any more signs of it either. So much for mixed training. Sometime I received a funny smile at the local shop but I couldn't remember any of the faces of the women from the training. Socially, it was a total disaster. I sold my house and moved to another city where I met my wife in the car park outside the city hall. We had known each other for years. It is not easy to find love and company."

"So why are you telling us this now?" Elsa looked a bit confused.

"Because I know that I am not the only one in this house right now with an aroused organ."

Elsa looked at the white dog and under the table. John smiled at Mary. Mary blushed. She put her towel right back down as it had come up and showed her knee.

"Is he right?" Elsa looked at Mary. Mary had a funny look.

"Am I right about it? No one should ever be ashamed of being alive!" Mary nodded and smiled. She sighed deeply.

"Do you really smell an excited woman miles away?" Elsa was curious.

"Oh, no. I was bluffing in that dressing room! I took a chance. I was a smoker for 20 years and have burnt away all my smelling nerves."

"What!??" You are lying??" Elsa got upset.

Mary took a quick deep breath as she was going to shout at John.

"So what? Our brains are made for lying! We think we understand the world around us. We dream when we are asleep and we have lots of fantasies. Especially about sex. Our brain presents its own pictures of the reality all the time. When concepts and figures aren't saturating enough it serves us with dreams and imaginations to complete the picture. Sometime it is correct but most of the times it misses. It is called Faith with a capital F. This has exactly the same function for intellectual evolution as mutations have for the evolution of biology.

"If I tell a story or paint a picture it is based on reality or a fiction. It doesn't matter how 'true' it is. It is the purpose of the message that is important. The Bible is

210

full of lies. Jesus didn't tell stories to make people believe in the facts. If we believed only in facts then Christians would say that the meaning of human life is to be beaten, punished and crucified. Jesus told stories to make people understand the message. He was a teacher."

Mary laughed. John continued.

"Philosophers have a hard time telling the difference between reality and concepts. Kant[19] spent years on the difference between concepts and reality. Concepts cannot be reality. Concepts are represented by electrical patterns between synapses inside our brain. You look at a mountain and think about it. But there is no mountain in your head. You look at a flower and you can see that it is dry. Then you maybe decide to give it water to recover, but you can be wrong, it can die from too much water.

"Concepts are not reality, they are imagination, but they help us to manage reality. That is how concepts and reality are connected. I lied to you to be able to disclose the truth. The truth is what works in reality. There was something going on in this room that we could not see with our eyes."

"You reckless bastard! I didn't think about it myself until you mentioned it. Don't you feel ashamed embarrassing me?"

"No, whats embarrassing mostly? Being honest about it or to showing distrust by hiding your true nature?"

"I wasn't prepared for revealing that yet I think."

"But it was OK to tell me you love me?"

"Sure, I am honest."

---

19 http://en.wikipedia.org/wiki/Immanuel_Kant

"I must tell you another thing. I can't smell everything any longer because of smoking cigarettes but I can't stop my nostrils fooling around."

"Your nostrils?"

"Yes, my nostrils start to vibrate when I come close to a hot woman. It took me years to understand what was going on. I had been living alone for such a long time and I thought that it had something to do with just a nervous habit that obsessed me when I met other people. I had no problem when I was in the army, but on the weekends on leave my nose used to freak out and I was sneezing all over. My upper lip curled and I couldn't speak clearly. Some of my army friends thought that I was snorting cocaine or something but I have never tried drugs. It was women. I got high on the taste of women. That's all. Learning this gave me back my self-confidence."

"Ha ha, I am glad I didn't follow you. I bet you looked like Jim Carrey."

"I see, I was right about you. I shouldn't have stayed."

"Oh yes you should. I was only kidding. It would have been totally different." Mary took his hand again and caressed it.

"You are a really nice couple, you two. I love to see you together." Elsa looked at Mary and John with gleaming eyes.

"I was tormented by the urge of my bodily functions. After the army I moved away to find a social function. I began studying economics at college. I lived in a small apartment and began riding horses to keep my body in shape. There were only women and girls at the riding school. Earlier in history, back in the centuries, riding and taking care of horses was a man's duty but today
212

you have a hard time finding men doing it. I began to understand what my nose was telling me.

"I liked to ride. I had a female teacher of course and she treated me so well. I had erections every once in a while up on horseback. She always smiled at me in the paddock. I think that the movements in the saddle were the cause. When jumping high fences I had a tough time in the beginning, because when I came down again in the saddle it was easy to land on my testicles and that hurts a lot. I had to learn a special technique to save my balls."

"So you still ride horses?"

"Yes, I love it. I have strong empathy with some horses. But I am not a chairman of the board in the local riders' association anymore. I had a great time with all the mothers in the organization then. I was the only male in the group. My nostrils went crazy at every board meeting. Every time I was at the riding school actually. But I must have been lucky because I could tell the difference between sex and love. I never got trapped into something naughty.

"Sex without love to me is like being hungry and having nothing to eat but canned dog food. I feel pity for all these people that fall for their lower forces. Molesting young girls or satisfying foreign frustrated housewives for their own lust has never enticed me. It seems like eating canned dog food to me. Backwardness. I think pornography where people are shown just doing things without empathy is disgusting. What kind of people pay for that? Do they eat dog food, too?

"People love to watch football on TV. The players and the teams used to be among the best and highest paid in the world. But in porn films, the actors are among the worst and cheapest."

"I just can't blame somebody for having different tastes even if they happen to like smoked herring or canned dog food. I think this is still a free country. You should have seen how the men on Papua did it. They wear penis protection. They can have an erection any time inside it without being embarrassed. I don't think they are retarded or backward."

"Yes, tell us more about your stay there!" Elsa woke up.

"I really will. I think I shall change my towel to something more convenient first." Mary went up to her bedroom on the second floor.

11 - West Papua

John could hear Mary walk slowly down the stairs. She was limping; he could hear by the uneven steps. But he forgot that immediately when she appeared in the door.

"Oh, how beautiful you are!" Elsa clapped her hands.

Mary entered the kitchen dressed in a handmade silk gown. It was pale brown and red with golden stripes.

"Yes, isn't it? My friend in Bali gave me this as a sign of our friendship. She said that I should wear it to my wedding." Mary turned around to show all sides of it. Elsa picked up her camera to take a photo but the automatic flash seemed to be dead.

"What happened to your foot?"

"To my foot?"

"I heard you were limping on the stairs."

"Oh, yes! I was walking barefoot most of the time. I got used to that with thick skin under my feet. One day I cut my foot on a small straw of grass and the little wound got infected. I took months to recover from it because it was in the raining season. Later when I fled from the army I twisted my ankle too, but that wasn't so serious I think."

"Can I see?"

"Yes, here. There is nothing there I think."

John examined her foot and gave her some massage. Her skin was soft and warm. It was barely tanned from the sun and John could see that she had been walking around a lot as there were no fluids retained at her wrists. Walking supports the transportation of fluids and gives the limbs a slim shape. Wounds and inflammations collect fluids to preserve the area from

215

violence and to support the healing process. He didn't feel any hotspots and there was no strange flicker in it. He decided that it would be OK. He borrowed Elsa's camera to see what was wrong with the flash and happened to take a footo.

John was used to horses and cattle. It was important to check their legs and hooves. The best way to find out was to touch by hand and look how they behaved in motion.

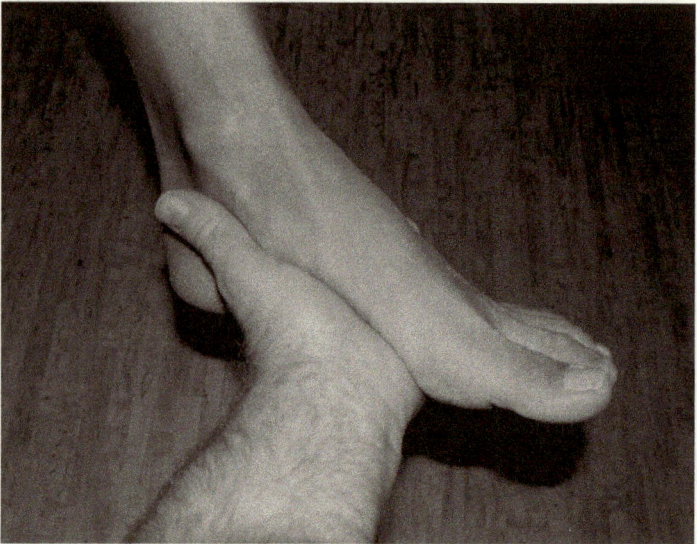

"I think your foot will recover. Now, let's hear about your trip to Papua."

"Yes, how did you come up with that idea at all?" Elsa asked.

"You know that I teach music and voice. I took a holiday to Bali and I brought my little MP3 recorder to make recordings of the music I could hear on the streets, at bars and in houses I passed. I tried to get in touch with people and wanted to hear them sing with their own voices. Not only because of my profession but also as a complement to the pictures I took with my camera. I love to listen later when I get home. Listening to the sounds creates an atmosphere that makes me feel like I am there again. It is much better than just pictures.

"Anyway, one night I met a man on the street. He was just standing there, leaning on a lamp post. When I came close to him he said: 'I have been dreaming of you'.

"I thought he was one of the thousand men that are looking for prostitutes and I tried to ignore him and pass by.

"'Wait,' he said. 'My people need you. I dreamt that I had to come here and find you. Now you are here. Let's go.'

"He made me curious and I followed him to a bar where we had a drink. He asked me about who I was and I told him that I was a music teacher from Sweden and liked to record local songs and music.

"'You must come to my people, then. We have a lot of songs. We sing all day long.'

"That sounded fantastic to me. I decided to follow him and the next day we took a flight to Jayapura on West Papua. There we found a man on the street selling tickets to a city in the middle of the island. In that city there were a lot of Indonesian military forces and we had to get a permit to walk out into the jungle as I was a foreigner.

"The permit let us walk south but we walked west for about 200 miles. That took us a week and we slept in abandoned cottages and we had no food. We met strangers of all kinds, backpackers and religious freaks. We saw guerilla soldiers. The Papuans don't want their island to belong to Indonesia. We were climbing high – I think we were up to 5000 feet. The jungle is misty and it can be very cold at night there."

"So it wasn't planned?"

"Yes it was, in a way. I had met another man from Papua two years earlier and spent a month on the island but I never made it into the jungle at that time. I met some locals and heard their music and I had a dream that I would go there again. So I had brought my little MP3 recorder but didn't know how to get in touch with them again. No wonder why George went crazy when I didn't come back as I said at the beginning. I sent a text message to my school and they said it was OK for me to stay some more. I had no access to the Internet on West Papua."

"How could the Papuans know you were on Bali?"

"Yes, that is strange, spiritual forces maybe? Many Papuans have left the island and maybe they keep in contact just by spreading talk in their local language, who knows? Someone recognized me and the talk spread undercover. They have over 350 different languages on West Papua. It must have been people from the same tribe.

"My friend followed me and guided me through the deep forests. Eventually we arrived at a village with people who never have seen a white person before. My friend introduced me to them and I was allowed to stay in the women's house. My friend disappeared, and there I was among them. A lonely white women in the wild bush.

"The natives didn't understand me and I didn't understand their language. So I sat down and waited. I had a little experience from my first trip about their habits to lean on. They gave me food, it was mashed

218

and boiled sweet potatoes. When they saw me eat and sleep they understood after a while that I was a real human and not a spirit. I spent four months with these people. Mostly listening and watching. Learning their language and their way of life.

"It was so fantastic. I didn't have to work. Many of them still believed that I was a spirit walking around. Over time I learned enough of their language to be able to understand some of their stories. It is so funny how the language makes you understand each other. In the beginning the only words I could understand were fire, rock, food, hungry. I had a picture from that that their minds were rather basic and primitive. Time went on and I learned more and more words. My understanding of their culture was deepening. I learned more and more of their way of living and their view of the life and the world. These people tell stories that sounds as alive as if they were from today, tales and legends that are older than we can imagine, they can be tens of thousands of years old. Just imagine how many dramatic levels you can find in tales of that kind. Our dramas from the time of Shakespeare or the Greeks are just soap operas compared to theirs.

"There were rats all around. The rats lived with them in the houses. When I was sleeping the rats came close and they tried to bite my fingers. None of the other women seemed to take any notice of the rats so I didn't dare to start screaming and fighting alone. I had to adapt to their customs. There were no place to wash your hands and the rats could sense the smell of potatoes from my fingers. I was never bitten hard but it was terrible to be so close to them. I sensed their little tongues tickling my skin. Uuuh!

"The people were really singing all the time. They began singing before they got up in the morning. All day they were singing together; different songs for every event. Breakfast was made on the fire that was rekindled from yesterday's glow. Sweet potatoes where boiled in the ashes. We ate it with our hands.

"It was a very nice way of life. After eating breakfast the women went out to get food. Mostly sweet potatoes that were farmed across the acres. Papua is an equatorial island so vegetables grow all season. The only seasons are more or less rainy.

"We were all naked but mostly wearing something around our hips and the nets that the women carried food in. The net was fastened around their heads and covered their backs. Men were naked but for their penis protection, painting and lots of fancy feathers. The climate is perfect for that kind of dress. Life was so peaceful there. I recorded their music and how their life sounded. I took pictures with my camera and filled my diary.

"After some weeks I began to find the rhythm, to be more and more comfortable with the situation. As I was a woman there wasn't much notice taken of my presence. I think it would have been different for a man. The men didn't take much notice of me but I could feel that I was watched all the time. Spies from other tribes or military agents. I could follow the women digging for crops, bathing in the river and taking care of the kids. The river was very cold as the water actually runs from a melting glacier on the top of the island. No fish in it but very clean water.

"Once there was a war going on between the men. That was frightening. My helper, a woman that adopted me, told me that I should take care and hide.

But I was lucky, our tribe won the little war, only one man got killed. I think that it was about someone being accused for stealing a pig or a making sex with a girl from another tribe on the next side of the mountain.

They had their own information system from a number of lookouts made of trees. A widescreen TV, or their own version of the Internet. They could see miles from these nests.

"The average age of the indigenous people living on West Papua is only 23 years and that is because so many of their children die early. If you look at it from that perspective their life is a disaster but they don't see it that way. Six kids out of ten die young. Those kids who are able to mature are very strong and healthy and pass their genes on to the next generation. This kind of life is normal to them. They are happy with it.

"One strange thing is that it appeared to me that they have no concept of time. They don't know what age is so it is impossible for them to understand a concept like average lifetime. Kids are kids and adults are adults. They have day and night and that is all. They don't worry about the next day. Their forefathers are present all the time. Their lifestyle is something that has been about the same for ten, fifty, maybe a hundred thousand years!"

"But you said that you recorded their music. May I listen?" John was amazed at her adventure. "This is better than living in the Lower East Side in NYC," he was thinking.

"Sure, I have got it here. My back packing is not unpacked yet. Hope the batteries are still charged."

She put on the MP3 player. There was no doubt that this was music performed by people that knew what they were doing. Daily practice makes it real.

"What did they think about that you where recording them? I've heard so much about primitive people being afraid to be photographed because they think their faces are falling off."

"No, they liked it. I recorded them and they could listen to the playback. They were listening and singing to my recordings and added even new choruses. It became popular to help me record their songs.

"But one day a man came by and he wanted me to record his friends' speeches and thoughts. They were singing songs about the Indonesian oppression and he wanted these songs to be recorded and broadcast to tell the world what was happening. I didn't understand that he came from the guerillas first and when I got the question about guns I decided to leave. I couldn't take the risk of being involved in their business. There were spies and soldiers everywhere in the jungle."

"What a thrill!" John was absorbed by her story. "But how can you say that they had no concept of time? That really puzzles me. To be able to sing melodies they must have a firm concept about which order the notes come in, mustn't they?"

"I don't think they see it as an order as they repeat phrases a lot."

"I still think that the time concept has to be there, but you could be right that they aren't so conscious of it yet. Europeans themselves have a lot to do with their own concepts, too. About money, social needs and environmental care, for example. I am very interested in time at the moment. I have been studying the works of Robert Pirsig, if you know him?"

"No?"

"He wrote a book called *Zen and the Art of Motorcycle Maintenance* in the seventies"

"Oh, that one! Yes. I read that but it was a long time ago. I don't think I remember anything but I think I've become more positive towards Zen Buddhism and meditation from reading it."

"I don't think the book was so much about that. If you want to know more about Zen you'd better read the book called *Zen in the Art of Archery* by Eugen Herrigel. That is a good one about Zen, I think. And I think more people are interested in money than Zen. Zen and Buddhism are old. Money is the modern religion and price is the modern God."

"So what about Zen and time?"

Mary let the MP3 player carry on playing at a low volume. It gave an exotic touch to the night. John felt like the Papuans were there listening. Elsa changed the candles on the table that had burned out.

"Pirsig wrote another book. It is called *Lila. An Inquiry into Morals*. He received a grant from the Guggenheim Foundation to write a book after he wrote *Zen and the Art of Motorcycle Maintenance*."

"I have never heard of that book. I think I must have a smoke first. Anyone for a drink?" Mary went to the stove to puff a little from a cigarette for a minute. She opened the cupboard and picked out two small glasses and a big bottle of cheap Polish vodka. John had forgotten that he had to drive the next day and accepted the invitation.

Mary moved over to John beside him on the sofa and filled the two glasses.

"Excuse me, but I have to go to sleep now. I am exhausted. Thanks for everything, Mary, this was a most memorable night. I would like to spend the whole night with you but I think you two can manage without me. You look so nice there on the sofa! Like a prince and princess. I wish you a really good night, young lovers. It is hard to be the third wheel at the table." Elsa cleared the table of the tea.

"Goodnight!" Mary and John said in a chorus.

"I am so pleased that someone calls me young," John, said, smiling, to Elsa before she walked away.

"Yes, if you speak loudly I can hear every single word from you. I have got ears like a fox. I like to listen but I am too tired to sit in a chair any longer." Elsa disappeared and left the door open to the room. John could see her undress in the semi-darkness.

"Cheers!"

"Chairs!" John emptied the glass in one draught. The vodka warmed his throat all the way down.

12 - Four Levels and Vodka

"So what about the time, Johnny?"

The clock in the kitchen didn't work. John picked up his mobile phone to see what time it was. It was already past midnight.

"Times flies, when you're having fun. A week ago you were in the middle of the bush. Oh, I think I can still smell the jungle around you."

"Don't be kidding me. You said you lost your sense of smell."

"Who will benefit from that, me or you?"

"I can smell you. I can feel the warmth from your body. Now, what about time? You said something about Zen and the motorcycle."

"Oh, excuse me. Yes. In the first book Pirsig wrote about the different views people could have of reality. He constructed something that is called a dichotomy, which is when you present some criteria and by those criteria you can sort things in two heaps and the criteria works like a knife that separates them from each other. The dichotomy he used was that he saw that either people have either a classic or a romantic view about anything. Two ways to see things, two perspectives that excluded each other. Either people saw a thing's function, that was the classic view. Or else they saw things in a romantic way that we could call fashion. That meant people who just liked to see things how they were and fitted together with one another without taking notice of the function.

"It was a big eye-opener for me because that made me understand how time was changing all the time, but there is always something that is timeless and that is the rules for the mechanical function of a motorcycle. The motorcycle is a combination of the actual state and the eternal function. By using this dichotomy I managed to see and understand both perspectives. That gave me a third perspective – the classic, the romantic or the third – from outside, where I saw both. There are eternal laws for how things work but there is also an actual state that you have to deal with. If a tyre is flat it continues to be flat until you fix it. Romantic people see the flat tyre and buy a new one while classic people see the way to fix it."

"So that was about the time?"

"Oh, no. It's much more. Believe me. I have discovered fantastic things! Just today while speaking to Elsa. She's really bright. She gave me a hell of a hard time understanding her questions. This was only the beginning." Mary poured some more vodka in their glasses.

"Skol, my dear!"

"Scoal for love!"

"After the romantic and classic part, Pirsig continued to search for another thing in his first book and that was a simple thing called Quality."

"Yes, hic. It must be a quality book." Mary waved her glass with faraway eyes.

"He was working as a teacher of rhetoric at a university in Montana. One of his colleagues thanked him for bringing Quality to the school, or something like that. Pirsig became obsessed by this word Quality because he couldn't find a proper definition of it. At the end of the book he finds correlations with all of the grand Ancient Greek philosophers and he declared that

226

Quality isn't a Thing, it is an Event. That is why Elsa said that about love and the erotic as a parallel."

"We are in an event just now. Is that erotic?"

"Wow, yes. Anything that happens between people that love each other. I can sense warm feelings for you in my chest."

"Mmm. Wait, it's a bit cold. Let me fetch a blanket."

Mary went into the room behind the kitchen and returned with a big grey blanket of thick wool. She wrapped it around them and drew her bare feet up on the seat. John was warm and Mary stayed close to his body. John put his right arm around her and breathed into her hair behind the ear.

"I happened to read that book quite early, when it was just new. I had a motorcycle, a Triumph Tiger, and I read the book because I thought I would learn some motorcycle maintenance from it. But that book took me into a new world. This little sentence, 'Quality as an event', followed me through the years and I was kind of obsessed by it. Mostly for fun. I like to understand how things work. I find it natural. But there are so many things in the world to understand. I have never understood women. That is the biggest mystery to me."

"Time. You should talk about time. I am not mystic. I am me."

"OK. But it is true that it took me decades to understand the classic connection between Quality, events, time and money."

"And music?"

"And music. Right. Music is the best. Truly. It talks direct to your heart."

"So?"

"In his second book, Pirsig talks about something that he calls 'the Metaphysics of Quality'. You see? He put another level of distance to the event that was called Quality. Now he placed the Quality concept in focus and put a more differentiated perspective upon it. He was sort of watching the Quality from outside. I'll try to keep it short:

"Pirsig showed that the whole evolution in this world, on Earth, is an event of Quality. It is made by a certain experience of Quality from the beginning to the coming end and he began to see some clear pattern in this process. He found the creator's recipe, we could call it. Quality as an experience, the world experiencing the meeting between the material and eternal conditions, Romantics vs Classics."

"Does he talk about love?"

"Yes, I think so. Or I could make some connections about that."

John bumped against Mary in a friendly fashion and raised his glass.

"Whoops! Empty again."

"Now listen carefully: Pirsig found that the evolution of life on Earth is divided into four different levels. At first everything was just physical and chemical processes. Physical and chemical material is the basis for this planet, this sofa and the whole universe. Physics and chemistry, like geological inorganic processes created this world."

"Du bist mein Sofa!" Do you like Frank Zappa?"

"Oh yes!"

"I can sing every word of that song. You know that I was born in Switzerland. German is my native language."

"OK. Lets go to the next level. Over time, the physical and the chemical processes on the Earth began to be so complicated that bacteria and cells began to occur on the planet. It took billions of years to start but it did. In time a whole spectrum of different biological species flooded the Earth. Using the physical and chemical substances for their own cause. This new level follows another type of conditional criterion from the inorganic physical processes. Clear difference isn't it? It is the difference between organic and non-organic matter."

"It is all made out of physical material."

"Yes, but it is not physics or chemistry that creates an amoeba. It is biology. Mutations, cell division and survival of the fittest. Competition against other species over a place in the sun."

"Aha! That is obvious and true. I just haven't thought about it in that manner. So a machine is following physical laws and a living thing is following biological, and physical laws."

"Exactly. Physics had to come before biology because the biological uses physics and chemistry to work. It is dependent on the earlier level to exist but physical processes can exist and run without biology."

"Aha. I see."

"Now. The border between these levels is shifting, there are always cases of trouble at the border but you see what I mean. There is something there that is very easy to understand if you just happen to think about it.

The next level is the social level. Pirsig found that there was a new level arising from the biological. A new level using the biological level in the same way as the biology uses and is dependent on the physical inorganic level. Social strategies appeared on Earth that use the biological life for its own purposes. Bees, ants, herds of antelopes, fish shoals and humans. Group strategies that benefit from the biological level but in a new way. A field of grass can be regarded as a group strategy to survive better in the face of football players. There are always a few plants that survive and can pass on the genes. Bees and ants have members in their society with different roles that can cooperate. In a social network and society, it is no longer important that all are similar copies. In social strategies there are different roles and there is a decisive advantage with these differences. Social strategies can't exist without the biology but the biological level can exist without the social."

"So that is the basis for human society. Social strategies and the founding of networks, tribes, societies and nations. When they make war on each other it is at the biological competitive level. When people try to build a federation because it offers a better economy than war, then it is social behaviour."

"Bravo! You are getting it fast!"

"Well it is not so special, is it? Most of this ought to be known already?"

"I am not so sure about that. In school shootings the victims use biological strategies. They run like stupid chickens and every individual becomes an easy target. If they instead stick together and act socially they can overrun the villain in seconds. Some will be shot but the more will survive and the loony is definitely the loser. I'd rather die for and together with my friends than alone and abandoned in a hole.

"Most people want to join working life but they have to compete to be part of it. There is competition for jobs, celebrity, for positions within the social level. Many are put aside and forced to be poor and homeless even if they still are doing their very best. People should have the right to be weak. Anyone should have the right to be proud of his membership in the social level. Regardless of position.

"Celebrity is mostly measured by the money you have. In some cases it depends upon the intellectual or cultural impact you have on the society. In very strange cases celebrity is based on the persons look, his or her biological structure. I am thinking of bodybuilders and photoshoot models. Millions are spent on looking good biologically to hide the fact that there is no real basis for celebrity behind it."

"I am getting old. I'd have no chance of being a model. My breasts are too long."

"I think you should be proud. It is your shape. Your individual body. Your contribution to the social level is not based upon your biological structure. You are a music teacher! We must be different. Naturally matured breasts, like yours, are more beautiful than all these cartoon-like balloons filled with toxic silicon that puff and burn at 42. Celebrity should not be based on biology more than in very special cases.

"It is like trying to arrange social parties running under biological conditions. How would it sound if only the best birds were allowed to sing in nature and all the others had to pay for a ticket to listen? Without ugly-looking people there would be no beauties and there are many more of us ugly motherfuckers than of them!"

"You are so ugly. No. Yes you are. We'd better make love."

"Yes, isn't that what it is all about? Love is to build federation, not war."

"I think sex is all about biology. I can't control my biology at all. Plus I am a bit drunk now. Oh! John! I am feeling so good! This is so nice. You are so caring and intellectual. I just can't understand how everything changes all the time. Just a few hours ago I was ready to commit suicide, then I was nearly killing you. Ha ha! Oh, what a day!" Mary crawled closer to John under the blanket. John filled the glasses.

"There is nothing compared to being together with someone I like in the night. It beats just anything. I really longed for you today when I realized that we should meet. I have been so ..." John caressed her neck to show how much he liked to be close to her.

"No more spear-throwing, OK?"

"OK."

"I hid the spears!" Elsa shouted from the living room.

"Shhhh, she's listening!" Mary whispered and giggled.

"Uh, there is more." John continued in a lower voice. "I have to finish. Now, we've had the physical inorganic, the organic biological and the social level. There is a last level that comes after the social level and that is the intellectual level. The intellectual level is the level of concepts, grammar, ice hockey rules, music theory, technical instructions and literature. Philosophical evidence. Cogito ergo sum. Anything that is above the social, using the social in the same manner as the social uses the biological. Social strategies can work without philosophical evidence, but philosophy and language need people that understand and use them in practice. Concepts are not interchangeable in the same way as members of society.

"Anyone can play a written melody any time. Written music is free from the social level. It can exist for thousands of years without being played, but it needs a player and a listener to be heard. Physics makes the sound work technically. Biology makes it possible for the fingers and the ear to distribute the vibrations into the brain. Inside the brain the intellect meets the music."

"Sure, music is the best. I am happy with my work. You are a real philosopher."

"Ah, you're flattering me. I am a comedian. If you can't laugh at it, forget it! Knowing these differences between the different nature of the four evolutionary levels will help you understand how the American culture has developed. At least regarding the American view of life in the 19th century."

"What?"

"Well this is just my own theory, but I use it to understand the difference between biological and social forces.

"Iceland was inhabited originally by people who fled from Norway because their first king, Harald Fairhair, introduced new common laws in Norway. A lot of people liked to be still free and under their own will as they were since the Stone Age so they emigrated to

Iceland. After a few hundred years it appeared to be most rational to make laws by a democratic process instead of consulting the Gods about what was right or wrong by practising Holmgang. The Gods were supposed to have the winner's opinion. In the book Njál's Saga there is a story about the famous Althing at Thingvellir, where the opposing parties instead of choosing two combatants had to take the suggestion that was represented by the majority of the attendants. This was the start of the era of North European democracy.

"The people in the medieval Europe were oppressed by a social reality, commanded by the churches, that had an insufficient basic intellectual analysis. Instead of a theory based upon intellectual truths it was based on fiction and faith in religion. You know how they treated scientists at that time. Instead of a clear scientific and logical definition of truth, faith in God was used.

"When scientific arguments are not enough, faith will take over in the end. Europe didn't work very well, witches were burned and millions of people escaped from the pressure from the religions and wars between competing beliefs. It was a social disaster. Galileo discovered the movement of the pendulum[20] and he was put under house arrest by the inquisition. Descartes had to flee to Sweden from the Dutch clergymen."

"How does that explain what happened in America."

"People who emigrated to America left the intellectually half-rotten civilisation in Europe. But there were no higher intellectual standards as it was mostly Europeans that came to America. So instead of starting the same fight in the new country, the

20 http://en.wikipedia.org/wiki/Pendulum

immigrants turned their confidence more toward the biological level: survival of the fittest. Every man cared for himself alone and had a minimum of social engagement. Freedom was regarded as freedom from social responsibility. Western movies. Lowest taxes wins my vote etc.

"But at the biological level we don't have much opportunity to choose. Martin Luther King had a dream that his kids would be judged by their character, not the colour of their skin. No one can choose his time to be born, when to be sick or struck by accidents. The biological level is unfree and should be treated equally by society. Health care should thereby be a common civil right. At the social level, on the other hand, we are free to choose but also responsible for our decisions and for following the laws.

"Common laws are at the social level. Any talk about justice for animals is pure nonsense. Animals don't gather together and make laws. Animals don't have to follow human laws. Animals don't have to pay taxes and they can go naked, yell at people, show their genitals and shit anywhere."

"Hey dogs! Listen! You are free to piss on this man!" Mary giggled.

"There were other ways to react against the lack of intellectual sharpness. Amish people conserved their whole lifestyle and abandoned thereby further evolution on the intellectual level. Hitler and the Nazis were too rational, dreaming of a new kind of super-intellectual government and had too little respect for our biology. Too much or too little is wasted. Extremism of any kind is bad.

"Robert Owen tried to start a new and better kind of society. He called it 'New Harmony', but it fell down on his limited economic understanding. His intellectual understanding of economics wasn't mature enough. He was bold enough anyway to introduced his own currency based on time[21]. A bill was not in dollars, the local currency was in 'Hours'. Instead of one dollar it said: One Hour. He didn't understand that money is not just time per se, money is saved time!"

"I have never heard about that man either. Boy, where do you find this sort of stuff?"

"This orientation towards the biological level gave a remarkable strength to the American way of life; however, it was poisoned with this intellectual void. That is why many Americans are as much Christian fundamentalists as the Muslim fundamentalists in Asia. Faith and fiction fill the intellectual gap when arguments are running short. But this is not valid for all Americans of course.

"We have the opposite too. The art of trade and barter, the common sense of fair trade has come a long way in North America. The refinement of the art of marketing and business has created the largest and most profitable enterprises in the world. Some of the most modern economists and philosophers are Americans. It is not pure chance that William James's Pragmatism[22] was founded in the USA. Pirsig's work also came from this need for an intellectual completion."

"Yes, but you should tell me about time. Are we there now?" Mary yawned.

"Yes we are. With this Metaphysics of Quality, this four-folded perspective on reality, warts and all, I have

21 http://en.wikipedia.org/wiki/Time-based_currency

22 http://en.wikipedia.org/wiki/Pragmatic_theory_of_truth

found that the lowest common denominator of the MOQ is time, saved time."

"Phew, now you sound like a mad engineer with his wonderful machine, but go on. You must be finished some time."

"I can think about this for hours, there is something in it that thrills me so much. Skoal my love! This is a wonderful night isn't it?"

"Yess, Schkoll monsieur! Hic. Oh, I have to drink some water too."

Mary went to the sink and filled a cup with water. She returned to the blanket and the sofa. Now she laid her head in John's lap but sat up immediately to save her head from swirling.

"Time is crucial in all music, right? It takes time to think. And truths are eternal, timeless. A good idea is the one that lasts forever. The last thing in mind of the absolute last human on Earth could be this: 'I had a dream of a better world'. Bad ideas like exaggerated headlines, lies and rumours in the press create time-sucking unrest. So much for the intellectual level."

"Right."

"And time is crucial in all social processes. Swiss train policy for example. Arrive on time, keep the pace to be able to cooperate at maximum, right?"

"Right mister teacher."

"Money is what it is all about at the social level. Money and celebrity, but money is the meter for celebrity value. Very few celebrities die poor. If a celebrity stays poor it seems suspect. Money comes from saved time. I can't explain that to you now but that is how it is."

"Time is money."

"No, time is not money, but money is saved time."

"Sounds the same to me."

"Don't worry. Next; I am going in the other direction now. In the biology it's all about getting power to compete against other species, survival of the fittest. Catch as much energy as possible in the shortest time. The winner is the one that gets the most food, the most air and space. Competition is all about time. To be the winner, the first. The freedom of the individual."

"Mhm, I can see that."

"Now we have the last and most thrilling. Have you tried to play with a ball, bouncing it on the floor and tried to keep it bouncing? Like players do with basketballs?"

"Yes, but it is hard work. I am not so strong."

"Sure, but you know the feeling when you get the right tempo and distance from the floor, how it feels easier at a certain level?"

"Yes I think so."

"That is how the physics works. All particles and superstrings, all atoms and molecules, all are energy in self-oscillation. The nature of all mass is energy that is trapped in different kind of stable states of self-oscillation. Like a sounding tone in a whistle. There are an infinite number of ways to oscillate. But for a form to persist, it needs energy. The most effective way that takes the least energy to continue to vibrate is self-oscillation. Self-oscillation is the easiest and most economical way and takes less time to perform. For the small lump of energy in a quark to stay in a stable state self-oscillation is a way of saving time. All other ways to behave takes more time.

"Mass itself affects time so much so it can deform space and cause gravitation. As long as nothing puts the oscillating energy out of balance it will continue to swing in a stable state. Just like tones in a flute or a vibrating string with a minimum loss of energy. The pendulum law. The sound of a Gibson Les Paul Custom. Time, time is the crucial part in the appearance of material too because it is all moving, an eternal event.

"I think that one day, scientists will find a way to distract the time, disturb the oscillation in crystalline metal structures so it will force the structure to move. The force of that movement will be so strong that it will be possible to carry loads. That is what the Tibetan monks do when they levitate. They just hum a little with the nose and fly away in the air. The flying vehicles you can see in Star Wars will be a reality and we will use it in spaceships."

"Wow! Is this true?"

"I don't know for sure but it sounds reasonable. We shall not underestimate the Force! I would really like to see that thing live!"

"So what is time then?"

"Eh, it is, well, time. Space in the time, no I don't know really just now ..." John's brain that was soaked with alcohol broke down and lost its function temporarily. Oscillation fell out.

"So you told me all this but still don't know? You said you would tell me about time, you spent a lot of time on that in vain. We could have done something else." Mary lost her interest in the whole thing and went to the loo.

John was humiliated. He knew that there was just a small piece missing. The last key to it all. He lost his faith for a minute and looked at the half-emptied bottle of vodka. He was drunk now and his brain was drained of concentration power. Thoughts ran around

239

headless in his brain. The electric light between him and Mary became fainter. Then his consciousness clicked on again, the synapses wakened, his brain flashed and ran into overflow again.

"Thermodynamics! Elsa said the exergy was the key to time! Exergy seeks its neutralisation! Which causes things to happen! Exergy is the power in the flute of vibrating energy in stable states which in turn creates all particles which are the base for all the material in the universe! Exergy forces events, exergy meets the natural laws and the actual state in the now. The time runs in one direction and every next step in the processes is based on the last step. Idealism meets Materialism!

Mary returned into the kitchen and lit another cigarette.

"So how is it going with the time?" She blew smoke into the void.

John smiled at her. "I love you Mary!"

"Don't be stupid."

"I am not stupid, I'm drunk. I lost control for a while. But I am happy. My mental crash made me feel stupid but I recovered a minute later. Time is – time."

"Yes, Mr Smarthead?" Mary killed the cigarette.

"Time is the space for possibility of change. It is the opposite of the Big Bang. The Big Bang happened and then time could begin. Time is the possibility of events, change, evolution and all. Without time there would be no sound or music. Time is crucial in both making music and making love live. It is fantastic!"

"Yes, I believe you but how does it help us? Now?" She leaned over the sink and swayed her hips.

"You are drunk too."

"Yes. I have had a hard day. Not the worst in my life but still. OK, I am happy. If you had not come I could have been dead now. Or I would have been alive but alone with an empty fridge. Which is worse?"

"I could have been dead now! The spear flew just an inch over my face."

"Ha, ha, ha! Maybe you deserved it. Oh, no! What am I saying? Please forgive me! I just can't keep my mouth shut. I am so glad to see you again Johnny!" Mary ran over to John again and crawled up into his lap. She drew the blanket around her and cried for a while. She was really drunk.

John held her gently and caressed her cheek. "Forgive me, I shouldn't have tried to talk about such a boring thing. But I think it is fantastic! Yes, it is!" John got upset again when he was thought about the last piece in the puzzle.

"Don't drink any more, please," Mary begged silently in his lap.

"There is just one more thing. Lust and danger, love and desire, is the perfect recipe. That reminds me of another story." John caressed her hair and neck slowly. "But we have time, don't we? There is no hurry, we have plenty of time. Love continues."

"Yes, love continues." Mary purred.

The cat was asleep.

13 - Signals at Breakfast

He was lying on his back in the sofa. The kitchen was dark. His kimono was wide open. She was lying with her suppressed weight on his chest. She was warm upon him. Her friendly softness tickled his fancy. John could feel her claws …

"Claws?

"Something is wrong here!"

John quickly awoke. The cat had taken up a sphinx position on his bare chest and her paws were attached to his flesh. The big cat's tail waved like a snake. The claws were alternately buried into his skin. She didn't seem to like being moved away.

John took a slow deep breath. He placed his right hand under her paw and his left hand slowly under the other. He massaged her paw matrix with his thumbs and moved the paw he had in his right hand slowly over to the left hand so he held both arms of the cat between his fingers. John then used his free right hand to gently caress the cat over her head and down her neck and back a few times. The cat purred. Her soft tail swept from the left to the right and back again. John caressed the cat again over the head, to the neck. In one sudden moment he grabbed by the scruff of her neck and grabbed her front legs to protect him from the paws with the other hand. The cat was taken by surprise but screamed wildly when John opened the door and threw her out of the house.

It was still dark. John went to pee. Back into the kitchen he turned on the light.

"A-Ough-rrr!" Three dogs sat on the floor beside each other in size order. The big wolf, the short-haired
242

white one and the grey snoring thing. On parade. They were all looking up at John.

"I seem to have made three new friends," John was thinking. "Common values. I defeated the monster. I had a plan. The cat has only claws and teeth. Intellect vs biology 1 – 0."

"At ease, friends!"

The dogs went back to their sleeping quarters. John went to the sink to drink a big glass of cold tasty water. He returned to the sofa and put the blanket over him. "I must be kind and take care of my biology," he had time to think before he fell asleep again.

John woke up to the sound of somebody working in the kitchen. His head was dizzy. He groaned loudly under the blanket.

"Good morning darling! Had a good night? Camping in the kitchen?" Elsa said in a soft voice. She was wearing a pale green gown made of very thin silk.

"Yes thanks, how about you?"

"Oh, I had a wonderful sleep and lot of silly dreams. I heard you throw out the cat."

"Yes, she woke me up."

"Cats like to be awake at night. I am preparing breakfast for us and then we are going back again. We have completed our mission. Mary is gone."

"Is she gone already?"

"There is a note on the table for you."

John sat up in the sofa and saw a piece of paper. He had to scrub his eyes to be able to read it.

To be continued …. That was all that was written on the paper.

"I didn't hear her leave." John could sense the regret.

"I slept so well last night. Oh, it is so quiet and nice here!"

"Have you checked her bedroom?" John wasn't sure that Mary had gone already.

"No, I am too old for these steep stairs."

John went to see. In the middle of the stairs sat the cat, ready and waiting. How had it come in? John must think about that. The big cat growled. John stopped. He was nearly naked. This was not the time to pick a fight with a cat. "If Mary is still up there she will be awakened by the scream and the cat is in a superior position now, well prepared for an evil combat." John decided to wait. If Mary was sleeping now she would maybe come down later by herself. John went to brush his teeth and wash his face. He dropped the satin robe on the floor and took a short shower to get free of last night's adventurous secretions. He tested his socks and underwear. It was slightly damp but John thought they would dry and get warm in a while.

"Ho ho, breakfast is ready." Elsa shouted from the kitchen.

John returned to the kitchen and the sofa dressed only in his underwear and socks. Elsa had made oat and apple porridge, boiled eggs and coffee. It was a tasty breakfast but there was a disturbing empty place at the table. John was not satisfied but decided to stay calm.

"Mary is gone, or is she sleeping? She is a real night owl and can turn day and night upside down. If she is sleeping now you cannot wake her. She needs all the sleep she can get." Elsa filled her cup of coffee.

"But she has to go to work?"

"She used to be free before lunch. That suits her sleeping habits better. She is used to working late with the many night courses."

244

"I understand, people working at bars and restaurants are the same." John let the porridge bring his belly back into shape. He looked at Elsa's soft breasts that showed under the silk.

"Ice!" Her nipples stiffened immediately.

"What?"

"Oh, excuse me I was just thinking to myself."

"About ice?"

"Please, it wasn't anything important. What are we going to do now?"

"I think we shall finish our breakfast and make some coffee for the thermos. Then make some sandwiches, pack our things into the car and go home again."

"OK, I was drinking some alcohol last night but I hope I can manage it."

"That is your problem. I want to get home safe."

"I think I had two glasses of wine and two glasses of vodka. That is four glasses. Each one takes about three hours to digest. That makes twelve hours before driving again."

"That also depends on when you were drinking it."

"We started at about six o'clock yesterday, that is fourteen hours from now, right?"

"But you were drinking vodka in the middle of the night. You two were fooling around on the sofa until three in the morning. How's your head?"

"A bit dizzy but not too bad."

"I think you should eat this breakfast and then take a sleep on the food. In case there were any more glasses of vodka. Bettering the margins. We don't have to leave before eleven to be able to drive in daylight. If we drive on without stops we will be back in five hours. That will be at four o'clock."

"Then perhaps Mary will be awake."

"Well then. I can take another nap too. I didn't get much sleep either."

"So you were listening all the time?"

"Sure. You two are more amusing than radio. Embarrassed?"

"No. Not at all. Privacy is nice. What is happening between me and Mary is mostly a biological matter and should be kept apart from the social level I think. Our business is private but I don't think that it will affect the connection between you and me. Anyone has got the right to privacy as long as it doesn't intrude on the social level. The social level rules, but the biological is the basis for the social level. You can't cook good food from bad ingredients."

"So you will accept infidelity?"

"What for?"

"You said that what is happening between you and Mary is just a biological matter and will not affect your other social responsibilities."

"No, I said that my connection with Mary is acceptable as long as it does not affect my other social responsibilities. Acceptance is a social matter. Infidelity doesn't exist at the biological level I think." John could see that Elsa's nipples had become soft and relaxed again.

"You can be sure that I will tell you if your affairs are intruding into mine. But so far I have no problem with it at all. You are both my friends and it is so nice to see that you like each other. It confirms that my relationship to both of you is good."

"We are not your sucking babies." Her nipples stiffened at once.

"What do you mean? Are you still drunk?" Elsa looked curiously at John. She was now convinced that she wouldn't let him drive for a while.

"Oh, excuse me, my mind is flying away again … You know, I think it is very important to take care of the biology. Sleeping is a good thing to do for your body, as long as it doesn't make you get to work late. When you are asleep, the social level is cast off. We must be able to disconnect the social to be able to sleep and recover. I have to wait for my biology to digest the alcohol in my veins to be able to drive socially correctly." John filled his cup of coffee and took another slice of bread.

"You say that you must forget your wife to be able to connect to Mary? Isn't that cheating on your wife?"

"Well that depends on what the social contract between me and my wife says. If she is number one, she will stay number one and as long as I don't put another on the throne I am not cheating. I think that the most common problem for a married man is if he makes love to another woman and takes the risk that there will be a baby. That child will have the right to inherit and by cheating the claim to an inheritance will be discussed. The mother wants to have a share of his daily time and income. That is definitely cheating."

"So you mean that if there is a child you are cheating but not otherwise?"

"No. I think it starts already from taking the risk. You know you can't control the biology 100% even by using a condom. Sperms and germs are very small and naughty little bastards."

"So how can you say that you are separating the biology from the sociology if you accept cheating on your wife? I don't understand."

"No, I am not cheating on my wife! I don't take risks."

"But you love Mary?"

"Yes, I do."

"Aahh!" Elsa nearly lost her temper for a second.

"Love is a feeling that confirms attraction and sympathy. It confirms our shared values! I love you too!" John saw that her nipples had become soft again. But her breasts were swaying inside her gown every time she got upset and shook her body. The contact between the nipples and the silk tickled her and caused them to get stiff again. John enjoyed the view.

"Don't be stupid! We are friends. I like you but I am not going to marry you."

"Who said that we should?"

"No one would, ever. Besides, you are too young."

"Can you see the difference between a feeling and a social deal?"

"Well, they are different of course." Her nipples were soft again.

"Feelings comes from the biology, our biological system. Emotions are messages from the biological system to the social and intellectual system. Feelings are signal substances that come from our glands inside our body. Signal substances that deliver important information to our bodily functions. Like hunger, when the level of energy, excuse me, exergy, when the level of exergy is low, signals are sent to our bodily functions to get more exergy. The signals make us hungry and the signal substances also tell fat cells to release the fat to be burned to sugar in the liver. The signals tell us to slow down bodily actions that consume exergy. We get tired and hungry from the message from our glands.

The glands are programmed to respond to the situation."

"But where does the feeling of love come from?"

"Do you believe in angels flying around in the sky shooting arrows in our hearts?"

"No. What do you think of me? I am not drunk!"

"Love and compassion come from our biological system but it is a combination of sexuality and sociality. It started already with the appearance of sexual reproduction that overthrew reproduction by parthenogenesis. Parthenogenesis is the way bacteria and viruses reproduce. Parthenogenesis leads to identical copies while sexual reproduction produces unique individuals, male and female and with different identities. The origin of sexual reproduction leading to unique individuals was the start of the social level because it demands cooperation to reproduce and defeats the destructive forces of time and age. A reproductive system that had major advantages before the pure organic level.

"A species with individual variations has better chances of surviving an attack from a homogenous enemy. The strategy that is easiest to detect where its weak points are revealed loses the game. The strategy that has the best defence system against the other wins. It's the 'war of the worlds' fought by the strategies from each level. For sexual reproduction to continue and survive, male and female must each have a signal system that informs individuals how and when to act and reproduce. These signals must be based on both biological fitness and social affinity."

"So you mean that we are programmed for love, to love a different person?"

"Yes. It must be so. If the signal system does not work, there will be no children or it will be children that have a weak signal system for love. Which gives weaker and weaker signals transmitted to the next generation and so on. The function of love is crucial for the human race. To learn how to live and survive, love must be the most important discipline for the human race. With a malfunctioning signal system for love, the human species will be depleted and doomed to extinction."

"I had no problem with my love of my first husband. My daughter will survive."

"Yes, and you liked your other men, too?"

"Sure. But we didn't have any children."

"No, for sure, at your age! But as I said, the feeling of love is not only sexual, it is a social message also. Because we are a socially cooperative species and we need each other to survive. When man was mostly organized in tribes and small groups, there must have been some kind of nice feelings of pleasure that told the individuals to stick together.

"Sticking together led to an advantage against other groups and species. That helped us to survive as a species because our group of unique individuals were the fittest. That is why it is important, as I see it, that sex and love have to be treated very, very seriously. Sex without a social feeling of love weakens the society genetically from inside. We can't just leave love wild in the streets."

"Mhmm. Why are you staring at my breasts?"

"They are beautiful. I like to watch your nipples change from soft to stiff."

"You naughty little boy! You aren't wearing anything on your own, at least from what I can see. You are still drunk! Shame on you!"

"Please, excuse me. I study them just because I wonder where the signals come from that make them change. That's all. Nothing sexual in that, is there? It is just something on your body that you cannot control. Do you believe me?"

"That is why you make me feel embarrassed. I feel naked when you say so." Elsa crossed her arms to protect her body.

"What's embarrassing about being naked?"

"I don't know, I feel weak."

"Believe me. I will not hurt you in any way. Please, relax. I am your friend. You are smart, beautiful and you are socially agreeable. I like to be together with you.

"It is a nice morning and we have a fine breakfast in Mary's comfortable home. We have time and space enough to live. I enjoy your company, trust me please.

"It is nice to be here, isn't it?

"Does it feel better now?"

John talked silent and slow to calm her.

She released her arms again and leaned back to straighten her hair on her neck.

"Maybe. I was of course used to being naked with all my men. We would bathe together. I would brush their back. I prefer clean men."

"But I am not your man?"

"No, it is not that. You are right that I got embarrassed for something that is out of my control. I want to be alone on the loo."

"It must be absolutely normal to not have full control of our biology. Isn't it? We all have our civil right to our own small secrets about our biological processes, don't we? Love and desire included."

"You certainly cannot control your own body functions, with your erections. I have seen that!" Elsa giggled.

"Yes, that is true, but in some situations it feels worse and in others it is more OK. When I am dancing, for example, there is nothing embarrassing about an erection when I touch my dance partner's thighs and feel their rhythmically moving body. No wonder some fundamentalists ban dancing, they just can't handle their emotions.

"But on a beach, with a lot of mothers and children it can be painful. I cannot make it rise, nor sink. These men with twelve-inch equipment must use a jockstrap I think, if they care at all."

"Your signal system is fooling around with you!"

"But if it was common knowledge that this is reality and that the continuation of a healthy sexual life is crucial for the survival of the human species, then it would maybe be more easily accepted and less embarrassing?"

"Doesn't it depend upon how frustrated you are. I mean if you have had sex enough with your wife?"

"No, that is not my picture. Not at all. I have both experiences from that. It can turn me on even more after we have made love. It is so nice when I am naked with my wife. Then I feel no shame for my body. I could be a pure naturist. But I think I would feel completely different being naked at a nudist camp."

"Have you tried?"

"No. I am sorry. But I think that it has to do with the mixed feelings between biology and sociology. I can be free individually but restrained socially, if you understand what I mean?"

"No, I don't."

"But think about this: I can go naked and show my organic individuality but hide my social preferences. When I am visiting my doctor, for example. If he sees a naked person. If you see a naked person, you cannot tell by what you see whether they are a republican or a liberal?"

"That would be difficult. I am not sure if any of them would show up naked at all."

"I think it is obvious that you can't tell a person's social function from the look of his body, isn't it?"

"Right; in face of the court and the death we are all equal."

"In face of the scale and the IRS!" John said like preaching.

"Oh, you're so dramatic!" Elsa made a holy gesture with her hands together.

"I mean that we are dealing with more than one type of signal system, the biological and the social. The biological relates to our bodily functions and the social has to do with our role in the society. They are different and must be treated as such but none of them is less important than the other."

"You said that the social was superior to the biological."

"Wait, I must think. What about if we imagine people wearing clothes but openly communicating their true social feelings versus another group of people that are naked but hiding their social signals. What is the difference and which is worst?

"Are nudists who run around naked all day long but hide their sexual signals really naked? Is it possible to consider skin as just another uniform? The penis protection on Papua maybe a very good idea? It is a pure mystery to me how they put it on?"

"Clothes are a way of hiding your biology, aren't they?"

"Wearing clothes is to be a liar you mean?"

"Hmmm, I don't want to be a liar, even if you like to watch my nipples." Elsa smiled and moved her body to make them sway.

"I love to, but that is of no big importance, is it?"

"You are welcome. It doesn't hurt anyway. Hey, there is a liberal view on being naked. No one can see to which social class you belong."

"OK, but that doesn't change it. That also sounds like a fraud, a social lie. Yes, that is really an argument for eligible lies in a social group. I think I like best to be naked with people I know well, where the social parts are already declared and where it is allowed to be natural, biologically and socially. Wearing penis protection, ha ha!"

"I feel natural with you, but don't touch my nipples! I warn you!"

"No problem, I think I know the difference between being social and biological. Social behaviour rules. Shall we go to bed, my dear?"

"Yes, but you sleep here and I'll sleep at my place."

"Naturally."

"Get sober!!"

"I'll do my best."

14 - Shoe Diving

At half past ten John was awake again. Elsa was still snoring in the living room. The dogs were waiting at the door. John opened it for them so they could take a look around outside and mark their territory. He went into the living room, took his suit, which was hanging on the chair, and got dressed. Elsa was woken by the sound of his clinking belt.

"Uuhh!" It was like a sound from a Haitian zombie.

"Ten-thirty. Time to get up and go!"

"What are you doing in here?"

"I had my suit here, on the chair. Did you have a good sleep?"

"Please leave me alone. I want to get dressed."

"Sure."

John went out to the kitchen and put the coffee pan on the stove to heat it. He made some sandwiches. Ate a banana and looked out of the window. The temperature had been going up and the ice crystals on the birch alley had melted. The twigs were dark red and dripping wet. White spots of snow in the fields. Good and bad news. Wet roads give better grip if the road temperature is above the freezing point, otherwise, slippy as hell. John wished that he could call some God to fix the temperature for him. "Better take care and watch the road," he thought.

Elsa came into the kitchen. They helped each other to clean up and put their things together. John took a look up the stairs. The head of the cat with half-open eyes was aimed at him from the top.

"I'll write a note for her." John took the note on the table and turned it around to write a short message. "I'll be back!"

They put their things into the car. Elsa checked that all three dogs were back inside again and closed the door without locking it. John wiped the water off the windscreen. He wished to see Mary's face and hand in a window to wave goodbye. He felt a pain in his chest when he put the car in reverse and turned his head away from the house. He already knew that a return to her was just a bitter dream.

"Ahh, it is so nice to be on the road again." Elsa held her handbag on her knee. She took a deep breath and sighed.

"I will do my best to keep us on the road." He drove carefully and tried the brakes. There was no sign of slipperiness.

They were going on in silence. The road was fine. John could see that in the lower parts the road could be frozen. The surface changed from shiny to matt so he took it easy. The weather was grey. No rain but moisture. The windscreen got dirty from oncoming cars and from cars ahead of him if he stayed too close. He was thinking over the events of the last twenty-four hours. The ride over the mountain pass. Elsa's perspective on energy and what he found out about time and money. He wished to just let it be digested and sorted for a while. It was so strange when he thought about the two names of energy, exergy, mass, which must be the same or whatever.

"Mass is convertible to energy, $E = MC2$, Einstein showed that." John had read the formula many times in popular science magazines. C, the speed of light, is a function of time, distance per time unit. John remembered the Lorentz-transformation[23] that tells that objects moving fast will have another view on the room. "Moving at the speed of light will contract the distance to zero. Light and natural laws 'move', propagate in the speed of light so in regard to the light's perspective, the room of the universe must be a singularity, or a field of now between the past and the future[24]."

The time dilation (the length contraction by high speed) $=\sqrt{1-(\text{percentage of lightspeed}^2)}$.

Speed (% of light speed)	Length contraction (%)
10	99 %
50	87 %
70	71 %
90	44 %
95	31 %
97	24 %
99	14 %
99,9	4 %
99,99	1 %
100	0 %

This means that, to the light itself, there is no space at all. The universe as 'light-room' is a singularity.

Exergy must be the same as potential energy, as it was called when he was in high school. Exergy must be the usefulness of energy. Usefulness must, by that, be the potential for transforming energy. Transformability. If a certain amount of energy can be transformed into another form then things are happening. The amount of transformable energy will decrease. But the total sum of energy is still the total sum, as no energy can be destroyed, only deformed. There must be two

23 http://en.wikipedia.org/wiki/Lorentz_transformation

24 http://en.wikipedia.org/wiki/Time_dilation

independent parameters in all pieces of energy; the amount and the form.

"The general conditions, the natural laws that are valid for these two parameters must be able to work independently on the energy or on just anything we know exist."

John worked with his brain.

"A natural law must have some kind of energy, too, and a form. It must have energy to be able to impact on other things with energy. A thing without energy must not exist.

"A natural law must have some kind of form to have a characteristic impact on form. It must be impossible to hit and hammer down a steel nail with a jellyfish! These natural laws are thereby defining themselves. Very funny!" John liked this parts of real working truths.

"Wonder if Elsa has thought about that? It would be impressive if she has." John felt a bit undereducated in the matter compared to Elsa. She had been married to a highly educated nuclear scientist for thirty years. John's wife was an artist and made paintings all day long. Colours and pictures can tell long and interesting stories. John had spent many hours just letting the pictures talk to him in their own language. His wife touched him through these wordless stories. He had no defence against colours. He could not resist her being herself. Listening to her reading poetry was the best. It put him to sleep only after only a few seconds.

"Yes! The paintings also have energy and form! Every single brushstroke, every single piece of pigment. The painting is a mix of energy and form, an expression of energy and form, formed energy."

This combination met him every time he looked at her works. He could remember many of her paintings from the period when she was working on them. Some were destroyed or changed but he had a good memory for these pictures and the process they were in. He had lot of time to look at them when he passed her workroom. The repeated looks at them trained his synapses to burn a copy in his brain till the next time he saw it so he could observe the difference and give a comment. His wife appreciated his participation.

After about one hour's drive the road was rerouted to pass a small village. Elsa saw a restaurant and yelled, "Stop, we must eat! Turn to the right here!"

John slowed down and turned into the road to the village. He parked in front of a little restaurant in the end of a big multistorey building. It was a combination of public house, police station, restaurant and chainsaw repair shop.

"I thought we were going to eat the sandwiches?"

"We can have them later. If we eat now we've got enough for the rest of the trip. I can show you a shorter way this time."

"I'm looking forward to that. So we are not going over that pass again?"

"No, because now I have recently seen it. This time we are going another way."

"OK." John turned off the engine and they went in to have some lunch.

For today's lunch they ordered rice and chicken and brought it to a table at the window. At another table three big policemen were having their lunch too. They were well fed with broad leather straps over their chests.

"This looks like a dangerous place to live in," she said after she had eaten most of her food.

"Why?"

"A police station with a good restaurant in the same building is not good. They'll eat too much and after their meal they'll go to sleep. Then the criminals can do just whatever they want. With a lot of crimes in the village the policemen know that they have a safe and steady job so they can keep on eating in peace."

"Aaah!" John was doubtful.

"The chainsaw repairman often tests his chainsaws outside and the sound is heard above all other sounds so the police will be the last to know when something bad is going on."

"Now I think you sound like Sherlock Holmes. There are places that are wilder than this. The place where I come from for example. No police at all. No cab drivers. No banks. No public house or library anymore."

Elsa laughed. "I know!" She went to the ladies room.

John got his iPad to check his mail and the news. Not much had happened. The civil war in Libya was definitely over, since Gaddafi's son had been captured. Unrest in Syria, the army shooting live rounds at civilians. Far away from Sweden. Snow at last, owners of ski centres were happy again. Some mail that he left unread.

He went outside and took a walk around the block to flush the blood round his veins. When he came back to the car Elsa was standing by it and seemed to be looking for him inside the building.

"I thought you were in the men's room?"

"I just wanted to get some fresh air before we leave. We have a few hours left." John unlocked the doors and they crawled into the car again.

"Ah, it is so nice to be on the road again!" Elsa said when they got back to the main road again while John changed up through the gears to take them on their way south.

"You say that every time."

"Hm, maybe, it is a ritual. It makes me prepared I think."

"I like to drive in your company. This is the second day and I've already got used to you. I was thinking about it when I walked around the block. I have touched your body all over. I have used your physical weight in a positive way. Those are the organic and the inorganic sides of it. I have met your mind several times, that is your intellectual side and I think that I have touched some of the deep points in your mind, right?"

"There is no deep in me, only darkness!" Elsa laughed. "I am a woman!"

"Please don't make a joke about it. I am serious. I think you are serious."

"I am serious about everything I say. I want to express myself and no one else's opinion."

"See, that is what I mean. I can feel that you are serious, open-minded. It feels like I am touching your mind unfolded, naked or clean. I like that very much. Personal confidence."

"I am honest, that's all. I think that it is everyone's duty to be honest."

"OK. What I was thinking about was this: I can touch your intellect, your body and your physical appearance. But how do I touch your heart?"

"You already do."

"Do I? How do you mean?"

"You are kind to my friends. Mary is like an extra daughter. You are a good driver. Being driven by you is sensual pleasure. You don't make me scared. You listen to me and take care of my needs. We are well suited.

You don't rush me and I don't have to wait for you for a long time. I was used to having to scream and argue a long time before we stopped, shut off the radio or got away after a stop. You are the most fantastic driver I have met. You touch and respect my desire."

"So love is a matter of sharing priorities?"

"How do you mean?"

"The feeling of love is based upon your prioritized issues, your priorities. Some people don't see anything other than the material side, the physical evidence of existence. They save hair or things from loved ones as objects for devotion, as a timeless fetish. Other people are more oriented to the biological side of love like sex, dance, smell or passion. A third category is when love is manifested by relations and connections, pride and honour. That kind of love is very strong but can be disastrous if the former grade of bodily functions are not treated well and in a fruitful manner. The fourth grade of love is manifested between people with similar intellectual values and priorities. Someone that cares about and works for the same kind of intellectual values as your own must gain your absolute respect."

"I think you are well suited in all these cases. None of them is more important than another. Your car, your smell, your care of me and Mary and your odd sense of humour."

"Thank you." John took her hand and caressed it.

"Prrrrrt!"

"What was that?" John looked at Elsa.

"I had to fart."

"IN MY CAR?" John stepped on the brakes and stopped the car halfway into the ditch.

"GET OUT! NOW! AT ONCE!!" John ran out of the car and to the right side of the car, slipped in the ditch but managed to open Elsa's door. John's entire energy reserve was released and he yelled at her to get out of the car at once. He opened the door to the back seat and ran around yelling for another second. Then he felt his throat crack up and he had to find a better way to release his anger. He had wounded himself by mistake several times before. He found a thick tree limb in the ditch and used it to hammer repeatedly on a big stone on the other side of the ditch until his arms lost their power.

Elsa stood and held the door so as not to fall. John could see that she was crying. He got mad again. Now because he felt so stupid about his way of acting against women. "I never learn," he was thinking. He threw the limb with the rest of his power straight across the road so it landed in the bushes. He had to get back his breath and came to a standstill behind the car to calm down.

"I knew it," he was thinking. "It impossible to rely on a woman, whoever it is. I try to be reasonable. I had tried to point out the reasonability behind any human action and then that stupid bitch does a fart in my car. I knew that something would happen, sooner or later." He was breathing more slowly. Elsa looked at him over the car and looked very afraid. She sniffed and her eyes were red. Tears were running from her eyes rolling down on her coat. John had a soft heart; he lost his anger and became sorry for it.

A school bus was passing. The Volvo blocked the road so the bus driver had to slow down a bit. All the kids on the bus could see them up close. John saw their faces and he could see that some were laughing at

263

them. A boy pointed his finger at Elsa. John tried to read his lips but he could guess that the boy used no kind words about her. In the middle of the bus John could see another boy and a girl who appeared to be afraid of what they saw. Maybe they had had some bad experiences of grown-ups that were angry.

John's conscience fell into pieces and it spilled out into the ditch. He didn't like to be responsible for scaring an innocent child. Shame fell over him. All his self-confidence was crushed into dust again. He must apologize. The bus disappeared along the road and John went slowly around the car to Elsa.

"Forgive me Elsa. I am so stupid. I couldn't control myself. All the kind and smart words I say are worth nothing when I behave like this. I am just a piece of shit."

"Yes you are! I am an old woman and I can't control all my body functions. I had to fart. It wasn't my fault."

"But you yell 'Stop!' for everything else?" John held her around her shoulders with straight arms. She looked quietly at him with her sad face. Elsa still held the door by both hands so as not to fall down into the ditch. She couldn't dry her tears as a result. John took a tissue from his pocket and dried her face. He slipped with his right foot into the bottom of the ditch. He felt the cold dirty water run into his shoe. Water all the way to the toes before he got back his balance so he could lift the shoe above the surface. Elsa giggled at him.

John went to the back seat and took off the shoe. Turned it upside down to let out the water. He took off his sock and wrung the water out of it. He placed it on the floor by the back seat over the shoe. He placed it in front of the opening from the heating system so the hot dry air would dry the sock.

"You certainly cannot control your own body functions. I have seen that!" Elsa cried.

"That doesn't smell!" John went back to help Elsa back into the seat. "I beg you Elsa, people farting in a car is the absolute worst thing I know of. It feels like somebody placing his arse into my face. Would you please ask me to stop next time you have to. Please! And it is not a certainty that I have an erection every time my trousers get buckled. I use to wear trousers with plenty of space and that makes buckles in the material when I lean forward."

"I know when I see an erection. I can see it move!" Elsa said in a proud voice as her better mood had returned once she was sitting comfortably again.

"You keep a good eye on it, don't you?"

"I am a lady and I have a right to be pleased by men with straight backs standing up for themselves. You shouldn't be ashamed of your temper. You did the right thing. Except for shoe-diving. Ha ha ha! Ha ha ha! That made me happy again!"

John had to drive with a bare right foot. He adjusted the current from the heating system so that most of the hot air fell on the floor to warm his foot and to dry his sock. The bare foot helped him to drive even more softly and gently. Elsa could look forward to another comfortable drive.

"OK, I think I can recover from that. Please tell me next time you have to fart. There is no problem in stopping and getting some fresh air."

"I'll do my best, partner. You are a good driver."

"What did you think about Mary's trip to meet the savages in the jungle?" John wished to change the subject. A sign told them that it was a long drive to the next place. That left a lot of time to talk about something else.

"Ahh. That was exciting. And that is so typical of her to change her travel plans. George must have been going crazy about that. This wasn't the first time she changed her plans. She does that all the time. Did you know she lived with the tinkers in Ireland?"

"No. I thought she was from Switzerland?"

"Yes she is. But she left home at sixteen and stayed with tinkers for years, all around in Ireland. They have no steady address but live in wagons pulled by horses. They are nomads. That is where she learned to play the flute."

"Sounds as if she likes to be close to danger."

"Why should that be dangerous? Tinkers must have a desire for life like anyone, I think."

"Yes, but a young girl with blue eyes can very easily be used and seduced by older and more experienced men." John had a flash. Mary's stay with the tinkers reminded him of a dark event that he would rather forget. It had a connection. He must think it over for a while first before he told Elsa.

15 - A Crawl Lesson

"Once I was young, too!"

"Sure you were."

"Yes. But this is special. Mary's story reminded me of what happened to me once when I was in Louisiana."

"What is so special about that?"

"It was a very strange thing. I have nearly forgotten it. Now I understand that I was ashamed about what happened. I have tried to forget it. I have never told this to anyone before. It's about meeting people in the wild. I have done that once too."

"That sounds good, go on please."

"I was visiting my friend Jeff in St. Petersburg, Florida. We drove in his car to New Orleans to listen to Frank Zappa and his band playing live. It was a long drive overnight. Jeff caught a cold during the drive so when we arrived at New Orleans in the morning he was really sick. We rented a motel room outside the town. Jeff had a fever and felt so bad. He couldn't do any more than just lie in the bed. I waited at the room, watching TV all day long.

"I got bored of that so I took his car down to the city and parked it on a vacant demolition site close to the French quarters. It was in November or December. I don't remember exactly but it was definitely far away from the Mardi Gras. It was early in the evening and there were almost no people in the streets. I walked around and looked at the buildings; the french windows, the cast-iron verandas and the small pieces of life I could see. It was not cold but it was not hot either. Perfect for a slow and easy promenade on an evening in New Orleans.

"I walked the streets where there were music bars. Different places in a long row beside each other. Different styles and different music. Fashionable and less fashionable. Large windows onto the street with pink and blue neon signs. Miller or Budweiser beer. Paper notes inside the doors. It was easy to look inside and get a picture of what was going on, or rather not going on. I thought about spending the night by sneaking in somewhere to have a beer and listen to some nice music. Most of the bars were open but there were no people. Most of the places were totally empty. It gave me a surreal feeling. That must have been because I was used to movie scenes and pictures from the Mardi Gras with crowded streets and people dancing on the tables. The stage was set, waiting for the actors and the camera."

"So you were a bit disappointed then?"

"No, not at all. I liked it. It was a bit weird. You remember I was not there for the festival. We were going to listen to Frank Zappa at the University Hall."

"So what happened that was so embarrassing? You got drunk and fell into the canal?"

"No. It was so empty everywhere, but I stopped at a small tiny place with a bar straight inside. There was some really nice soft blues music coming out through the open door from a real live band. Not just a lonely guy with a sax or a clarinet. I saw a single woman inside so I stepped in and went to the bar. The place was fresh and clear inside, nearly no smoke and a bit perfumed. The air felt more like in a barber's shop. The only guest at the place was a black lady in a short pink dress at the bar, sitting on a stool and talking to the black bartender.

"I took a stool next to her, to be the next one getting served. Their talk gave me some time to watch her. She was middle-aged, about forty I think. Big fuzzy hair with an embroidered red silk ribbon holding it together so it was pointing like a broom straight up. She looked pretty wild. Small but thick golden earrings. Big breasts, they were very big. She was big all over. Her hands were broad and she was wearing a complicated ring on every one of her brown fingers. The nails were painted clear red, like blood. I was convinced that she must be a prostitute. I had some thoughts about these hands, where they had been and what they had been doing.

"After a while the bartender turned to me. I asked for a beer with not so much alcohol. I didn't want to take any risk with Jeff's car. The bartender smiled at me. As it felt like I had disrupted their talk I turned to her to apologize. She looked at me with her dark eyes. I was determined not to fall for any tricks from a prostitute but when she looked at me and smiled, my gaze got stuck on her almond-shaped eyes. I forgot everything and just couldn't say anything else but 'You are beautiful'. You must forgive me for that Elsa. I was a lonely guy."

"Of course, that is the most natural thing to say to a beautiful woman. Go on!"

"You are beautiful." John gave Elsa a kind look.

"Thank you!" She smiled back.

"I remember this very clearly, but there are pieces missing. Anyway. Now, listen to this Elsa. I began to talk, we began to talk, I told her that I was from Sweden and that my name was John Smith. She laughed out loud at that and she said 'Hi, I'm Lulu! I run this place. That man there, Zeke, is my younger brother.' She pointed at the bartender as he walked down behind the bar closer to the band. 'Sure' I was thinking, every artist choose their nickname. I thought that by 'run this place' she meant that this place was her working area, where she picked up her clients.

"I said I was alone and a bit bored in the city. She laughed again and brought her big hand down hard on my thigh with a slap! That hurt a bit. 'Ha ha ha!' She looked at me and laughed. I didn't dare to complain so I smiled back and played tough. Then she took my left hand and examined it. I thought that it was just another trick. 'Now she will tell me my future for a dollar.' But she just looked at my hand and caressed it with her pale brown fingertips and said that she enjoyed my hands.

"I was working in construction at that time; that gave me strong hands but I had quit some weeks ago so they must have become softer. I didn't understand what was going on. Then suddenly she placed my right hand on her thigh under the edge of her skirt and returned to her drink."

"I like your hands too, they are soft, and, strong." Elsa said thoughtfully.

"We didn't say any more. She was listening to the music and I joined in. It was a very good band. They played so softly and perfectly together. Like they did this every day. The music came from inside themselves. It sounded like they were not just playing but more like contemplating today's fishing or something, bam, boo bam, ta ta baa … in this empty and uncrowded place. It caught me.

"Well. Lulu was a professional. She moved closer and let my hand come closer upon her thigh. I liked the contact with her skin but was not prepared to rent a prostitute in my solitude. This was just play for the moment. Her skin was soft, hot and dry. I could feel

270

how it vibrated when I moved my fingertips to the music slowly along the inside. On the street it was quiet and empty. No people, no cars. The bartender was standing at the other end of the bar listening to the music. His hands were busy with some glasses. I caressed her thigh. She showed no resistance. She smoked.

"I explored the area with my right hand and held the beer with my left crossed over the active one. By the end of a melody I had advanced to her inner secrets and now I was sure. No underwear! Definitely a pro. Great! Now, where is the pimp that will beat me up and take my money if I refuse her offer? Of, course I had an erection at that moment. Oh, that one was great! But what was I to do next? I don't think I had enough money in my pocket to pay for a night with her. I didn't know what to do. I had never met a prostitute before so I had no experience. But I had met many girls before, naturally, so in that sense I had a complete toolbox to handle the situation. This was huge. I have never met such a big little baby snake before! It was the size of a fingertip, I promise!"

"Are you sure that it wasn't a man?"

"A man with a small thing like that should not call himself a man, I am sure about that. This was a very horny, top-of-the-pop aroused, woman, nothing else."

"So then you followed her home and spent all your money?"

"No. We stayed at the bar. It was so nice there with the live music and cool mood. I treated her the best I could and she really enjoyed it. I tried her desire by moving my fingers a millimetre away from her and she followed. She moved closer over the edge of the stool and let me go on with my service between her thighs. The night was still young. The band was playing so

271

nicely. Blues all the time but every melody was new to me."

"So I guess, you are going to tell me that she eventually had an orgasm at the bar?"

"Oh, yes. I rolled my fingertips to the beat of blues. She rocked. She made noises with her nose and her mouth. She sounded like a purring cow to me. A heavy moan coming up from the deeps in her. She had her eyes half open but didn't look at me much of the time.

'Ohh, my- G-o-od!' she whispered to me. After another slow second she took a long deep breath and started to laugh, a thundering laugh, 'Ooo-AH-HA-HA-HA-HA! OAH-HA! OAH-HA-HA-HA-HA!' It must have been heard all over the music and out on the street through the open door."

"That sounds natural to me, to laugh I mean. You don't sound natural."

"Sure. After the laugh was over she hit me in my back with her big hand, 'Schmock!' so I nearly fell off the stool. She must weigh hundreds of pounds, I was thinking. 'What a punch!'

"'Hi Zeke, give us another drink!' The bartender looked at us and came back up again. I dried my hand on my trousers. Then I saw that we had got company."

"Here comes the pimp!"

"No. It was a young girl with black straight hair, of my age. She was very beautiful. She was wearing a thin pale yellow skirt and a light brown leather jacket. Not much jewellery. Slim and curvy. Red lips and long red painted fingernails. She stood on my right side and I was sure that she must know how I had treated my new friend on my other side. Lulu said, 'Hey Chica, here is something for you! He's got dinah-moe hands!' The girl turned to me and took my right hand that I just had used on the big lady."

272

"She must have been chic, that little girl!" Elsa added.

"Yes, but to me that was just another artist name. Chica examined my hand with her fingertips and held it to her cheek and then to her breast. She said 'OK. Hi!' and we began talking. I told her about the same story again, that I was a lonely guy from Europe and was here for a concert by Zappa. I told her that I enjoyed the music at this bar just as much. She didn't say much more about herself, maybe I was glad to talk to someone else that seemed not to be in the boxing business. I told her that I played the diatonic accordion and it would be nice to get to listen to some real local zydeco or Cajun music while I happened to be in this area.

"She said that I was lucky. She was going to drive her mother home from a barn dance somewhere outside the city. Her mother sold pancakes at the place. I could follow her there so I could get to listen. I thought it was a great idea. When we prepared to leave, Lulu waved to say goodbye so I turned to her again. She buttoned up my shirt and opened it a bit. 'Wham!' another hit with her right fist with all these rings. Now at my chest, but not so direct, even if it hurt, more like a slide. Her finger rings cut my skin and it began to bleed. She smiled in friendly way at me, clapped my face and buttoned my shirt again. I was just a green newcomer to this place I didn't know how to react. I just smiled back at her like a lost stupid white boy from the country.

"Chica took me out on the street to her car. That car was not just a car, it was a golden spaceship! A Pontiac Catalina from the beginning of the sixties. Stained but metallic-gold-coloured and a dirty white convertible top. It looked so funny next to the yellow markings in the street that marked the parking space. This car was just too wide for these narrow lines.

"We jumped into the wide front seat and she drove us away. She was a good driver and the ship floated away around the corners. I tried to complain about the cut on my chest, but she said that I should be glad. 'You are a lucky man,' she said. She gave me some tissues to take away the blood. She looked at it and said that Lulu knew what she was doing. 'You must have treated her well?' I answered that I tried my best. 'To get rid of her,' I was thinking to myself.

"I don't remember much about the way to the barn dance. When we arrived I saw hundreds of cars and trucks. Signs with the letters NRA, blah, blah, blah, Barn Dance, Promotion or Celebration or something. Chica told me that NRA stood for National Rifle Association. That was the reason why everybody, I say everyone, was carrying a weapon. Revolvers and guns. I saw rifles, more of them, in the back windows of the parked cars. And there was booze. A lot of people I saw were blind drunk and carried plastic gallon cans of homemade alcohol. It was just like home. Except the guns."

"Sure. I know the area you come from. No wonder why they call you Indians."

"Chica led me into the barn and introduced me to her mother. She was not as cute as her daughter. She was as short as Chica, but round, fat and with a wild hairdo that was more like the big lady at the bar. Her mother scared me with her expression as she grinned and start laughing at me. She gave me one of the last thick pancakes, covered by maple syrup. After I had it she invited me to dance. I didn't dare to say no.

"She took me into the crowded dancing hall and it was a real party going on in there. Big signs. Red, blue

274

and white paper decorations. Cowboy hats and high-heeled leather boots. People shouting and laughing, walking in and out. The music was high. It was just a regular country band playing as far as I could see. Guitars, drums and some fiddlers. There was a guy with an accordion playing. But the music was so loud and all the noise around made it impossible to listen seriously to him."

"You had a dance anyway. I have never danced!"

"Yes, but this was some dance I didn't know. She was very strong and she held me tight like a bear. She could have lifted me up off the floor if she'd wanted to. I just followed her steps. She seemed to be happy. We danced a waltz and I think it was some kind of polka, waltz again and some slow foxtrot type. It was damned hot in there and we got sweaty. Her smell was strong but not bad. The salt in the sweat hurt my wound.

"I was playing the defensive game as I was one of the few without a gun in my belt. There were so many drunk and armed people around. But I didn't hear one single shot during the time there. There must have been some kind of strict discipline running in the chaos.

"We didn't stay more than about an hour I think. Chica and her mother put together the things and we got back into the Pontiac. Chica's mother jumped into the front seat, too, so I had the place in the middle between them. Chica carefully backed out the spaceship from the port and began to drive her mother at home. I was a bit excited over attending the party but disappointed about the music.

"I must have been thinking about how Jeff was doing too. Him sick in the bed at the motel and me on this pleasant adventure. There were no mobile phones at this time so I had no opportunity to tell him what I was doing or where I was. I didn't know that myself. He didn't know where his car was parked if I were to get in trouble, and I had the keys.

"I had a good view of the road from the front seat and of how Chica was driving but all these turns, signs, small roads and bends in the dark made it impossible to remember the road. I didn't try either. It was dark so I didn't even know if we were going south or north. We were far away from New Orleans, that was certain. I had to stay confident that Chica would drive me home again after we had delivered her mother."

"So you were lost?"

"Yes, I had to admit that I was lost, but I thought this was still better than just waiting for Jeff to recover. I heard that Chica and her mother used another language between themselves.

"After about half an hour's drive in the dark, she stopped the car with the headlights still on and said: 'Get out! Now we're going to take a bath!' Chica and her mother went out of the car, stripped their clothes off and jumped naked into a small river. I was still sweaty and followed their example.

"I swim out in the dark, fresh water and it was so nice to get rid of the dirt from the barn dance. I turned over on my back and let myself float, carried by the gentle dark stream. I looked at the stars in the sky. I imagined that I was hanging in the water, caught by the gravitation, looking down at the stars in the space down under me.

"Chica and her mother were already up again. They began to laugh hysterically. I turned around and asked what was so funny. They laughed even more and after a while Chica managed to breathe. 'You are not supposed to stay in the water too long. There use to be alligators around!' In the same moment I felt

276

something alive against my foot and I panicked. I have never learned how to do the crawl but just then I crawled like Johnny Weissmuller. I didn't stop waving with my arms around until my entire body was up on land.

"Chica and her mother were laughing even more. They couldn't stand up. Her mother sat down on the ground laughing. It could have been a small little fish or a twig that I had felt with my toe. I felt like an idiot again, of course, but what could I say? I was still alive."

"And you learned to crawl."

"No. I still don't know how to do it. Anyway, we were wet. We had no towels. I worked hard to put on my trousers again and had a hell of a time with that, naturally. They got stuck all the time. When I finally had my trousers on, Chica and her mother were already sitting in the car and they honked the horn at me to jump in. They were naked and had just thrown their clothes into the back seat. I felt stupid. They were laughing.

"Two minutes later Chica passed a timbered bridge. She parked the car beside a rubbish heap and that was the place where her mother lived. I got out of the car and could see a lot of junk. Broken cars, ploughs and harvest machinery. Some small sheds and a bigger wooden grey shack with no paint between the big trees."

Elsa smiled and looked out of the window. The forest was thick. No alligators in the frozen creeks here.

"So what happened next? Now when you were out in the wild."

"Yes. What happened was this. I followed Chica and her mother into the shack. It was more comfortable inside than it looked outside. Chica and her mother put on some casual wear, some sort of dress to hide their bodies and began talking in their own language. I could see that they were probably speaking about me. Chica's mother maybe thought that I was her boyfriend or something. I sat down and waited for them to be ready so we could go back to the city.

"It ended with me getting drunk, really drunk. Her mother gave me a small drink first and then we talked, ate something, fish or meat? I don't remember. Then some more to drink and after a while I had no control. They were laughing at me but I began to get used to that. I was the brilliant and funny guy. I remember it was like a late party but I didn't know what was happening.

"To cut a long story short ... I was seduced by Chica and then by her mother. I woke up in her mother's bed. Later in the night two more women showed up and the party continued. I was filled with food and drinks and kept in the bed where a lot of things happened. The other two women were Chica's grandmother and Chica's aunt. They were Indians.

"This was an Indian tribe and these four women were the only members in their tribe. They were living on this island and had done so for ages. They told me a lot. One of their ancestors was the only survivor of his tribe from the battle of Wounded Knee and he found this place to hide. He had also brought some gold that he had stolen from the white army. That gold had been used to live a good life on the island for a long time.

"I asked them about their men, where were the men? Chica told me that she had some brothers, too, but in this tribe all men were fighters, running around all the time and got killed.

"They had another speciality. They were very skilled at making fishing hooks and knives. Very sharp knives that were used for hunting and fishing. The knives were made of pieces of old cars. In the old days they had to buy iron which could be more expensive than gold.

"The tribe was a matriarchy. The gold was also used to pay for the girls to go to schools so they learned how the white people were thinking. Boys did not go to school. They learned to make sharp weapons, fight and die. It scared me to death when they told me. I was prepared for the boys to come home and cut me into slices and feed me to the alligators. Chica assured me that would not happen. How could I be sure? I had no alternative other than to trust her."

"Stuck like a schmuck!"

"Chica told me that she use to dress like this when she was here but she had a job on an army base as a meteorologist and a nice and decent apartment in the city. Her grandmother said that she had been working with a secret project regarding the A-bomb during the Second World War. She had been an assistant for some of the scientists.

"She meant that she had an affair with both Einstein and Oppenheimer. 'They put a bet on me but I seduced the both of them and took the money! I gave them an offer they couldn't refuse,' she said and laughed.

"Late in the evening next day, Chica took me back to civilization in New Orleans."

"So you were out in the wild with a meteorologist and her mother. I am thrilled! Nothing to be ashamed of I think."

"But don't you see? It was rape! I was raped! What could I do against their razor-sharp rings and knifes?

I'd had enough already of that. You must understand that! Imagine that if it had been a lonely girl that met some men instead at a bar. Following a man out to a barn dance and then straight out in the bushes, doing the same things. That girl would have been all out of help. It would have been first-degree rape. I was defenceless and completely exposed to their will. A man raped by four women. So humiliating! The police would have laughed themselves to death if had they heard my complaints."

"Ha ha, maybe you deserved that from the way you treated the woman at the bar."

"Would you have said that to your daughter?"

"She would never do that to a man."

"Now, this is not the end of the story, there is some more. Chica left me in the town and we said goodbye. Kisses and all that stuff, you know. But she never gave me her name or the address of her apartment. I guess that I was just a sudden adventure and that was all. I don't think I miss her, either. Anyway. I went to find the car and drive back to the motel and Jeff. When I came to the demolition site I saw a group of boys fooling around by the car.

"Two of them were working on the door trying to break into it. I shouted for some attention from the neighbourhood but the only thing that happened was that the gang turned against me. A big guy came up and grabbed me from behind. A dark long-haired boy in front of me asked me if I was the owner of the car and if I had the keys.

"'It would make it much more easy to steal the car,' he said. 'The door wouldn't have to be broken and I wouldn't get hurt.'

"I was close to peeing in my pants and I really longed for Chica and her brothers at that moment. I didn't answer fast enough. I couldn't say a word, my brain just locked.

"The dark guy pointed a knife at my chest. He saw the dried bloodstain on my shirt. The big guy pressed my arms back so the cut on my chest opened. The wound began to bleed again and made my shirt wet from my blood. The new colour made him curious.

"'Hey whitey, why are you bleeding already? I haven't started yet!'

"The other boys came closer to look. I felt like a sheep trapped by a herd of dogs. The boy with the knife opened my shirt with his knife. He just cut the buttons with it. Then he took a closer look at my cut. He jumped back.

"'Oh shee-iiT! It's Lulu! How do you know her? Let him loose!' He ordered the big guy to release my arms. 'Stop, put back the hubcaps! Get off the car!'

"The ring widened. The leader of the gang backed off to the left side of the car. He took a look at the door where they had been working to break in. He tried to rub away the marks with his bare hand and smiled mysteriously at me.

"'Sorry mister, just a mistake. We just had to watch your car and to keep it safe in case someone tried to steal it. Looks like we stopped them, right?'

"He put a couple of five-dollar bills in my hand. My mouth was still dry as a desert but I began to understand that this gang was very afraid of Lulu. I told him that Lulu and Chica were my friends.

"'Chica? My sister? Oh no! Oooh shit! She's gonna kill me! Here, take this knife. Be my brother and don't tell her anything about this little fuss. I didn't hurt you, did I? No! You're Lulu's little friend. Lulu's friends are not my enemies.'

"He looked down at the ground and found the buttons from my shirt and gave them to me. He kept the knife. 'Buttons loose easy, right?' I had no chance to complain.

"At this time I had no more nerves to lose I think so I got back my voice and tried to be in charge again, so I said, 'OK suckers, get lost! All of you!' and they disappeared like rats in the dark. I jumped quickly into the car and drove away. I knew that they could return at any minute and do just whatever they wanted with me.

"Back at the motel the room was empty and Jeff was gone. He had a backstage pass and he didn't want to miss the chance to shake hands with and talk to Frank Zappa. I took a long shower and checked the cut and it really looked like a double L. I was marked like cattle. I missed half the concert."

"Two Ls for double luck."

"I am not surprised when I read the news about other people getting drunk and lost in the jungle. It is easily done. I will never follow a stranger out into the unknown wild again. I have never told anybody about this before. It hurt my pride to be seduced and mugged so easily."

"But you liked Chica?"

"Yes, and no. She fooled me, or she did that together with her mother. Maybe it was her mother's idea. Who knows."

"So it was more like eating canned dog food?"

"Or worse."

"Sorry to hear that you had such a bad experience of women."

"It was not entirely bad. I'm thinking about Chica's aunt. She was different. I liked her better. She was really different. She was darker but she also had different skin. I remember that now. They had a fireplace in the shack with an open fire inside and it was very hot in the room. They were dancing naked around in the light of the fire and singing.

"The others got sweaty but Chica's aunt didn't, she was still dry. She was the most horny of them, also, and I liked her best. Yes, she was good. Ah! 'Sweet memories of love!' She was to die for. Or maybe it was as usual, the victim falls in love with his watchman."

"So you have some wild seeds growing in Louisiana?"

"Maybe. Who knows? I don't think I am interested in finding out. How could I?"

"They may try to find you?"

"But I was raped, I can't be held responsible for that?"

"Maybe to give your share of the gold?"

"I think the gold was sold and done long ago. Chica's car was gold-coloured but old. This was in 1984 and the car was from the beginning of the sixties. It must have been more than 20 years old.

"Her aunt told me a strange thing, I remember. She must have been some kind of shaman or medicine woman of the tribe. Yes, I think she was the leader of the little tribe."

"Isn't the oldest the leader?"

"I don't know much about Indians and their traditions. I am no anthropologist. Forget that. But she showed me a thing that I remember. I have thought about that sometimes."

"Her aunt gave you her phone number?"

"No. They had no telephone, no electricity either. She drew my lifeline."

"Your lifeline?"

"Yes, the line that must be crossed by a sword to kill a person. She draw her finger from the top of my head slowly between my eyes, along my nose over my mouth, my neck, my chest, down over my body while reading a long string of words. Eventually she held my genitals. It was like, uhm ... I can remember the sound and some words but I don't think I understood much of it.

"'Wakan-tanka blows his whistle when I think,' or ask for something. When I was looking for something it was Wakan-tanka's sight I was using. When I try to speak it is Wakan-tanka's voice I hear and so on. Wakan-tanka's drum is played in my chest when I breathe, and it was something about my courage. When I was digesting my food in my stomach it was Wakan-tanka's body. When we made love and new babies was also a tribute to Wakan-tanka.

"She was different."

"That sounds like the Indian chakra wheels."

"Aha? Never heard about that. I have never been into Hinduism. I think that she did it to me so I wouldn't be so scared. It made me feel better. Much better. I have thought about her drawing the line at times when I have felt bad. Just thought about it. There was no prayer or anything. She only did it to me once."

"I think it's time for some coffee now."

"Good idea. I'll stop at the first good place I find."

16 - Emotions at a Distance

John found a small road that went fifty yards to the right into the forest. He drove to the end and turned the car so it was pointed towards the main road. Elsa picked up the coffee and gave John a cup and a sandwich. They became silent while their coffee warmed their insides. The surrounding trees were dripping wet from the mist. The sudden silence was intense but relaxing. John could hear Elsa breathe slowly. He wondered if it would be possible to hear her heart beat also. He could hear his own blood run in his own veins. In some vein that passed close to his ear. 'Fo-osh, fo-osh, fo-osh'. A perpetual sound that followed him night and day.

"How is your foot from driving naked?"

"Oh, no problem at all, thanks. I have hot air blowing on it so it is warm and dry. The accelerator is covered by soft rubber."

"What about your hands? How can they feel so special?" She said after a while.

"I don't know really. I have never had any others." Elsa took his right hand in hers and tried to find out. She looked curiously at every point, tried every wrinkle.

"I can't see anything special. But I like the feel of them."

"I like the feeling of your hands also. How do we know that your hands aren't felt the same as mine?"

"We would need another observer to decide that."

"We need a third party to tell the difference between two independent values?"

"Yes."

"So you were the third party when I was talking to Mary?"

"Hm."

"And if I as an observer am trying to find out the characteristics of anything, then I am some kind of third independent party between two objects. One object to compare with, as a scale, and another object. Everything I look at is compared to something else?"

"Well. If you compare an apple with a pear or just weigh the apple, yes. Kant was discussing his desk in front of his pupils. He showed how impossible it is to know something about the table it self, 'Das Ding an Sich' (the thing in itself[25]), just from the look of it as all you knew was just your own sensations. But by putting another table upon the first table it is possible to tell something about it, 'Das Ding an Tisch' (the thing on the table). Because then you are a third independent party that watches the relation between the table upon and the table under. We can change the relation by turning one of the tables and they can change place. That is what happens when you put something on a scale or compare it to a ruler for example."

"The scale I am using here can be my feelings about something I think. The scale is constructed of my memorized elements from earlier experiences, bad and good. If I look at a sandwich, for example. My feelings and memorized experience say it is looking good. I, as an observer, trust my feelings and decide to eat the sandwich."

---

25 http://en.wikipedia.org/wiki/Noumenon

"What are you aiming at? A new kind of therapy for observers?"

"No, I am just curious. I like to experiment with my thoughts. Like playing with bricks and blocks in my mind."

"And who are you, behind the observer?"

"I am the one that choose."

"You are the chooser?"

"I choose between opportunities."

"And how do you know what to choose?"

"I consult my experience. I experience my feelings."

"And where do the feelings come from? How are you sure that it isn't the feelings that are telling you how to act?"

"Because I am free to follow them or not. It is an act of balance. I can let my body drop down from the gravitation or I can strive to hold my body upright. Evolution taught humans to stand and walk upright. Those who did not became the last in the game to be among the fittest."

"So you think that the opportunity to be an upright standing animal was there all time?"

"Yes. I think so. If life is created on another planet, in another galaxy in the universe, I think that all the conditional opportunities are in place from the beginning. But it is a difference between ideal opportunities and real opportunities. It is ideally possible that a cat can be realized on that planet. Ideally, because the natural laws are the same there as here. But the reality has to be sufficient. The chain of events that has to occur to end up in a cat is a long chain of events. A lot of material objects have to be realized. Billions of years of chance events are behind this, our world of today. This world could have been totally different. But I think that there are some things that would be the same."

"Like what?"

"Concepts of time. Reproductive processes as a way to get around the problem with depletion of organic processes. By regeneration, the process can continue in new fresh copies. The distributed programme for the process confirms the use of the concept of time. The time-saving. I can see that saved time is the cause of evolution as those who are best at saving time win the competition for gathering maximum energy per time unit and become the strongest."

"You came back to me. You didn't stay with Mary. I am the strongest."

"Oh, no. Please!"

"I am older than that Indian woman. Please loosen your shirt and show me your back."

"Why?"

"I'll show you. Pull up your shirt so I can reach your back. You can lean forward on the steering wheel."

John followed her suggestion. He drew up his shirt up to his neck to show his bare back. Elsa released her safety belt and moved closer. She began to scratch his back with her right hand very gently from side to side working from the top and down and then up again.

"OOooaaaa-oaauuh!" John groaned deep. John felt her fingertips and nails claw his back. They released a million small rockets of sensual colours and vibrations. Warm streams of pleasure invaded him from behind for every stroke she made. "Oh, this is fantastic! Oh oh oh, Elsa! I am yours! Forever … I … love … you." He groaned even more. He lost all of his barriers against her.

"Ye-es, what about this young man. Now you know a bit better what an experienced woman can do. I know how to bring a man to the floor on his knees," she said with triumph in her voice.

"Now I hope that you will be a nice little boy and drive me home again and not yell at me anymore, right?"

"Yes, yes, aaahh!" John was both deeply pleased and surprised by this simple treatment.

"If I had known this before I would have put up a little business for women. 'I'll scratch your back for your pleasure!' I would be rich as they would come back every week."

"How do you know that you would stand up in the competition? Anyone could do that!"

"Yes, maybe, but I don't think I would let just anyone itch my back. You are good!"

"How do you know that I am honest?"

"I can feel it! Oohh, don't stop. Please, just some more in the middle!"

"I can tell you that your business would fail. Women don't fall for this little trick as easily as men."

Elsa stopped and pulled down his shirt again and helped him tuck it into his trousers. She giggled. "I can see that you are honest."

She was right. John leaned back again and breathed. He wanted to get out and stretch his legs but he had only one shoe at the moment. He pushed the button to wind the window down and let in some air.

"You got dynamo hands, lady!" John smiled at Elsa. He was thinking about Mary. He wanted to call her but she was probably busy working at the school now.

"Sure, I knew that all along."

"How do you know that?"

"I have worked hard all my long life so my hands are strong. I have worked with live animals, children and soft materials. The nerves in my hand are well trained. Working with textiles demands a very exact action with all your fingers. It is important to exercise regularly so I do my programme every day with my hands." Elsa showed how she exercised.

"Hands are the first thing a newborn baby feels from the world outside the womb. Every newborn baby should have the right to meet such lovely hands as yours to feel welcome. I was supposed to become a midwife."

"I remember when I was about three years old. I realized that I was I, that I had my own thoughts. I was not sure who the others in our house were. They were very tall and I was short. I thought they were aliens from space that had cameras and spied on me when they were not there. It made me afraid when I was alone and I had problems on the toilet. Until one day when I heard Edith Piaf on the radio singing 'Milord'. I decided that it could not be aliens singing such a nice song. It made me happy and made me relax. I remember so well how I sang it high and loud sitting on the ring. 'Ta da da daa da da!'"

"It would have touched her deeply to know that she helped a little boy with her song."

"That melody still follows me. I think that was what made me into the musician I am today. I tried to play this song on every instrument I came close to. The trumpet wasn't easy though."

"Pianists have lovely fingertips."

"I am playing the accordion, is that OK?" John played a short sequence on her thigh.

"That's good. I think you are a good player. Ha! But you're not going to play on my accordion anymore."

"Maybe we should roll on again."

John put up the window and started the engine. He turned south on the main road.

"Ahh, it is so nice to be on the road again!" She sighed.

"No matter what road it is?"

"No, just any road will do. It is my nomad blood. Sometimes I think my mother must have been cheating with a man from Lapland."

John tried to keep silent but the caffeine stimulated the linguistic centre in his brain. He was still a bit curious about the comparison she tried to make between their hands. They began talking again while driving.

"That was a funny thing. Before, when we talked about our hands." John raised his hand to emphasize his words.

"Was it funny?"

"Yes, I realized that I had never thought about how it could be to have another hand. In fact, I don't think I could know ever because it is nearly impossible to change hands, to try another hand. It is just like asking someone, 'How does it feel to be a black person?' He can hardly have any other experience to compare with."

"But he can see how it is to be white." She put down the sun shield to look at herself in the mirror.

"Yes, socially, but he does not know how it would be for himself to have white skin. But I think I was more into the numbers. To say anything about one thing you must be able to compare it with another. There must be two things to tell a difference."

"And a third to observe the difference from outside. If you hold my hand and you think it is hot it may be so because your hand is cold. You only know the relative temperature. The need of a third observation point corresponds well to the Zeroth law of thermodynamics, which is about three objects. If one object is thermally equal with the two others, those two will be of equal temperature with each other."

"Come on, that is rather obvious, isn't it?"

"No that means that temperature uses the same scale anywhere in the universe. We have identical natural laws everywhere in the universe."

"You mentioned the Zeroth law?" John's curiosity seemed never to end.

"Yes, the scientists of the 19th century first founded law number one, which is that energy cannot be created or destroyed. The second is that the temperature of an object can only change from hot to cold by itself. When they found that this new postulate about equal temperature was more basic they put it before the first and to avoid changing names they named it law number zero of thermodynamics."

"So there are laws in the universe and there are energies in various shape sand sizes. These laws tell us how this energy will behave? Which came first?" John slowed down at a crossing where Elsa pointed out that they should take a left. The next road was narrower and looked like it was an older route.

"Who, the chicken or the egg?"

"Was there energy first and then somebody wrote laws and then the Big Bang occurred as a starting of the party? The egg was first because the chicken is the result of an evolution of species that uses eggs as a means of reproduction."

"I don't remember."

"Well, no, you are not that old." John had to think for a while. He had realized that there were amounts of energy and that energy can have a form that can change. "What was the difference between amount and form? A hot object must have more, a larger amount of energy than a cold object. But the form is more about numbers, isn't it? Not the size of it.

"If you talk about one lump of energy or two or more. The existence of more than one of something means that there must be relations and differences. The chance to compare needs two objects, and a third independent observer. How to put energy apart and together again is one thing and what relation they have to each other during the time must be another."

"Are these three laws of thermodynamics independent of each other?"

"Of course, or it would only be one law. In fact, there are four laws of thermodynamics, still. I remember most of what my first husband taught me."

"Four? What is the fourth?" John was surprised again at Elsa's insight into these things. To discuss with her was more fun than asking Wikipedia.

"The fourth tells us that there is a point zero of entropy. Where no change can go further. The temperature is absolute zero and there is no disorder at all."

"Wow madam, you are really full of wisdom!"

"Ha! It's only small pieces from what I learned from my husband. You can find it all on the Internet. I used to go to my daughter or to the library to find out before you arrived with the white computer. The reason I wanted to have a computer of my own was to have access to my own personal mail and to be able to use it in the middle of the night."

"I understand. But I do not understand. First, there are the same natural laws everywhere in the universe. Energy cannot be created or destroyed but it can change its quality from total usefulness into total uselessness. This transformation takes time and it creates time, I think, so at the end of time there is the same total sum, amount of energy as there was in the beginning at the Big Bang. What I do not understand is how this usefulness should result in nothing? If energy cannot be destroyed, shouldn't that decrease in usefulness result in something else that is useful?"

"How about time?" Elsa seemed to enjoy testing his thinking abilities.

"The time? That must be the second useful part, but at the end of time there is no time left. Time and exergy must be at maximum in the beginning."

"I mean history. History is produced by evolution."

"Why not? Yes, that fits better. The refinement by evolution is driven by the depletion of the exergy. In the end we will have no exergy left." John looked around as if he would be able to see the end of time.

"In the end we will have no exergy left but full entropy or total disorder."

"The universe will be more like a dump you mean? Full of useless rubbish?"

"Principally yes."

"But what about all experience, all knowledge, all skill? Mustn't there be an opposite to entropy like the energy–exergy case? Couldn't history and knowledge be called Extropy?"

"Theoretically all information will in the end be so chaotic and useless so that it will be of no value."

"And the opposite to that is the absolute truth? The perfect crystalized base for all knowledge?" John felt that he was maybe getting something there.

"And what is that? 42?"

"42?" John was stunned.

"Douglas Adams wrote that in the book *Hitchhiker's Guide to the Galaxy*."

"I saw that in a cinema. I didn't understand much of that film. I fell asleep in the middle."

"Neither do I. I think Adams wrote it for fun. I didn't laugh. My husband enjoyed it a lot. I still don't know why."

"So what is the meaning of it all, then?"

"The meaning of the book?"

"No, I mean the meaning of life. What is the meaning of evolution and all?"

"The meaning of life is to be life. Period. The meaning of evolution is to be evolution. Period."

"Oh, oh. But what is life?"

"Life is not death."

"But why do we worry about life? Why do some love life and others hate it?"

"Because if it wasn't worth loving, hating or laughing at, then we would be dead already."

"So the emotional system keeps us alive you mean?"

"Sure. If it wasn't so nice to make love with your beloved friend, there would not be many children. The human race would have been extinct, long ago."

"Love is good, hate is bad." John tried to sing it as if it were a ballad.

"No, hate is good, because you hate things that hinder your life from being good."

"More emotions like …"

"Hunger, frustration, anger, jealousy, friendship. Are there any emotions that are not about life?" Elsa had to think.

"But how about reason. If you act according to reason, then there should be no need for emotions."

"And what is the fun with a life without emotions? I prefer emotions to reason!"

They arrived at a new crossing and Elsa pointed left again. The new road was bigger.

"We saved a few miles on this track. Now it is only about 60 miles to the next place."

"I hope you are right. There's not much petrol left." John saw the yellow alert blinking at the petrol gauge.

"You said you had a spare tank in the trunk?"

"Yes. That is enough for 30 miles so there shouldn't be any problem."

"I think we better call for help. Stop a car or something."

John noticed that there was not much traffic on the road. It was Saturday today. No business or work traffic. No trucks. It is easy to drive when traffic is light. But a bit lonely.

"I think you are right about emotions!"

"What emotions? Are you in love again?" Elsa sounded suspicious.

"Yes. No. I love life. I mean love makes me live my life. I am the one who chooses among the opportunities I have. I am free to choose among opportunities. I choose the alternative I think is the best. The one that I love best. Reason can help a little but my emotions tell me if it was the right choice."

"I am glad I chose to go with you. I have a good life." She sounded very satisfied with the situation.

"Me too. Time goes fast in your company. I can see that on the milometer. We are going fast today without speeding. We will be back at your home in a few hours."

"Then I will beat you!"

"Beat me? What have I done now? Are you angry for something?"

"No! I will cook a good meal and then we shall play cards again! I will not let you go before I give you a real match."

"OK. I accept the challenge. I like to be beaten by you. Your pleasure is my pleasure!"

The road was wide and smooth. No ice and a clear view. The car worked fine and the temperature inside was comfortable. John put on the radio and they could hear a voice present Lord Tanamo playing 'I'm in the mood for ska.'

17 - Red Boots and Little Lies

John was looking forward to being in Elsa's kitchen with good food and a card game again. This road went through a forest with no end, it seemed. The forest changed from big trees to small trees. Uphill and downhill, lakes and small creeks. Mile after mile. The time and the road were eaten by the front of the car. While the petrol gauge seemed to get helplessly stuck at the bottom.

"We don't have much petrol left." John pointed at the orange alert light.

"Shall we stop and get help?"

"I think we can wait until the engine stops. The petrol gauge is not too exact and it can show up wrong. It happened me once that I thought I was out of petrol. Then when I filled it up I could see that there must have been gallons left. I saw that by the difference between how much I filled and what the tanks holds when empty. There is room for 75 litres and if I could fill up with 65 litres there must have been 10 left. That is enough to drive another 50 miles."

"We went to Egypt once in the sixties by car. We had an old Volvo estate car. We brought more petrol than luggage in spare tanks on the roof. There were nearly no petrol stations at all between Algeria and Egypt. Oh my, that was hot. We sold the car down there and took a boat back to Europe."

On the next uphill stretch the engine started to choke a little. John knew that this was the first sign of petrol shortage. The pipe hole for the petrol was placed at the front of the tank and on uphill stretches the petrol ran to the back of the tank.

"I think we'd better stop before the next hill and fill up now. We are getting short of petrol already."

"That suits me fine. I have to pee again. And maybe fart a little." Elsa smiled a friendly smile at John as a gesture of her accepting John's desire for social behaviour in a car.

After the peak of the hill John could see a parking place ahead. He slowed down and released the accelerator to save as much petrol as possible. They stopped at the P-sign and Elsa went into the bushes to take care of her biology. There was a little slow stream on the left side of the road.

John went out limping on one shoe and one bare foot. He opened the rear door to check if his sock was dry. It was pretty dry but the shoe was still very damp. He decided to leave the shoe by the heating exhaust but tried to find a better position for it to get dry from the hot air.

John limped back to pick up the spare tank and fill up. He hoped that it would not be more than 30 miles left to the next petrol station. He had no other reference points but that was his hope at the moment. It was not the first time he had driven this road but the last time was a while ago and he had not got sufficiently used to it. He knew where it started, where it ended and had memorized some spots along it.

He opened the back door and was glad that it opened upwards. There was a steady rainfall and the door served as a little roof. He had to move the luggage. Elsa's bed-things in a big long sack were really heavy. John thought that this lady must be strong, carrying such a heavy load without complaints. He moved all the things to the right and then to the left but couldn't find the spare tank. That was strange.

He lifted the floor under the luggage, where the spare tyre was located, to check for the tank. No spare tank. John took a step back and tried to keep his perspective right. The tank was not so small. It must be there. He checked again. He opened the rear side door and checked under the front seats. No. There was no spare tank at all. A feeling of anger and despair filled him. Frustration ruled now. He did his best to stay calm and not freak out.

"We are out of petrol! The spare tank is gone! How could that be?"

John sounded angry. He tried to not accuse Elsa of anything but as he didn't believe that he himself could have moved the spare tank, someone else must have taken it. An evil force made him suspect that maybe Elsa had placed it on the ground when she packed and forgot to put it back in the car. "Did you see the spare tank when you put your things into the car this morning?"

"No. I don't remember seeing it. I know very well what it looks like. I've always kept a spare tank in my car." Elsa sounded trustworthy. "Do you think someone stole it when we were at Mary's place?"

"I didn't lock the car." John felt stupid. He didn't know anything about the neighbours at the farm, but why should they steal from each other?

"Maybe you should call Mary?"

"Why? She can't take her car and drive here just to give us 5 litres of petrol. It takes 20 litres to drive here and 20 litres back again. Bad budget in such a project. Besides, it would take her a lot of time too. She must be working now and leaving her job would cost her even more and I think she needs the money." John tried to sound reasonable but the thought of having a talk to
300

Mary again tempted him. Just because he was longing for her voice again.

"You can call her. You can stay in the car with your bare foot. I'll stand out here and stop the next car and ask if we can buy some petrol. Most drivers keep a spare tank in their car."

John took his mobile phone and looked up her number. John was glad that he picked it up yesterday.

"It's Mary."

"Hello Mary. It's John. How are you?"

"Oh, hello Johnny, I am fine. I am a little busy now but you called on a break. Lucky guy! We can talk for about five minutes, then I'll be busy again."

"Thanks a lot for last night. It was so lovely."

"It is me that should thank you. For all the food."

"We left some money for you on the kitchen table."

"Oh, that's great! I really need money. I must buy petrol for my car so I can get to work until next payday. Then I will pay you back."

"Please don't bother. It was a gift."

"Oh thank you! By the way, I had to borrow your spare tank so I could start my car in the morning. I got a text message from my friend Ollie. I hope I didn't cause any problems with that?"

"Oh. No problem. I have a lot of petrol and credit cards from two petrol companies. Don't worry." John was lying to her but why should John worry Mary about their little crisis?

"You see Ollie sent a message to me in the middle of the night: 'I am sitting here alone staring into the wall.' I had to send back a message to ask what was going on. Then I decided that I had to go to him at once."

"In the middle of the night?" John felt jealousy burn in his heart.

"His son had an accident. I had to help him. Was there anything else? I think I'm a bit busy now."

"No, I just called, to say, hello, and that we were alive and well, as we didn't see you in the morning before we left your house." John wanted to say "love you" instead of "hello" but the mention of Ollie made it more difficult.

"Well, thank you and bye then. I have to take care of Ollie!"

"Now? Aren't you at work?"

"No, I am with him. In his house … In his bed actually, ha ha ha! Thanks for all the food and have a good time with Elsa! Please call next time when you are passing by. I missed you, Johnny!"

"Sure, I will. Have a good time you too, both of you. Bye." John answered very politely.

John was humiliated and crushed for a second. His sight dimmed and the sky became dark. He knew he had no right to request her attention or fidelity. But his heart had its own opinion. Could emotions from an old memory, feelings triggered by the memorized picture of an old unsatisfied second, keep on teasing his reasonability? Forcing him to perform such stupid actions as to desire a woman that it was impossible to share a real life with?

John knew it was impossible. He was already married. He didn't need any more women in his life. Still, he couldn't refuse the opinion of his heart. "Is it possible to love more than one? Is this only biology versus sociology?" John decided that it wasn't practical anyway. Reason cooled him down. "Maybe another day, in another life," he was thinking.

Elsa stood by the road and looked in both directions to be ready to stop the next car. John sat in the car full of emotions that rolled around in his body. Alarm bells ringing and the sound of foghorns rolling between his ears. He felt stupid again. "What a weekend," he was thinking. "If it begins like this, how will it end?"

He looked out of the side window. He wanted to roll it down to tell Elsa that he knew why they didn't have any spare tank. He hesitated. The car was getting cold already and without petrol he could not get any heat from the engine. He had to think about was best. He had lied to Mary about their situation. John didn't want to upset Mary as she appeared to be in a situation that deserved peace. But Elsa would tell her later about what really happened on their tour. He was convinced about that.

Mary, and Elsa, would eventually realize that he lied about such a small thing. They would not understand what reason he would have to lie about such a small and trivial fact. His little lie would drive a wedge into Mary's confidence in John. Forever. A lie can never be washed away. John's lie was a declaration of lack of confidence in Mary. That he would decide by himself what should be called truth or not. She was deserted, left on her own, by John's decision, to believe in his description or not. Next time she would not be confident in his story, whatever it would be.

John realized that this was bad, very bad. How could he misunderstand this little circumstance to be biological and not a social matter? Or was it that her situation was social and his situation without petrol was more material. Nothing to bother about, just like a small personal problem like acne or superfluous hair in his nose?

Elsa would surely tell her anyway and reveal the misconduct. If John had called Elsa sitting on the loo he was sure she would tell him where she was even if

John wouldn't reveal that kind of fact himself. He remembered one time when he called a person that sat on the toilet, answering and pretending that he was at his office. John could hear him hold his breath in an unnatural way. That was so disgusting.

John decided to never answer his mobile phone in the loo after that. To not answer was a better way than lying to keep his privacy. He should not have called Mary. That was what he should have done. But now it was too late to repair the mistake. It was a desperate attempt and he had failed.

A car came by and Elsa managed to stop it. John saw her talk to the driver. It was cold inside and he was happy to get petrol and get away. The car drove away and Elsa returned into the car.

"He only had diesel and this car runs on petrol, yes? I am cold too. I have to stay inside for a while until the next car comes." She shivered a bit.

"Wooosh!"

"Damn! It came from behind! I didn't see it. You must keep your eye on the mirror!" Elsa looked angrily at him. John felt ashamed of the mistake he had made. It didn't make him feel more confident. He decided not to tell her about his call to Mary, yet. He didn't know how he would tell Elsa that he had lied to Mary. Elsa would probably not like that and the wedge of mistrust would grow and come in-between him and Elsa also.

John looked at the stream on the other side. The rain fell on the water. The surface was covered with sudden rings that grew wider and disappeared. John saw how the exergy, the power from the meeting between the falling drop and the surface caused a wave that spread out from the starting point in all directions. As the energy in the wave lost its power, it became weaker and after some seconds it vanished. The amplitude of the wave must be spread out by the fact that the diameter of the circle grew at an exponential rate of π times two the distance from the centre. The bigger the diameter, the greater the force needed to keep the height of the wave. A constant or diminishing force couldn't hold the wave's height. The exergy from the collision was spread over a longer and longer wave and it vanished. That is the natural behaviour of waves from raindrops on water. John had seen it thousands of times.

"Times! Time! Yes, time is round!" John shouted suddenly. Elsa jumped up in the seat at the surprising outburst.

"What are you onto, young man? I thought we were out of petrol. Time is the only thing we've got plenty of. Regarding me, anyway."

"Processes take time, time is round! Any process has a start and a future. The future is known and unknown. The known is the surface but the direction is unknown. The process can take any direction. What has happened so far is inside the circle and the future is outside the circle. The now, the exact now of the present process, where the event is really happening is at the top of the wave. Between the past and the future! We are at the top of the wave all the time!" John shouted excitedly in the car.

Elsa looked at him as if he was mad. She was cold and blamed John for being out of petrol. Yes, she wasn't responsible for the petrol situation. It was John's responsibility.

"Listen," she said. "Now it is your turn to stop a car."

"I have only one shoe!"

"You have got two shoes. One of them is dry and one of them is wet. Those men I took care of after the World

War didn't bother about a wet and muddy shoe. But you can borrow my shoes. What size are your feet?"

"42."

"Oh, you lucky boy. Mine too. Here take my shoes, they will help us get the petrol we need."

She took off her sharp red leather boots and handed them over to John. They were calf-length with a zip at the back. John took off his dry shoe. He had to take off his sock too as the boots were a little small. He put them on his bare feet. They were still warm from her.

John went out and stretched his legs. He was unused to walking in high-heeled boots but after a little walking his feet got used to them. He listened for any sound of a coming car and watched the stream again. The rain was uneven. The drops that made rings on the water appeared very suddenly and it was hard to see the very beginning of a ring. After a while he could hear a car approaching. He heard that it was coming from behind him so he went to the that side of their car and prepared to stop the car by waving his arms.

A four-wheel-drive truck, a big Chevrolet stopped. John was glad because he was convinced by the sound that this had a petrol engine. He went to the driver's side. The unshaven driver opened his window and lifted his cap an inch.

"Trouble?"

"Yes sir! We are out of petrol and someone took my spare tank so I wondered if we could buy some from you. If you have a spare tank, so I can just fill up enough to reach next petrol station."

"OK!" The big driver opened the door and got out on the road. When he closed the door he saw John's liberal outfit. The red boots shone like stoplights to the cowboy. He smiled at John, spat on the road, looked at

306

Elsa in the car, opened the door again and got up in his cab again. He shouted out through the window as he started his car: "I don't serve fags! Ha ha ha!" John heard him laugh while he drove away with his window closing.

John became mad again and couldn't answer but there was nothing he could do. He was glad that he hadn't got beaten up. He went back to the car and took off the boots, gave them back to Elsa without a word. He decided to put on his own dry and wet shoes.

The next car stopped after 20 minutes. It was a lumberman in a Japanese minivan. John could hear from the sound that this was a diesel engine so he had no hope of petrol this time. John had another idea – that he could hitchhike to the petrol station and try to hitchhike back again with the petrol. But that would take time. Elsa was alone and cold in the car.

But he was luckier this time. The lumberman had a lot of chainsaws in the back and the chainsaws ran on petrol mixed with oil. Not the best but it was possible to drive a car on it. He helped John to fill up with the drops he had left in each one of the saws. They poured the petrol into an opaque plastic container first, so he could see how much they could find. It was about five litres and they decided that it would do until they arrived at the petrol station. His mobile phone rang. John had to wait while he was answering. When he was ready he put the phone into his pocket again. He looked at John's shoes.

"Why are you wearing a dry and a wet shoe?"

"I had a little accident earlier today and I have nothing to wear instead."

"Hmm." The lumberman helped John to pour the petrol into the Volvo.

"Thank you very much, sir! How much do I owe you?" John was determined to pay him for the petrol.

"200 kronor!" John coughed, but the next second he opened his wallet and gave him the money and thanked him again.

"Thank you, sir. You know, that was cheap!" The lumberman looked askance at the crazy white-collared city man. But he was satisfied by the deal anyway. The lumberman was prepared for some negotiation and soft talk over the sum before the deal but this one must have loads of money in his wallet to be able to pay 40 kronor per litre for oil-blended petrol. John could see the lumberman dialling a number on his mobile while he drove away. "He seemed to be a busy man," John was thinking.

He went into the car where Elsa was seated with a map wide open. He put on the engine. John checked the mirror and saw a thick white cloud spread behind the car. He released the clutch and the car accelerated along the road. A tail of smoke spread over the road behind them.

"Ah! It is nice be on the road again!" Elsa sighed deeply.

"Yes, that problem wasn't easily solved. It took us an hour to fix." John was wondering whether he should tell Elsa about his little lie to Mary. He had to consult his strategic mind in this case. Strategy wasn't his strongest side anyway. He had to imagine the different possible scenarios and evaluate which seemed most appropriate. He decided to tell her the truth. After all it wasn't a big lie and a new lie could make it even worse.

"I called Mary!"

"Yes I know. I told you to!"

"She left the house early in the morning!"

"Yes, I know!"

"You knew that?"

"Yes, she told me that she had to leave. She had to go to Ollie."

"Did she tell you that she took my spare tank?"

"No."

"Well, she took my spare tank so she could fill up her car and go to her job she said but she was with Ollie."

"They have been good friends for years. Now that George has left Mary they can keep on more freely. That is good for both of them."

"I didn't mention that we were out of petrol when I called. I didn't want to make her feel guilty for it."

"Ha ha, you stupid boy. What could she do about that? You said it was alright yesterday, didn't you?"

John dropped the subject again. His feelings had had another blow. He had tried being honest and been met with newly disclosed facts. How could he trust Elsa after this? Or was he entitled to insist that she should tell him everything all the time? He hadn't asked Elsa about what had happened in the morning so he could hold himself to blame for not asking. She knew what she knew and didn't seem to feel responsible for John's information status. He had tried to be reasonable but apparently there were more things going on around him than he could handle.

The road was parallel to a railway. They passed a slower, heavy-loaded train going south. They came to a crossing and John decided to keep up his speed going onto the crossing and drive over before the red lights started as the train must be close behind them. When the car ran over the track they bumped around a bit. When the car landed again on the other side of the railway track a red light blinked on the instrument board.

"The car is equipped with a sensory system," John said to Elsa to calm her down a little from the bump over the crossing.

"I don't know what that red lamp is about. Probably the oil in the engine jumped up inside so that the oil pump got no oil for a second. That lowers the oil pressure and the red light comes on."

"I don't want to have any other problems for a while now. I am just getting my feet warm from the last one."

"I was thinking of the similarity with human biology. Biology in general must be equipped with a sensory system and red lights when things get risky."

"You think that is the reason why we get red in the face when we are angry?"

"No, I think it is the reason why warning lights are red!"

"So where does the green light come from? Sickness?"

John smiled at Elsa and made a sick face at her.

"No, I was just thinking in a more functional way. Our biological system has evolved since the first bacteria and cells, billions of years ago. Their survival depends on the way their processes are handled. The biological process is free to act in a number of ways. It has different strategies for different situations. To choose what strategy to use it must be able to receive information from the surroundings, evaluate it and send signals to the cells to adopt the correct strategy. Even if it is done instinctively, it is a managed process. Biological systems have warning lights, but far more advanced than those in the car."

"You had no warning lamp for your spare tank."

"No, that was my mistake. I take risks so as not to have to go through a long checklist every now and then when I drive. I don't want to risk my life, but small risks like parking fees, pressure in the tyres I can live with."

"Don't play with my confidence by taking risks with me!"

"I promise you, I will not take unnecessary risks in your company. By the way, we are close to a condom factory now! I have been there in my job."

"The pope should know about that! He would surely ban it immediately."

"There it is!" John pointed to the left.

They arrived at another railway crossing and John kept the speed up again to get across before the red lights and the train. The car bumped again and Elsa shouted out loud. All lights on the dashboard were on now. John slowed down and tried to understand what had happened.

"What sort of driving is that? First you talk about safe driving and then you drive like mad through a railway crossing twice in a row?"

"I wanted to beat the train. To save time."

"To save time! You are really stupid! I can take the time to watch the train. I love to watch trains passing by and count the wagons. Now you have destroyed the car again!" She was angry now. John was ashamed over his stupid behaviour. This time it appeared to be really serious. Nobody was hurt but something bad must have happened to the car. He drove slowly into a closed campsite by a big lake and let the engine idle.

John checked the lamps. The oil lamp was dark so it was safe to let the engine idle. He could see that the headlights where dimming a bit so it must be something to do with the electricity system. He drove on into the campsite and turned the car so it was pointing at east, away from the wind. He shut down the engine.

"It is something with the electricity. The generator is not working I think. It could be the fan belt that is broken."

"What can you do about that?"

"I don't know. I have to go out and have a look first." John released the bonnet and went out in the dusk to have a look. Elsa came out too. She had a little lamp in her handbag that she gave to John.

"Here, you can connect it to the battery to make it light."

"You surprise me again. I never had such a lamp in my car!"

"Didn't I tell you I was an experienced driver myself. I think I have been driving twice as much as you. Don't you think I have been stuck with malfunctioning cars before?"

"Can you see what is wrong with the car, too?" John checked the fan belt. It was not broken but a bit slacked.

"The fan belt is too slack to drive the generator. You've got no power to the battery. In an hour it will be dead."

"We must adjust it then." John looked at the generator with the light and he could see that the adjustment bolt was lost. The generator hung on the bolts that attached it to the engine. Without this little bolt it was impossible to stretch the fan belt. It would fall back again and the belt would not be attached tightly enough to be able to drive the generator. John gave up for the moment. He let down the bonnet and they stepped into the car again. John shut off the

312

headlights to save electricity in the battery and tried to start the engine again. It started without a problem but the generator lamp was shining red. He shut off the engine again.

"We can drive. The engine works, but we don't have any light. We cannot drive in the dark."

"If we can't get any help then I guess we have to spend the night at this place. It would have been better if the campsite had been open for the season."

"But now we can stay without having to pay." John said in a sarcastic tone. He didn't like the idea of staying in the car for a whole night in this cold weather. His shoe was still wet and cooled his entire body.

"I can take a walk back to the condom factory and see if there is anybody there. I need a walk anyway. You can stay in the car."

John sat in the car and saw her walk away. His mood was low and he began to be tired of the trip. This could have happened anyway but he might have been closer to home. It was still about three hours' drive down to Elsa's and then he had two hours more to get home. Now it seemed like he would not be home for dozens of hours. Or days. Or ever.

18 - Bubbles in the Train Light

John watched Elsa disappear beyond the railway. The situation was depressing. He felt that barriers were arising between them. He wondered if she would return. He decided to call his wife.

"Hello John, how are you?"

"I am fine, but the car broke down! I have no lights on the car so I cannot drive until next morning when it is daylight."

"So where are you?"

"I am about five hour's drive from home. I have to spend the night here!"

"Sorry for you, but that is no problem for me. I can wait. I am working on my own. The kids are in Thickholt so they can take care of themselves."

"I'll try my best to come home tomorrow, or on Monday."

"You do your best. I know you always do. I am busy with my paintings. See you, honey. Kisses. Take care!"

"See you!" John shut off the phone to save the battery and leaned back to think over the situation. He didn't understand that he was depressed.

John heard the bells ring at the crossing and he saw the gates drop down. After a minute he could see the heavy light from the engine light up the railway. The train were closing in and the light got stronger. He could see the raindrops as falling spots in the light from the train. A long slow train passed. The cars were low and he saw a huge dark block of some sort of material on each of them. Maybe steel blooms. It seemed to be a heavy load.

John could feel the ground shake to the rhythm of the passing cars. The ground must have some resonance and the train was working like a fiddle bow on a string. The rain was heavier now. He looked at the drops falling into a pool of water in front of the car. He began to freeze and thought about Elsa wandering around in the dark. The raindrops were heavy and fell fast, so fast that the collision with the water created a bubble, a perfect upper half of a sphere, in the widening and vanishing ring. It looked interesting.

Once the train had passed it was rather dusky again. John couldn't see much more in the dark than the red blinking light at the railway crossing with its rising gates and the lampposts far away at the condom factory. He continued to think about the falling rain against the water surface. Some bubbles were blinking red. He imagined the picture in the dark. It had to be something that could light up the dark. He thought about the sparks in the generator that initiated electromagnetic waves around it.

"A bubble has three dimensions!" John sat up and became aroused. His brain accelerated and the pieces fell together in a fantastic order. He got tears in his eyes from the excitement. The mighty impression made him feel small and powerless.

"A collision in three dimensions creates a time bubble in 3D! You need three points to create an area and four to create a volume! A flash in the generator creates a three-dimensional electromagnetic wave that spreads evenly in three dimensions in the room. Gravitation comes from mass that bends the room by retarding time in three dimensions so planets get their spherical shape. The pendulum seeks its equilibrium position, closest to the centre of gravity. Time goes slower close to a material body and that makes things fall against it as it saves time to be closer to another body in the time–space.

"Drops of water are round because of the even surface tension that is working evenly in all directions. Time makes spherical bubbles in the space of a possible future. The meeting of the laws of thermodynamic and the energy starts events, processes that use exergy to keep on. There must be a space of possible future that allows the process to continue in time.

"As long as the process satisfies the existential conditions it will continue. By dividing the conditions into three dimensions I can see the picture clearly. Energy meets the laws of thermodynamics and has the freedom to evolve in time. As long as the process is fulfilling the conditions in three dimensions for its existence in three dimensions it will continue, otherwise it will vanish.

"The conditions are mass, form and something else." John was sure about the difference between mass and form, but there must be a third. "What is the third that is not mass or form?"

Mass and energy level is equal. Before when they were out of petrol the form of the car was OK but there was a lack of energy in the tank. Now he had enough energy to reach a petrol station but the form was not satisfying for driving in the dark. In both cases the car was useless until it was fixed or the conditions changed. The car had a low value at the moment. It would take time to fix it and he needed money or time to have it fixed. With some money, saved time, he could maybe pay someone else to do it. He had had to pay 200 kronor for the chain-saw petrol that was in the car.

John took up his iPad and started up the map application to check how far it was to the next petrol station. He got a surprise when the blue needle dropped in the middle of nowhere. They were stuck in the deep green world with no name. He wrote 'Petrol station' in the search field and pressed on the 'Search' button. Immediately a blue curvy line appeared, the scale of the map was changed and he could see that it was 23 miles to next petrol station.

John was surprised at how useful this little thing could be. Light, very complicated inside but easy to handle from the outside. A perfect combination of mass and form.

There – he had it at once!

"Value! Value is the third dimension! The combination of mass and form gives the Value. Value depends on one process, one events relation to another. In addition to the conditions for real existing objects with energy and form there must be a third independent set of conditions that are directing the value and the relations between separate events and processes!

"Conditions that are free from mass or form, but only applies the relation between existing objects with any mass and any form. These three sets of conditions are working together independently and are the source of all existing matter. They are even the basis for themselves!" John felt like he had found the Holy Grail, sitting there stuck in the cold car in the dark rain.

"Energy, form, value. That must be the basis. It demands an ability to see things as events, a process in time that must meet three different conditions to keep on. Something without mass does not exist. Something without form doesn't exist either. If it is something that has mass and form but it is useless, then it doesn't have any value. Like a flat tyre, or a flat dog on the road. No good."

John tried to find something that didn't have these three dimensions. He thought about particles and atoms, molecules and substances. They all have mass, a form and value. The elements had all of them a certain specific mass, an objective form and its characteristic value. Any combination of energy and form that saves time will exist as nuclear particles.

The scientists working at CERN and with other particle accelerators are hunting for the impossibilities to be able to see the limits of the possible. Hydrogen and oxygen have a high value to each other as they can combine and create water molecules. Water has a high value to organic processes as its form gives a magnetic function so the water molecules can link together and dissolve other chemicals. The connection is relatively strong, depending on the temperature, the amount of heat exergy in it. As a fluid the water can change form

318

and creates drops and waves in the sea. A sailor is forced to keep the balance by the Archimedes' principle to keep the boat floating, but he is free to sail in any direction as long as the sea is deep enough.

Organic processes have their own strategies to manage their economy. They must have energy to exist, light, heat, inorganic material and water. Too little and too much destroys the balance. The form can be just any form that fulfils the mathematical and geometric requirements. Every organic biological species has its characteristic value. Its taste in the view of other biological species. Wolf likes rabbit. Rabbit likes carrot. Carrot likes houmous.

Competition for the material resources in time and the possibility of finding new forms by mutation creates new and stronger, better, strategies with higher value for the next event.

To win, any strategy must be successful in all three dimensions. It has to be expert about its mass managing process and its economic behaviour. It has to be expert in form: mathematical and logic construction. It has to be expert in how to manage the surroundings: its constructive or destructive value to other processes. Too much or too little in any direction is fatal to the process. Keeping the balance in all three dimensions is the winning recipe for a process with a stable pattern. Imbalance kills the process. The dynamic, never-ending balancing act between the three is what makes the process continue.

This balance must be what Pirsig described as a stable pattern of quality. For instance, the intellectual static quality of a message depends on what words are used (mass), in what order they come (form) and how well they are expressed to and received by the listener (value). Too much or too little in any of these three factors leads to an intellectual pattern of low quality. When rhetoric works, when it is a message of high quality, it works as a bridge between the sender and the receiver. They begin to cooperate as a new event, a new static pattern of value.

All biological structures have accomplished a characteristic strategy recorded in their DNA that knows how to keep this balance. That is why John's body is filled with signals from its deepest biological strategy centre that work to manage his biological process so it will be able to continue the competition and survive among the fittest. That was what it was all about. To survive as an organic structure. Not just for the moment but forever. His biological strategy learned billions of years ago that sexual reproduction was a perfect method for overcoming the problem of processes depleted by age. Sexual reproduction however requires the capability to cooperate with other unique individuals of the same species. Primarily of the other sex in order to be able to reproduce.

Social structures have had the same kind of evolution, following the rules of the three dimensions to keep the balance of mass, form and relative value. Social structures have evolved from the biological level but have advantages over biological structures that reproduce by splitting themselves into direct copies. Identical copies are an easy target for viruses and simple hostile strategies while sexual reproduction results in mutual variations. A virus attack can't easily kill all individuals as there is too much variations in the group. There is usually a marginal group that is immune to the virus. The virus can adapt to this by changing its structure faster but that is not the same as being a species with wide reciprocal variation.

A social group also benefits from this mutual variation and wins in the competition. Beehives, for example. Concrete gets stronger just because of the different size of the grains. Smaller grains fit better and fill in the spaces between the bigger grains. Humans societies benefit from different individual members with different positions inside the group; leaders, hunters, mothers, soldiers. Teachers and medical doctors.

The economic basis of a human society is the saved time gained by mutual exchange of specialities. By trade and barter the total amount of time taken to produce the values is shortened. Time is saved by the organization of human society. The commonly gained resources are shared so every member can express his value at its best in the organization. Wars between different societies and structures are fought and the winners are those who have the best balance between mass, form and destructive value against their enemies and constructive value to their friends and followers.

John could follow the whole line of evolution this way from the inorganic, through the organic and biological up to the social and the intellectual level. It was all about how to save time, to keep the balance between mass, form and value. It is all made of some kind of energy. As long as the form and value follow the rules for it, it will be able to go on as a stable and continuous process. The dynamic process behind the evolution, the perpetual change in mass, form and value in every event, expand the time until the end. Inside the sphere of every single ongoing event is the past and outside is the future. This would be an excellent graphic model for understanding any change. Every event, as a part in the process has its own time, beginning, history and possible future, age and profile. Like a cosmic rain in 3D. John could listen to it now and the hair on his neck rose in pleasure at being a part of it. Now he knew exactly what to do.

"This must be like meeting God," John was thinking.

"No, better than God! I meet the universe in myself.

"I stand here at the fundaments of the universe and I am one that chooses!"

John took his iPad and put on the music player to relax his mind. His calculation was that if the battery in the iPad died it wouldn't affect his odds of survival too much to survive. He chose a playlist with old music. 'I Know Why' by Glenn Miller and his band from 1942 filled the car. He leaned back and drew the blanket from the back seat over him.

Suddenly the right door was opened and the light in the coupé went on. Elsa jumped into the car with a white paper bag in her hand.

"Hello again! How do you do young man?" John was awakened by her brisk voice.

"I am fine, really fine. I think I fell asleep for a minute."

"What time is it? Oh, I must have been away for three hours! Uuuhh, it is cold in the car but it is worse outside! Brrr. Here, I brought some food for you."

She picked up a load of sandwiches and put them on the board in front of her. She had a bottle of milk too. She picked up her bag with the old coffee and the other leftovers they had brought from Mary's.

John took a sandwich and a cup of lukewarm coffee. He shut off the light to save the battery. They sat quietly in the dark for a minute listening to the soft music from the iPad. Now it was 'Oh, So Good' by Glenn Miller. He could hear Elsa breathe and he heard from her breath that she wished to talk.

"You were away a long time?"

"I went to the condom factory. It was closed, of course. It is Saturday evening. But I knocked at the door as the lights were on and was let in by a cleaner. Her name was Frieda. I told her we had a broken-down car and needed help. Now, you will hear something fantastic! She heard immediately that I was talking with an accent so she asked me if I was from Denmark. Then she told me that her mother was Danish too. I asked her how they could live so far away from all honour and pride.

"She invited me to follow her home when she was finished with the work. I helped her get ready and then we walked away to her home close to the factory. There we met her mother who was about my age. She was a bit suspicious at first but when she heard that I had a problem with the car she invited me for coffee. Yes, she really was Danish. I told her the whole story about our trip up till now. We had a really good laugh at your meeting with Mary yesterday!"

John did not find it so amusing as he did not know what they had said about him, in what way Elsa had pictured him. But he had to stay confident in her goodwill to him.

"After my story and laughing together we were good friends and she told me her story, how she had come to live at this place. Her name was Christine. She told me slowly and backwards that she lived with a man Franz Ulger."

"'So you fell in love with a German boy?' I said to her.

"'Yes, and after the German occupation it was not socially appropriate to be a nice Danish girl who was together with a German boy. So we moved to Sweden and we found this place far away from the civilization to live our life here. I have never returned to Denmark since then. My relatives still cannot forgive what I had done.'

"'But you did no wrong,' I said. 'How can love be a sin?'

"'Well, we didn't meet after the war was over. It happened during the German occupation. You know how it was. All these soldiers put together on army bases and almost no women around. That kind of arrangement is asking for sexual trouble, isn't it?' Christine was honest with me.

"'But I can forgive you, or I still don't think I have to. To me it was not a sin.'

"'Yes it was. It was very strongly and morally understood by us not to fraternize with the enemy. Don't you remember?'

"'But we were humans, civilians. We were not soldiers. Where is the line between civilians and soldiers? Every Danish person had something to do with the German soldiers in some way. We travelled by the same trains. I sat in the same wagon as German soldiers many times. They bought food from us, was that a crime? We breathed the same air, we walked on the same streets. We drank from the same water wells! Was it forbidden to talk to them? No!'

"'Yes. Girls fell in love with Germans and there were babies born.'

"'Yes, I know. But it was not only German boys who did that. My mother warned me about being too

324

intimate with any man before I got married. How little she knew! But I still think it is wrong to let a war come between people that fall in love with each other.'

"'When the war was over, we had peace. No one should fight and no one should be regarded as an enemy. The violence must stop. There must be a chance for the soldiers to be forgiven, otherwise there is no peace yet. All parties must lay down their weapons when the war is over. You cannot continue the war with such evil weapons as social rejection and intolerance. The Danish people must forgive. They goddamn call themselves Christians! They must be able to forgive.'

"'After all the terrible things that were disclosed after the war. How they treated the Jews and all. No one wanted to have any connection to the Germans. They were really hated. We have talked about that many times me and my husband, dear Elsa. We can't force them to forget. I am sorry. We must forgive them. All conflicts have parties with different view on the facts. You have your picture of it and they have theirs. Telling the so-called truth is not always the best thing to do. It can lead to an unsolvable conflict that hurts more than it gives.'

"'Then I told Christine that I had a relationship with a German, too, after the war. We met in Germany when I volunteered. I had to leave him for the same reason as she had trouble. My mother would have died from shame if I had returned with a German. I was so glad that he had survived the war. Sigmund was enlisted for Stalingrad but as his last name was Zucker he was the last in the list of 33 and there was only room for 32 in the local troop so he was sent to the Luftwaffe in Denmark instead. That was how we met. He learned to speak Danish during the war. I thought he was from Denmark when he shouted at me in the queue for the soup. I was speaking German but he heard my Danish accent.

"'Hurry up! Time's running and we have no children!' he yelled at us in Danish by the canteen. I laughed so hard I nearly peed in my pants.

"The German soldiers were asked to help de-mining their own minefields or walk home. There was no transport arranged for them. He had to walk back to Hamburg from his base in Denmark. He was not alone."

"Christine went on, 'My husband had to go to Stalingrad. But he was lucky, if we can call it that. He survived anyway. Until last year. We had a good life here, we have a healthy daughter. She still live here and with this condom factory ... I am longing for grandchildren!'

"I told her that it couldn't depend on that! A man must be free to use it or not. Ha ha ha!"

"Here, look at this, we got a present too! She heard that we would spend the night together!" Elsa had been served food by Christine. Frieda had even given her a promotional pack of condoms from the factory, a piece of card with six different types attached.

Elsa put on the light and showed him the condoms.

"I am not going to try any condoms on you!" John said with bread in his mouth.

"No, for sure! You are a decent man and I am not cheating on your wife!"

"Exactly right." John swallowed the coffee.

"But I can think about spending the night with you. It is cold as hell sleeping alone in a car. I have my bed-things in the luggage. Please help me with the back seat so we can make a bed in the back." She stepped out and opened the rear door.

"You know a lot about cars, don't you? But it will be a firm bed. We don't have any mattress. Only some blankets and your bed-things."

"Ha, I am always prepared for the unknown. I have a mattress in my luggage. It is an inflatable mattress!"

They helped each other to make up the bed and John had the pleasant task of blowing air into the mattress. It was about three inches thick when it was ready and wide enough for two. It took a good while to blow up. When it was filled, Elsa crawled into the back. She undressed half-lying-down and placed all her things in the corners. John thought she looked like a seal crawling out of its hide.

"You must take off your clothes, too! It is dangerous to sleep in your clothes when it's cold. The sweat will chill you."

John followed her advice and hung his clothes over the front seat so the trousers wouldn't get more creased. He turned the light off and crawled down to Elsa. It was already warm and cosy under the wide and thick quilt with the wool blanket on it. John tried to find a comfortable position and laid his head down. There were no pillows. He put his arm under his head but that hurt his arm. He tried to place his head on the edge of her pillow but she moved him away.

"I have no pillow. This doesn't work."

John sat up again. It was cold outside the quilt but he had to have something under his head. He put on the light again and looked for something to use.

In the middle of the front seats he saw the six-pack of condoms. John took one of them and blew it up. It was soft and he was convinced that the rubber was tested at very high pressure. He made a knot at the opening of the condom. He wrapped his shirt around it and there he had a perfect pillow. He showed Elsa his innovation.

"Better use a condom for yourself!" She grinned at his creation.

"Dout, Deeee Dout, With a condom all over my body, I can feel completely safe!"

John sang a tune while he stretched his arm out to shut the light. It was a melody by Robert Broberg from the seventies

He laid down his head slowly to try the pillow and now he was ready for the night.

19 - The Dimensions

"Are you ready for sleep or would you like to talk for a while?"

John asked gently, lying on his back with his hands crossed over his chest.

"I can talk. After all this is Saturday night and we are free." Elsa lay on her back, too.

"While you were out. While you were with your Danish friend, I think I found the Holy Grail."

"What? Here? That is from an opera by Wagner, isn't it?"

"No, I once had an old red Volvo estate car made in 1953. I painted the car ruby red and called it Parsifal. Just for fun, it sounded medieval and mighty. Later I found out where the name came from. Parsifal was a fool that happened to stumble over the Holy Grail in an old legend. King Arthur and his Knights of the Round Table were searching for this legendary item. It was the cup that was used at the Holy Communion. The legend also says that it was the cup where some of the blood from the crucified Jesus Christ was saved.

"I read that Joseph of Arimathea saved this Grail and escaped to the end of the world to keep this relic safe away from the Romans. He would have travelled to Iona, an island off the west coast of Scotland. I took my red car and drove to Scotland to have a look for the Grail. I couldn't find it, of course, but I managed to fall in love with the principal's daughter when I visited the monastery on the island.

"I suspected that the Grail was saved from the Romans but Joseph didn't count on the Vikings that robbed it from the monastery and eventually dropped

329

the Grail into the North Sea after drinking too much mead. My quest ended in Fingal's cave. Later, on my way back the car broke down on Mull, one of the western islands."

"And now you say you have found the Holy Grail here? That sounds strange, doesn't it?"

"OK. My quest wasn't too serious. It was more an excuse for travelling around in Europe with an old car with space inside for nice young girls. My story was more a means for starting conversations with young women. That worked fine, then. But now, I mean I found it not in reality but more in principle."

"Like a picture of it?"

"Sort of, yes."

"You have found sort of a picture. I think it sounds more like you have made up another story again. But go ahead. It must be better than watching the TV at this cheap hotel." Elsa prepared to listen again.

"All the stories, operas and tales I heard about the Holy Grail interested me. I think man has always tried to find the final solution for all questions, the key to the universe and the answer to all prayers. The theory of everything. The grand cure for all diseases and like."

"Tell me what you found instead."

"Remember what you said about thermodynamics?"

"Sure. It is you that should remember what I said about thermodynamics."

"I said that I had a hard time accepting that there is a difference in mass as energy and energy as exergy, the usefulness or the quality of the energy."

"I have no problem with that."

"Yes, but you say that the amount of energy is constant. Energy cannot be created or destroyed. Right?"

330

"Right."

"What you call exergy, is the useful amount of energy and that is changing from usefulness to non-usefulness."

"That is the entropy that grows."

"Yes, but they are different!"

"How do you mean?"

"I mean that the amount of energy is one thing, the quality of the energy is something else. One lump of indestructible energy can change from useful to not useful. Still it is the same amount of energy. The universe is changed from useful to not useful."

"Amount and change is different, yes."

"The interesting thing is that natural laws, they are the same everywhere according to the laws of thermodynamics. These laws must have at least two independent dimensions, then. One regarding the amount of energy and how addition and subtraction must be something of absoluteness. An amount of energy is fixed and must be considered as an absolute matter. Two lumps of energy that stick together in an addition must be the exact sum of the two as no energy between them can be created or destroyed. No part of the two separate amounts of energy can sort of overlap the other and nothing extra can come in-between them."

"I understand."

"The other dimension, the one that is independent from the amount of energy, is the quality of the energy. That you call exergy. The form of the energy is changed from useful to not useful. Right?"

"Right, I think you said it before."

"Yes, I must repeat it for myself too. I am still not sure whether I have the right words for it. Anyway. The natural laws that are behind amount and form must consist of two independent sets of conditions. They are working independently from each other and affects anything in their own aspect.

"Take for example an isolated system, a locked room with air and some wood and paper in it. The laws about amounts say that there is a certain sum of energy in this isolated container. To change the amount you must either add or subtract something. There is no other way to change the amount of energy in it.

"Now say that we had included a mechanism that makes the wood and paper catch fire. We will have a fire in the system. The wood and paper will change its form and become useless. The exergy in it will decrease while the entropy increases. The paper, wood and air change into heat and coal and carbon dioxide etc. It is still a perfect isolated system which means that no energy can be added and no energy can leave the room."

"You said that before."

"Yes, but the form of the energy in the room has changed. It has changed and this change is following another set of natural laws. A set that is independent from the set for the amount of energy. Not only the second law of thermodynamics, but it's following standard chemistry like coal and oxygen that reacts into carbon dioxide etc. That is something other than addition or subtraction of the amount of energy."

"So you realized that there is addition and there is chemistry? Bravo! Are you applying for the Nobel Prize with that? I can tell you are a bit late."

"No, please don't nag at me. I mean that they are different!"

"That sounds reasonable as coming from someone who names his car Parsifal."

"Please Elsa, I am serious! This is only the beginning. What I found is why they are different. Just wait. There is more!"

"I should think so. Like what?"

"There is a third independent set of conditions and that is the set of natural laws that are about how lumps of energy correspond with one another. The Value of anything. The energy in the room has a relation to other lumps of energy. If you compare one with another it can be regarded as hotter or colder. There is a set of universal conditions for the Value of things, the Value in relation to other things. How things fit together."

"But what is the point? It still sounds obvious to me."

"I found that time is the key to it all, because it is all happening at the same time. We have three different and independent aspects of just about anything all the time. That makes time three-dimensional."

"Ahhmm, now it begin to sound more complicated, but I like that. Go on, please."

"We know that everything there is can be regarded as an event, a process in time. Everything you find has some energy that is statistically proven to be there often enough to make it exist as a real object. If you can measure it, it is. Everything has energy, it has a form and it has value. It has a time history. It has a beginning somewhere in time and it will probably end sometime or change into something else.

"We observe it in the now, at the border between the past and the future. All particles, all chemical reactions, physical activities and social actions are something that is really happening now. The now is a perpetually changing wave rolling from the beginning to the end in the future. I saw it on the surface of the stream where we were out of petrol."

"You saw what in the stream, a fish that farted?"

"No! I saw a picture of time! The rings that come from the raindrops."

"Aha! I know how they look. But I have never seen them as pictures of time."

"Now imagine that there is something happening in space. Like the drops that hit the water but now something that acts more like a spark in the sky. This does not create a ring on a surface but a bubble, a perfect sphere around the spark, growing just like the ring before, in three dimensions; up-down, left-right and east-west. Imagine how the sound wave spreads from a bell in the air that is hit by a hammer. The sound spreads all around the bell out in the air as a bubble, at the speed of sound."

"Uhhh, fine."

"Now imagine that we have three independent sets of natural laws that work together, affecting anything in the universe and with the same time component. Regardless of which time we are talking about. Everything we are looking at has a start point and a now where we can observe it and an end where it is not any longer.

"Three independent things are happening as long as it exists. It has an amount, it has a form and it has value. Everything there is, is at the meeting point of these three dimensions. Seen from outside the now is just a bubble with a history. Seen from inside the now is an infinite area of future possibilities."

"What has that got to do with us and the Holy Grail?"

"I dropped the chase for the physical Grail when I understood that most of the stories in the Bible were just stories. The important thing in the Bible was not
334

the facts or content but the message. The stories don't have to be real historical events. It is the message in the story that is the important thing."

"So what did you search for then?"

"I read that the Holy Grail was a metaphor for the understanding of the conditions for life. Life was carried in a cup of divinity. So I began to search for this kind of a cup of understanding, God's 'Recipe for the universe', that carried life."

"You really aim high, young man."

"Yes, that is why I think it is such fun. I found the answer when I was waiting for you. It is all about an act of balance between these three forces. Too much or too little is wasted. In all three dimensions. Anything there is has to be 1: enough, 2: logic and 3: appropriate if you see."

"No I can't see anything. It is so dark in here. I can feel you."

"But you remember what I said about time. Everything is about saving time?"

"You said so."

"I was really stupid when I drove too fast through the railway crossings. I tried to save time, but I caused us a problem and we lost time instead."

"Yes that was very stupid of you. You scared me."

"I am very sorry for this inconvenience I brought to you. Can you forgive me, please?"

"If you hadn't done that I wouldn't have met Christine and her daughter Frieda. I forgive you anyway. It is your car. I feel fine now in this bed with you."

"It is all about saving time and time evolves like a sphere from the start. Like the water ring, but now as a spherical bubble. The three dimensions seek to be balanced with each other. Have you seen a lava lamp?

You can imagine how a drop of water moves to try to keep perfectly round. That is the important thing. To stay perfectly round. A good thing, event, process or anything is one that is well balanced in amount, form and value."

"Ahaa. But how do we know if it is in or out of balance? It sounds very abstract to me."

"We are, luckily not at the beginning. We have a lot of experience of this search for balance already. Our biological system has evolved according to natural laws for millions of years. Our emotional system is already prepared for this business. We just didn't happen to know it, until now."

"I'm not really sure yet."

"Any kind of biological species is a living process, right?"

"Right."

"A biological species has a DNA system and stuff that tells the cells how to act in different situations, all to survive and prosper as well as possible. They learned it in the school of Survival of the fittest."

" Yes."

"The biological system sends signals to its parts on how to react in various situations. Sometimes it has to take care of the amount, sometimes it has to take care of its form, its structure. Other times it has to communicate, to take care of its relation to the surroundings. That keeps the balance in three dimensions."

"But how would we know how to keep the balance in something we hardly understand? I can't really see any time-sphere around me!"

"We already have a sensory system. The trick is how to learn how to read it."

"I have no problem with my feelings."

"Yes I know. You are a good woman. But you remember Chica's aunt, she drew the lifeline on me?"

"Yes."

"A three-dimensional sphere has six poles. Up, down, left, right, east and west. The three independent sets of natural laws are working in each direction, like types of invisible light crossing each other, or like streams or magnetic fields. In opposing poles the force works actively on the one hand and on the other it is passive, with or against the conditional field. Regarding the amount, for example, you can act to gain or lose weight. You want to eat but at the same time something else wants to eat you. Regarding form, you can get in better or worse shape without changing your size. Regarding the relational value, you can value or be valued."

"Six poles."

"Yes, six poles of emotional signals of what to do to keep the balance."

"You must give another example. I am interested but this was a lot in one bite."

"OK, let's take a single cell, one of the smallest kind of organisms. The cell needs to keep its amount of energy or it will starve to death. It has some kind of measuring system in its DNA. That system starts the alarm when supplies get low. A biological warning light goes on and the cell starts to work to provide more energy. That is, to get energy, increase its amount of energy. At the opposite pole it is about the amount, too, but here we have signals that indicate that it has too much of something and must shed some of its belongings. Those are two of the emotional poles in the sphere.

"The next dimension, which is independent from the first concerning amount, is about the form of the cell, how it is organized and so on. Here we have two opposite poles: one for getting more organized and the other for a more rational composition.

"The third is about how it is related to the surrounding and what the surroundings look like, what it is worth, its value. Whether the organism can affect the surroundings or how it can be affected by another organism."

"I didn't understand the last bit."

"Well take myself as an example. I have instinctual emotions that tell me to eat or stop eating. I have instinctual emotions that affect my physical composition and position. I also have instinctual emotions about the surroundings; I want to say something, I find words, arrange them in a certain order to form a message. A message works if it has the right words in it and they are pronounced in the right order. The feeling that the message and the communication work, and the feeling that I want it to work, are in the third dimension. Listening is at the other pole. You know yourself how frustrating it can be to not get time to talk or do things sometimes?"

"Oh, yes, like now." Elsa sounded frustrated.

"What would you like to say?"

"I don't want to talk but I think I must fart. I can't sleep with a belly full of gases. I feel so embarrassed about that after your outburst today. I think I have to go out for a while."

"Please Elsa, I think I must apologize for that once again. I don't think we have to be so strict about that. When we are sleeping I am sure that none of us is able to control our bodily functions as we are then unconscious. Our biology has to work freely. It must be allowed to fart during the sleep to be able to have a good and relaxed recovery, don't you think?"

"Yes."

"I can roll down the windows just a little on both sides so we will have some ventilation. Maybe you can do it outside the blankets as long as you are awake. OK?"

"Yes."

"And try to do it silently, OK?

"Yes. A sneaker."

"I have to get out anyway because I don't want to pee in our bed. Can I borrow your toothbrush?"

"Yes, it is in my plastic purse by my feet. There is toothpaste too."

John found the things after some fiddling and stepped out of the car. It was cold outside. He noticed that the wind had turned from west to northwest and it was stronger. John was warm inside and felt invulnerable against nature. He went down to the beach to find water for the toothpaste.

He stood naked in the dark and felt the icy wind blow around his body. The blood in his feet was automatically shut off to preserve his inner temperature a little longer. His penis had shrunk to a minimal size and he had some problems getting rid of his urine. The wind blew against him and some of it splashed on his legs. John walked out into the water to wash it off. There was frozen water glazing the rocks above the water's surface. He listened to the wind and the waves.

This was a big lake but it wasn't the sea so the waves were small and had a strange sound. Just a small whisking against the stones. John listened more closely to the water. It wasn't even like waves. A sound more like a running stream in the wind. Was there another train or a car coming? He looked to the right but saw no lights in the forest. The sound in the strong wind became clearer and louder.

It was rather dark around him. He thought that it sounded like something coming towards him. It was not the water, it was not waves, it was ICE! He saw a wall of white shiny ice and broad ice floes come sailing up very fast in the wind straight towards him. John had to run out of the water in panic. He dropped the toothbrush. The thundering ice wall forcing layers of thin ice floes with sharp edges before it hit the shore. The ice was crushed against the stones and the higher land. It followed him a long way up. John took cover behind a thick birch and breathed out. He wandered around in the dark for a while before he found the dark green car again and jumped in under the blankets.

"Oiiih! That was cold! You are wet too! Did you pee on yourself?"

"Don't worry, I just washed. But the wind was cold. Please let me warm up by you. It won't take long to get warm again."

"You like me when I'm hot don't you?"

"Oh, ye-eh-es-s!" John said shivering.

John was warmed by Elsa's radiation by the contact of her burning skin with his stiff and icy body. He shivered for a long time before he could feel his muscles begin to relax and return to normal function. He turned around to get warm on the other side. They said nothing but touched each other through their different temperatures. She gave and he took. They laid side by side with her back to his belly. He held his right arm around her and rested his head on the condom.

When John felt that his feet were beginning to get warm he knew that he would soon fall asleep. He wondered if Elsa had fallen asleep already but her breath was quiet. He waited for the sudden movement that comes when somebody falls asleep.

"I am not going to sleep yet, if you think so," Elsa said with a clear voice. No sign of tiredness.

"Do you want to talk some more?"

"I want you to draw my lifeline."

20 - The Sound of Rain on the Roof

Elsa lay on her back. John on her right side. He raised his right arm slowly under the quilt. He searched carefully, found her face in the dark and touched the top of her head with his index finger.

"Wotan blows his whistle …"

"Wasn't it Wakan-tanka?"

"No. He is for the Native Americans. Ours are Wotan. It is the same guy but with our name."

"Fine, go on with the game anyway." Elsa corrected her position.

"Wotan blows his whistle and when you think, it is his music you are making. Six poles in the music, strength, harmony and expression. Can you see them?"

"Too loud and too quiet is wasted, that is two. Too complicated and too simple, that is four, right?"

"If you say so, yes." John held his finger still on her head.

"Expression? Can it be too much of that? Beauty, yes, and ugliness is easy."

"I think beauty lies in the dream of perfect balance of all three dimensions."

John continued to her eyes. He held two fingers softly on her closed eyes.

"Wotan blows his whistle. He hides but you know he is there. How does he look?"

"He is … huge. But not too big. I must see enough to be sure. I know when something is missing in the picture. There is a lot of details too. This is harder. I can't see what I don't understand or have not heard about. I believe in what I see but not in what I cannot see.

"That's six again. Two about amount, two about order and two about what it means …its value … Oh God, Oh my God! Je-esus!"

"Oh, I am so glad that I am not religious! It is so beautiful! I see colours!"

"In the dark?"

"Yes, I see it in colour! Oh, it is like watching a colour film for the first time! Concepts are in black and white. But my feelings about it are in colour!

"From deepest black to blue and lilac, when I think about amount or something missing. Order is red, mostly, brown. Meaning and message are yellowish, orange to bright white.

"Aah! Now I understand why it is called enlightenment! I can feel my thoughts and my heart come together!"

"You are crying. Your eyes are wet."

"No I am so happy! This is wonderfulh, bhut de tears run intoh by dose. I bust have sobethig to blow by dose idto."

John gave her a paper tissue from the compartment in the door.

"Next, please."

"I think you can put your hearing and your sight in the same place, they are both passive in a way but you are using them."

"I think so too. It is wonderful to sharpen my hearing. When I can hear what I am searching for. And it is awful to be annoyed by a scream. Next, please."

"Wotan lights a fire and the smoke is all around you. Thick, coloured smoke that tells you what?" John drew his fingertip very slowly along her nose.

"I try to breathe without choking. Sniffing for nuances. Smells that I have known since I was a kid. I've never forgotten the smell of my first puppy. And

343

the medicine I had to take, Yeech! I am getting surprised over all the new perfumes and long for the yet unknown."

John continued to her mouth and placed his fingertip on her bottom lip.

"Wotan is talking through your throat. What is your answer?" John continued the movement across her chin and followed the outside of her throat.

"I must speak and I must keep quiet sometimes. I choose my words and I learn new words and languages. There is a meaning in what I say and I have to ask about what I don't know."

John's hand moved in under the quilt. It was cold outside and warm under it. He showed Elsa how to hold her arms along her body so he could continue the line. He started over from her larynx and moved his hand slowly between her breasts.

"Wotan plays his drum. You are listening to the sound and the rhythm."

"I can hear the power in the beat. It gives me courage to breastfeed my baby. It makes me so happy to work and I would like to dance together with my family. It makes me understand what is right and wrong. I am prepared to fight for my rights against my enemies. Ahh, I feel so alive when I am angry! There is happiness, and there is sorrow and trouble."

John's finger stretched the line down to her belly above her navel. He could feel her heart beat. She was breathing deep and slow. Something ran with a bubbling sound inside her. The wind from the north shook the car.

"Wotan plays his drum even harder. He hides in the grass, in the wind, in the forest and in the water."

"I must breathe, I must drink and eat. Too much and too little is wasted. My belly knows the difference
344

between good and bad taste and it can make me sick. The food gives me power and I am weak without it."

John went on down her warm and soft belly with his finger. He reached her pubic hair and continued slowly until he covered her secret damp flower with his hand.

"Wotan plays his drum more slowly but more heavily. It teases your lust and joy." He could sense her flower unfold slowly.

"Oh, I know when I need a man. When there is something missing. I know very well when it is the right man and how to treat him well. That joy I feel to be together with the man I love. I am so glad that I have never been forced into it. Wotan would be proud of me."

"Me too. I think the line is finished. Did you like it?"

"I am very pleased, thank you. I counted them all."

"Them?"

"The poles."

"How many?"

"42. Adams was right."

"Apparently."

"Wait, I'll tell you when you move your hand away."

John listened to her breath and felt the winds suddenly shake the car. He could hear the waves meet the melting ice floes that were washed over by water. Elsa stopped breathing for a second and sighed. John could sense her hair tickle between his fingers and the rising tension inside her thighs. She relaxed and breathed through her nose. John waited for her next move. He thought back over their trip. Ups and downs. Her findings at the lifeline. The ice at the beach. Mary, Christine, oil-blended petrol, food, the fan belt, the light, the motor needing electric power to start. He made another attempt to move his hand but she took his arm and held it in place.

She whispered. "Please wait. It is so lovely to have you there. I can come again."

John let her stay in her warm dream. He enjoyed the close contact with her. He was warm all through now and he was far away from the trouble in the lake. Another wave rolled through her and she giggled quietly. No sign of getting tired. His arm was still held in place. John moved a little closer and put his head on her shoulder. She nodded his face with hers. John had his ear tight to her skin. He could listen to her slowing heartbeat. She changed her position to the left but kept his hand locked. John turned more to relieve his hips and put his leg upon her right leg.

He listened to her heartbeat and began thinking about what melody he could play to her beat. He imagined that he was playing the trumpet in a swing band with Elsa on the contrabass. Trada da daa da daa trrra da da dah. He tried to find a rhythm that fitted her breathing and her heartbeat. A bell began to ring. A red light blinked and lit up the campsite. Soft light came into the car. He saw her closed eyes close to him. He could hear a train coming closer.

"Please relax now, just hold me. I can do the rest of it myself. Your lovely hand there is enough. I am finding the balance between force and rhythm."

Elsa whispered between the red light waves. John held his hand in place, relaxed and alert to any sign of change in her female tissue. She moved her knees apart and together. He listened to her breath. When the train came closer John felt the power from the weight of the heavy carriages transmitted by the vibrations of the ground into the car. Her hips started vibrating and joined in the dance.

John began to think whether he had any instructions to read about the electrical system of the car. They must be in the glove compartment, under the other papers he used to carry when driving. He knew that there must be an old road map from McDonald's there too. The map was over fifteen years old and there were roads built since that weren't on the map. "To find the right way was a kind of sport. GPS systems were for losers," he was thinking. He wanted to have it in his brain. Being lost a little was just a thrilling spice to the daily driving. He suspected that the GPS system could send his location back to some server, too, information that could be sold to his boss so he could see where John was driving for real.

He was wondering whether the little bottle of green repair colour would still be usable or if it had dried up. It had a code number for the colour and if he wanted to replace it he must quote that number to match the colour of the car. The number was stamped on a plate under the hood. He thought it must be 606, which stood for Classic Green. But he should check that in the morning to be sure.

Sometimes he put sweets in the hatch that he used to pick up from the information desk on his visits to companies. His passengers used to open the little door and search for something interesting. So it was good to have something for their pleasure in place. John liked to please people. Elsa was in a nice state now. But the electrical system in the car was harder to please. It demands perfect organization to work. The exact length and quality of the wires all the way around. Any little breach compromises the whole circuit so that it won't work. Fixing electricity is mostly about finding something that is broken. It could be a wire or a loose coupling. More waves coming.

John had read a lot about electric coupling systems. He remembered when he was introduced to the DIN[26] system at school. It was a technical wonder and he read all he could find about it. He went to the library and had them order catalogues and technical preparatory work. He had to learn the German language just to be able to read them. The pleasure of learning the technical perfection aroused him.

"Ungh!"

Things that worked together. Pure mathematics materialized into real moving machines. It had something eternal in it. The train was gone. The red light was gone. The bell didn't ring any more. It was dark in the car. Elsa was still moving. She had found a stable state of permanent motion. She was in a higher level of self-oscillation. Waiting for the next train to come. John stayed patient.

"Nnnnhh, ooh. That was really something coming from inside," Elsa moaned after a while. She breathed deeply for a while and giggled. "You really have the hands to my taste, young man." She held his arm still in position and talked leisurely, and was thoughtful between every sentence.

"It is like all my life happened only to end up at this place tonight.

"Now I know that I can die. I know that I have lived, and loved.

"I was thinking about my dear Sigmund. He must have suffered. My mother told me to not let any man come too close before I got married.

---

26 DIN Deutsches Institut für Normung

"What a fool I was. But we couldn't find any prophylactics at that time. I was not ready to have a child with him.

"Biologically yes, but not socially."

"I love when you come into my hand. It is like you are giving away some of your secrets. You let me come close to you."

"Your hand fits well."

"To your well."

"Well done, thank you mister, but now I want to listen to music. After all it is Saturday night. What time is it?"

John picked up his iPad again.

"8.27."

"What kind of music do you like?"

"I'd like something by Zarah Leander. I remember me and Sigmund ins Kino in Cuxhaven. Es war eine … Oh, excuse me, I start to think in German when I think about Sigmund."

John tapped the icon for the YouTube app that looked like an old TV set from the fifties and typed in 'Zarah' into the search field. A lot of clips appeared on the screen.

"Oh, yes I'd like to watch TV! Can you find a song called 'Kann denn Liebe Sünde sein?'

John added the word 'liebe' after 'Zarah' in the search field. The screen was filled by hits and there it was!

John pressed the play button.

"Oh, so nice! I want to see all her films! This will be a nice Saturday night after all. We have lots of time to have fun. The night is still young."

They watched the video. Elsa knew the words and hummed to it and waved her feet. John picked up some of her luggage to place behind their backs so they could lie better for movie watching. John arranged the cover of the iPad so it could rest on his belly. He had to hold it with his bare arm and used his thumb to manage the actions on the screen.

They watched movie after movie on YouTube. Elsa wanted to hear every song by Zarah twice at least. Then she asked John to find more old German hits. He searched for 'Marlene Dietrich', 'Edith Piaf'. Elsa wanted to see Lotte Lehmann sing 'Der Rosenkavalier' by Strauss but they only found a short clip sung by Pavarotti. They went on to 'Andrews Sisters', 'Glenn Miller'. Elsa was so happy and watched with her mouth open like a child. After about an hour a new train passed. The bell rang, the red light blinked and the ground rocked their bed. John wasn't sure how long the batteries in the iPad would last. He began to be tired of watching.

"I think I have had enough of this for the moment."

"Oh. That is fine by me. I brings back so many memories. Good and bad."

"So what are we going to do now? I can sleep but then I might wake up too early in the morning, when it is still dark. We can't play cards in the car like this, can we?"

"I can draw your lifeline! Put away the things and lean back, my dear."

"OK. Nice idea." He could feel his heart beat harder. He lay down and let his arms be placed at his sides and closed his eyes.

Elsa put the index finger of her left hand on the top of John's head and began reading.

"Wotan blows his pipe and when you think you can hear his music. Six poles in the music, strength, harmony and expression. Can you hear them?"

"I know my land of memories. It is wide but not borderless. It is like an island in the dark and I don't know what is outside. New things are coming to me like snow from the sky. There are things that I want to forget and there are things I shouldn't forget. I try to put them in order. Some things fit into the pattern I already made, other don't.

"It fills me with joy when I find something new that makes the machinery run. I am very sorry when important memories are lost. Forever … like cracks in an old plate that I had used for eating many times through my life. The hunt for missing pieces is very clear and well known. In the opposite direction is the struggle for hiding my secrets. That is about the amount, the sum of my concepts.

"Next is the form. The feeling I get when something is wrong and I must solve it. On the other side are the times when I feel that something threatens to make the logic fall apart. The third is about value. What I think is important to the world. My opinion is counted as we live in a democracy. I have to accept that we all have different opinions about just about anything and still everyone thinks he's right.

"The majority sets the framework of what will be considered right and what should be considered wrong. The minority must accept what the majority thinks. Or else, if the minority is to decide, there are just more who will have to accept another view. I read and listen to other peoples opinion and they put a value on my different perspectives.

"A president must understand the connection between GDP, health care and justice. One saves time, the other uses the saved time and the third is the guarantee for a fair deal that satisfies our inorganic, organic, social and intellectual desire.

"All are important but to keep the balance you must have a sense of balance. In a business it is easy to decide if the current focus should be put on increasing the balance sheet, reorganizing the company or emphasizing on the marketing to show its value. Professional 'balance-dogs' will be recruited."

Elsa continued and held two of her fingertips on his closed eyes.

"Wotan blows his whistle, can you see him?"

"Yes I see him. Everything I see has energy and power. Light is energy. Pictures are made visible by light. Too much light or too little disturbs my sight. I can find or make pictures myself if something is missing. I get angry if someones hiding something for me and curious if I someone gives me a nicely folded present.

"About form: a wrong picture is easy to detect. I am so fascinated how we can know each other by our faces. How embarrassing it is to not recognize old friends or ascribe to them the wrong social connection. While playing a board game such as chess, I can see the possible moves as pictures. But all the possible draws blind me. I really like to be surprised by new pictures of the world.

"Third, value; it can be very annoying with a picture that I don't understand. Other pictures make me think that they tell us all we need to know, like a high definition picture of the planet Earth made by Suomi[27].

"I am very sorry, but I don't have the same colour sight as yours, Elsa. I see different colours with my left

27 http://en.wikipedia.org/wiki/Suomi_NPP

and my right eye. I've never known which are the correct versions of red and green."

They continued the game. John was very amused and found long answers to every question. He had lot of time and wanted to explore the poles carefully and exactly. Elsa was patient but had to rest her arm some times. She kept her hand where she had come to. John wished that he had recorded what he said but as he knew that this was based on a simple system it would be easy to reproduce.

Elsa continued along his lifeline. Finally, she slowly reached his erected organ. She held it tenderly, rested her arm on his hip and whispered into John's ear:

"Wotan blows his trumpet of pleasure."

"My joy brings me to my beloved. I flee from the dangers in the darkness and diseases in the dungeons. I dance in front of the fire and let the red light show my shape. I meet my child's mother and rest my meat in her caressing cave. The sound and the power of the trumpet brings my lust and desire for life over to her. I listen to her answer by her song. My power and my dance moves find the balance. I open the door for my children to walk through and enter into life."

Elsa let her hand stay where it was. John sensed how the blood was pumped to make him as hard as possible. The nerves were all outside to direct the process. Outside the wind caused the car to shake a little. It was raining again. The drops of water hit the roof of the car and the sound from every collision spread in the car. John could hear where every collision came from. They were many and spread all over the roof. He could even hear the sound of drops falling on other things outside the car. The total sound was mixed into a white noise of an infinite number of sound bubbles. Each one with its own time.

"I think I need a towel or something if I come."

Elsa was quiet for a while.

"We can use a condom. I can put on a condom for you. I am not letting you come into me so I have to do the work of cleaning up the mess. But I can put on one of the condoms. Then it is just a matter of taking it off, making a knot in the end and throwing it away outside. I've done that before."

"OK, go ahead. But the night is young. No hurry please. I know what I am doing."

Elsa released her hand and turned around for the six-pack. She had to turn on the light to find it. She opened it and picked a strange green thing with lot of wrinkles on.

"How can someone believe that a woman would like to have such a thing inside her? Better to use it like this."

She put it on, the condom with its contents more like some kind of a handle for a household appliance. She shut the light and lay down again on her right side under the quilt. John drew up his right leg so it made a tent with space enough underneath. Elsa held her left hand on the handle prepared for the work.

"How many poles?"

"43."

"43? You mean Douglas Adams was wrong?"

"No. 42 plus one.

"No, not that one.

"I am the one that chooses. There are an unlimited number of choices between the poles. It is the discrepancy between how it is and how it could be that makes things happen and that can be in any direction."

"I think you are too smart for me. Can I stay here with you tonight."

"You are so welcome."

"Thanks."

"I like this. We have lot of time, don't we?"

"Yes, I can rest my arm on you. I am not so used to doing this with my left hand. The other has more than 80 years' experience."

"Please, suit yourself. I am not in a hurry. I have never thought about it as something that has to be done in eleven minutes. Every second of this is sacred. Find the balance between …"

"But if I fall asleep?"

"I will wake you up, like this!"

"He he he, I look forward to that."

"I thought about how the men of the churches had to live in celibacy. That must have been a real pain. I know what happens if I wait too long."

"I don't think any one of them could stay in that celibacy. The only men who can are the impotent old leaders of the church. I think they invented this dogma of celibacy for the young priests mostly by being jealous over the younger men's physical power and potency.

"That must be a fine way to demonstrate the old men's power in the hierarchy, to punish and destroy these young men's ambition to find true love in life. Poor young men. You know that I lived together with a priest for ten years. He didn't like the celibacy at all. He was a horny and happy beast!"

"Don't you think that celibacy causes a perverted sexuality too? Ejaculating at the sight of the Madonna or in front of the crucifix?"

"After what I heard there is a lot of perverted sex in the monasteries, yes. Just like eating dog food, or worse."

"There is no dog food in here."

"I think that is true, yes."

"I really love to spend the night like this with you. I can feel it inside, in my heart."

"Me too. My nipples need your attention."

"Shall we wait for the next train coming? I am standing at the station waiting for the train ..."

"Be my passenger."

"I will."

"Need a ticket?"

"No. This train is free. Would you like some soft music?"

"Yes, why not. Something old-fashioned maybe, the kind that I like."

John opened the iPad again and found an album with Nat King Cole. 'Nature Boy' filled the cabin. Elsa knew how to balance. John lost his own balance and drifted away.

21 - Frieda's Place

Someone knocked at the window. John awoke. It was daylight and he saw a woman outside the car. Elsa woke up too.

"Oh. It is Frieda! Good morning!" Elsa opened the back door immediately and crawled out to talk to Frieda. She wasn't bothered about being naked, but picked up her dress from behind her and put it on outside the car. Elsa's hair was in chaos pointing in all directions.

"Good morning, both of you! I brought some breakfast for you! Did you have a nice sleep? I can see that the night was one of pleasure, ha ha!" She saw the green condom on the ground.

"I didn't know you had room service at this place, ha ha ha!" Elsa stepped around to get her limbs awake. "But there is no toilet here, I think."

"Yes there is. I run this place and there is my office. Just hold my things, please, so I can open up." She opened up and let Elsa use the toilet room.

John put on his clothes and crawled out of the car. He had been sleeping totally unconscious all the night. He didn't remember any dreams at all. His stomach was well awake and it alarmed his constitution when he heard the word breakfast. John picked up the used condom and threw it in a litter bin on the wall.

He followed Elsa and Frieda into the cabin. She opened the shutters. The daylight came into the office. Elsa put the coffee thermos on a small table while Frieda took her office chair to sit on as there were only two small chairs to use at the table.

"So you had a good night! Both of you?"

"Yes!" Elsa and John answered simultaneously.

"We played games and watched TV all night in the car. It was a wonderful Saturday night, wasn't it, John?"

"Yes, unforgettable." John smiled and looked at the bag of bread that Frieda was opening.

"This is a place for pleasure, I promise you. I've had it for about twenty years now. My mother thinks I am crazy but this is the life. It is my life!"

"But it is not the season for tourists right now, is it?" John tried to see it from a straight business perspective.

"Tourists only come in the summer and they drop by very suddenly so I can't count on them."

"So how come you say that this is your life if you don't make any money on it? Where is the customer value?" John took another fried egg sandwich.

"Good point! I didn't say that I made any profit." Frieda smiled widely. "You know that I live next to the condom factory. When it was built here it was because the local government wanted to put some kind of industry here to create jobs for the unemployed people in the area. That was me and some guys from the woods. The local government tried to support any enterprise to establish something that made it possible for us to get a job and not have to move to some suburb.

"It began with just repacking the condoms but I was too young then. It was ideal as it was so close to the railway. The condom factory was already established in Thickholt but some difficulties with the landlord forced the owner to find a solution and then they decided to move the production here, too, and that's how it started to be big business."

"And then you and the boys were employed and were happy all together?"

"No, not at all. None of us were qualified for that work. They had us trained at the beginning but most of us got bored of the whole thing. Some of the guys were so embarrassed at touching something that should go on another man's penis that they ran away after a few days. Many of us, even me, are hunting a good part of the year and that takes time. Full-time work is hard to combine with the hunting season. There wasn't many suitable jobs at all. Most of the skilled workers at the site in Thickholt followed up from the city and have a good life here. When they long for the city it is not far to go there for a weekend."

"But you clean the factory?" Elsa sat in her dress but nothing underneath. Her legs showed and her feet were bare.

"Yes, and that is enough for me. I don't need so much money to make it here."

"You said that this is your life?"

"Yes, I am so glad that you seem to understand. I knew at once that you would when Elsa told me about an odd couple like you, planning to spend the night in a car just here! I would have charged you if I hadn't met Elsa last night."

"It was not planned. We have trouble with the car. It was an emergency." John was finished with the sandwiches and had a half cup of coffee left. He leaned back with a satisfied expression.

"But why didn't you call the phone number on the big sign on the wall behind the car? I could have let you sleep in real beds in a well-tempered cabin?" John's face turned with a funny smile to Elsa. She looked innocently back at John.

359

"Didn't think about it, sort of," John mumbled, blushing, with the mug to his mouth.

"But you said that this is your life and you sounded so convinced about it. That must be something for us to hear." Elsa changed the subject over to Frieda again.

"Oh. That is easy. They tried to train us in how to produce condoms. We also learned why it is important to produce condoms. That was my first contact with true sexuality and I learned about the freedom to choose when to have a baby instead of being ruled by your biological nature. Before that, sex was just something that I was alone with. I didn't have any boyfriends and my mother was a bit old-fashioned. When they built the factory these cabins were brought here for the workers to live in and I got job as a 'general maid'. It was said that I would clean up and keep the keys when they were at home at weekends. All the workers where men of course.

Men have certain needs too. I learned that, especially in the factory training. My mother went crazy but I didn't care. I served the men and they were very happy with my work, day and night. I got to know the boys in the neighbourhood too, in due course. I guess that rumours spread so at the end of the summer when the factory was built I took over the campsite. There were no vacancies at the weekends for a long time. I sold food, I took care of their laundry and called the social services. In fact, I did everything a mother or a wife should do except one thing."

"Except what?" John was thinking of her not being a prostitute.

"I didn't get pregnant. Thanks to the condoms. Thank heaven for this marvellous invention. No bugs or germs at all. I had to be careful about that, too."

"But do you serve just any man? What if they are mean or naughty in some way? Aren't you afraid?"

"That is no problem here. I am never alone in this place. I get full protection from the other boys. There is a golden rule here and that is 'Don't fuck with Frieda!' They take care of me like I was their mother or daughter."

"Maybe it was some of your friends that we met when we were out of petrol."

"Probably. Most people around here know each other. They'll soon find out that you have spent the night at my place."

"Is that a problem for you?"

"No not at all. I am glad to meet some other people. It is easy to be bored anyway."

"Maybe we should play cards? Do you like card games?" Elsa's enthusiasm shone in her eyes.

"No thank you. I have more work to do. I shot a deer on Friday and it is time to butcher it. Before that I have to do my books. I do it all by myself. I don't like to depend on anyone else." Frieda began to put the things together. Elsa and John understood that she wanted go back to her work.

"Well, thank you very much for the room service. How much do we owe you?" John stood up and searched for his wallet.

"Oh no, don't worry about that. It's on the house. You gave me a nice story to tell my boys."

Elsa thanked her further and hugged her. John went back to the car to put together the bed-things and the back seat. He had to deflate the mattress to be able to roll it. He opened the valve and left it in the back of the car to empty from the pressure from inside. He went to the front and opened the bonnet to examine the situation. Frieda came by and had a look at the car.

"So what is wrong with it?"

"We have lost the adjustment bolt for the generator so it cannot hold the tension of the fan belt."

Frieda took a close look. "I don't think I can help you with that kind of bolt. It is very special bolt as far as I can see."

"Yes, I have enough electricity in my battery to start but we will run out of light so we have to drive in the day. But we will be home in four hours so it's not a big problem now. That is why we had to stay overnight."

"But why don't you put something else under the generator? I would use a stick!" Frieda bent down to the ground and gave John a thick wood stick. She picked up a big knife from her belt so John could carve it to fit between the compressor for the air conditioning and the electric generator. She helped him to bend the generator up so the fan belt had enough tension.

John could see that Frieda had strong muscles. He was a white-collar worker who had to ride his horse regularly to keep his body in shape. She worked hard all day long. For her this was just a little fall out from a regular day. John guessed that she would probably have solved this in three minutes even if it was dark. John blushed again as his manhood was disturbed. Frieda saw that and gave him a firm, friendly hug. John could feel that this woman also knew how to treat a man. He liked her immediately. "Where is the weaker sex?" he was thinking.

"You must stop here next time you go this road."

"Promise, I'll be back." John gave Frieda a friendly smile and his business card, just in case.

John got into the car and started the engine. It worked as normal. No warning lights were on. The fan belt made some noise. He pressed the accelerator to check if anything was wrong. He let the engine idle and went out to close the bonnet but Frieda put it down with one hand as she passed around on the other side to go back to her office. She said goodbye to Elsa. Elsa put her things together in the back and they were ready to go. Frieda went into the office and closed the door to avoid too much of the white smoke from the exhaust.

John drove up onto the road and geared up slowly, leaving a big cloud behind them.

"Ah, it is so nice to be on the road again!" Elsa sat with her handbag on her lap and smiled at John. "Isn't it?"

"Yes. Now I have to drive very carefully with as little petrol as possible to be able to reach the petrol station. The oil-blended petrol works fine but it makes so much smoke."

"And I had such a good sleep last night. I was totally biological! Everyone should have the right to have a good sleep every night!"

"Maybe. When I have had periods of bad sleep for some reason I have felt like I had caught fire the next day. I had to burn my spare energy. But there was no fire department to call. If a house is on fire the fire department comes immediately but if a human is on fire it is his own responsibility to put it out. That sounds strange, doesn't it?"

"What do the insurance company say? They are the ones that have to pay the damage."

"Bruce Springsteen recorded a song called 'Fire'. But that is about love."

John tried to look back but saw nothing but a white cloud in the mirror.

22 - The Value

"So what's the object for today? What are your preferences, your desires and what is most valuable to you?"

"I want to get home, that's all. I will cook a good meal for you. I want to play 'Evil of the World' and beat you up."

"OK, that sounds reasonable as long as you don't mean you'll beat me after we play."

"No. During." Elsa had a cruel face.

"I want to get home too. Arriving at yours is just a part of my object for today. First we have to find a petrol station and next find someone that can help us fix the missing bolt for the generator. Shouldn't be too impossible.

"We have some petrol in the tank, enough to drive for a while. The generator is charging the battery but I am not sure how the fan belt will do with just a stick to keep the tension. We have had breakfast, thanks to Frieda. We are healthy and had a good sleep. What else?"

"We are friends! I really like to be with you. You are the perfect mate for a trip like this."

"Thank you. I like you, too." John took her hand.

"I can see that." Elsa smiled at John and looked forward along the road again.

They passed over a hill and they could see a big lake far away in the forest. As far as they could see there were only forests, for miles. The sky was blue and the sun had left the horizon on its way up to the left.

"I really hope that we can find a petrol station before the tank is empty again."

John picked up the iPad and the map app was still on. He could see a blue line with a blue needle head that moved along the line.

"Look, we are tracking ourselves!" He gave the iPad to Elsa so she could monitor their route.

"How does this work?"

"I searched for the nearest petrol station on it and it gave the way to it from where we were last night."

"So I will be your co-driver using this? I can tell you when the next turn is coming up."

"That will be fine. You will be a good co-driver."

"That depends on you."

"How do you mean?"

"Whether I am satisfying your expectations of a good co-driver, I mean."

"Anything but farting will do!"

"Aye aye, sir!"

John's brain woke up again.

"Goodness!

"The value! The value must depend on what it is related to! Value cannot stand alone. It is all based on relations. Anything has an amount of energy and a form, but its value depends on other objects with energy and form. Some things fit together and others don't."

"I hope I fit in this car!"

"Yes you do, my dear. The main object for today is to get back to your apartment again. The choices we make and the value of today's activities is based upon that. The activities we perform are the form, the strategy to get home and we need energy, petrol and food and a working car to do it."

366

"We need a road too."

"Yes. And a satisfactory traffic situation. Every second is filled with surrounding events of all kinds. A moose is living his own life in the forest, fulfilling his natural life. If it happens to cross our path we may crash. The combination of our car and the moose is no good. We must avoid that."

"No accidents, thank you! No more Big Bangs!"

"Accidents happen. But I will try to do my best. There is no such thing as 100% guarantee against accidents. We cannot control everything. There must be risk and forgiveness."

"I wish you could forgive me for farting in the car yesterday. It was an accident. I lost control."

"OK. I forgive you. You couldn't know that it was beyond my expectations."

"What do you think about Christine?"

"What would I think? I didn't meet her at all."

"She said that we must be able to forgive our enemies, even if the enemies are our friends that can't forgive their enemies in turn. We must forgive those who can't forgive."

"Sounds a little complicated but it must be technically right, mustn't it?"

"We must forgive the German people for believing in the Nazi propaganda. We are, as they were, after all, only humans."

"I have no problem with that, I think. They were fooled. Are we too?"

"Humanity has been fooled by leaders throughout history. I think even a leader is often fooled by his own dreams. He just doesn't know any better."

"You mean that we should also forgive Hitler and the Nazis?"

"No. Everyone must be responsible for his conscious choice. You can have any opinion you want but you can't hurt other people because of your private opinion. That is going too far because that is infringing on the other's right to have his own free opinion, just like you. But I think it is possible to understand how a people with a social strategy, the cultural form of a society, can make mistakes on its way to becoming better.

"We must remember that human civilization has evolved from us being just apes with a big brain. It is still evolving. This is not the final state of human civilization. In the next century our descendants will create a totally different society from today. I hope they can forgive us our mistakes and be thankful for the small steps we made."

"You mean that British cuisine is just a step in evolution? I wonder how Darwin would put that?" John thought about the time he had spent in Scotland.

"I am thinking about a lot of things that are not so good, like terrorists and missionaries that are as blinded by their lack of insight about the difference between biological needs and social responsibility. When I was living together with the priest I met many church people and they appeared to be just as bewitched themselves as the pagans they tried to convert. I think they have a good heart deep inside but somewhere there is something that they misunderstand.

"Why do they preach to innocent indigenous people in the jungle instead of the people that burn down the forests in Brazil? It is like they have had some kind of accident in their morality. We can't blame them for that error in their understanding but we must blame them for their choices arising out of that. They are not stupid,

368

but they were unlucky when they tried to think. Just as we must accept that our civilization has grown from being intelligent apes, we must accept and forgive that we are not all super-smart and educated from the beginning. There must be a human right to be stupid and not to understand common law."

"As long as it doesn't hurt another person?"

"Or the insurance company. The law is no longer the prime determinant for social behaviour, it is the fine print of the terms of insurance."

"You bet!" John could see in the mirror that he had some cars following him that had difficulty in overtaking him because of the smoke, so he pulled over to the side to let them pass. The drivers used their horns and waved their hands at him. John interpreted it as a thankful gesture. He checked the petrol gauge. The needle was stuck to the left with the yellow warning light lit. Elsa was busy again with the iPad. She had found out how to use the Internet on it.

John geared up again carefully to save petrol.

"I have to keep the balance between energy, form and value. By balanced pressure on the pedal I get the best value out of the process for the moment."

"How do you know when you are in balance?" Elsa looked at John with curiosity.

"I think it is impossible to know that by my conscious mind. I must use my feelings, I think. If I tried to control my process with pure intellectual understanding it would be impossible because I have got no intellectual sense of the balance. I can understand what the balance is about but I have no intellectual tools to measure it. I can't just measure every drop of petrol with my conscious mind. I want to do my best but what is really exactly the absolute best?

"I'd be better off losing my conscious control and trusting my feelings. If it goes too far my feelings tell me how to change it. There must be some margin for action in-between. My emotions about amount of energy, form and value are easy to separate. I think I have got a good sense of size, order and proportions already. I realized that tonight, when you drew my lifeline. I just had to put them together in the right places."

"My feeling is that there is not much of a margin for the petrol."

John could do nothing apart from hope for the best. It couldn't be worse than yesterday anyway. At the end of the straight he could see a blinking blue light.

"Look, maybe there is an accident on the road ahead?"

"It is the police." Elsa put down the iPad beside the seat and looked ahead.

"It is no accident, it is just a police car with the blue lights on at the road. Maybe a car or a dead moose down in the ditch?"

John slowed down a little when they came closer but didn't want to seem too curious. A police officer stood beside the car. He raised his hand to stop them and indicated to John to stop behind the police car.

"Good morning, sir! Can you show me your licence, please?" John gave him his card.

"What it is? An accident or what?"

"I am asking the questions here, mister. Could you please get out of the car for a moment." John opened the door and got out.

"We are out of petrol!" Elsa shouted from inside.

"So how can you drive then?" The police officer said to her with a smile, bowing and looking into the rear of the car.

Another officer came by. He looked at John's shoes.

"This must be the wrong guy. He doesn't have red boots."

John blushed. "Hey listen, we really have problem with the petrol. Could you please tell me how far it is to the next petrol station?"

"Sure. We can! The next petrol stop is just about one mile away from here. I suggest you don't fill up with oil-blended petrol."

"We just wanted to know what kind of people you were. Here is your licence sir. Have a nice day!"

They police officers smiled at each other and went to their car, turned off the blue light and drove away. John was not too happy about their attention.

"I must forgive them, I must forgive them," he said to himself.

"These officers were really nice men. They are so beautiful in their uniforms. They look so powerful and strong with their muscles and their guns. They looked so happy!" Elsa said with twinkling eyes.

"Yes, they were happy. I think we made their day. Our value in their eyes was just a bit different from what we think, I guess. The petrol station is not too far from here." John had to concentrate on their mission.

They turned left at a crossing and came into a very small village with only two houses and a petrol station. Everything seemed to be oriented around this waterhole for automotives. A shed with a long row of used snowcats outside told them that this was an area with deep snow in the winter. John filled the tank and saw that they must have had about a glass of petrol left when they arrived.

The pump meter showed 75 litres, exactly as much as there was room for according to the papers for the car. John did not trust these papers' liability as to the exact material truth, or even that of the pump meter. But he was glad that they had made it this time. The margins seemed to be on their side this time. Elsa bought some fruit and John paid for the petrol. He asked the person behind the desk if there was any possibility of fitting a new adjustment bolt for the generator on his car.

"You can try a garage just by the road when you enter Pale Valley. Look for a sign on the roof on a house with the word 'Racing'. That is about one hour from here. I have heard that they can even help people on Sundays sometimes."

"Thank you sir. I'll try that."

"We are going there anyway. It's on our way home." Elsa said. She wanted to use the Internet again and picked up the iPad while John started the engine. The white smoke disappeared after a few seconds and he had a feeling that the engine had become more powerful and responsive.

"Ah, it is so nice, to be on the road again!" Elsa said with her vision glued to the screen.

"It is nice to be on the road again with a full tank. In about an hour we will see if we can fix the generator. But I think we will make it home anyway. The fan belt seems to be tight enough to load the battery."

"Hmm hm." Elsa was busy. John put on the radio. He found a station that played old jazz music and blues. Andy Kirk and his band was playing a melody called 'Say it again'.

"See why I like this music?"

"It is from your time?"

"No. They are very skilled. They had no expert equipment at that time. They had to rely on their own practice and expertise. The music is so human!"

They had an easy and peaceful trip to Pale Valley. The radio station was playing only old classics from the thirties. John enjoyed the impressive beat. The road was very fine and straight. The sky was high and the road was dry. After half an hour Elsa got bored of the Internet and looked at some of his picture albums on the iPad before she put it down between the seat and the gearbox again.

John could see the red garage with the 'Racing' sign far away. He drove up to the door and got out to check if it was open. He could see some light inside. He knocked and tried the door. It was open. John went in and could see two mechanics standing by a car but they didn't seem busy with it. He asked them if they could help him with the adjustment bolt.

"What kind is it?"

"Volvo, a '96."

"And what kind of engine?"

"B23, petrol."

"Hm, hm, well I'll open the door so you can drive straight in here." He showed John with his hand. John went out and started the engine to drive the car in. He turned off the engine and released the bonnet. John told Elsa that he thought that they could fix it and prepared her for waiting in the car or, if she wanted taking a walk outside.

"How long will it take?"

"I don't know, but I would guess an hour or two."

"Bonk!" The bonnet was closed and the mechanics indicated to John that he could back the car out again.

"What's this? Couldn't they fix it?" Elsa looked worried. John followed the instructions from the mechanic. He backed out and was prepared for more trouble coming. He got out of the car and went into the shop after parking up and asked why they didn't fix his car.

"We did! You could drive it out, couldn't you?"

"Yes, but I wanted to have it fixed with a real bolt, not just the stick that I put there myself."

"Go and have a look if you don't believe us. You see we are trained racing mechanics. We work fast. Our boss is a Chinese expert on fighting techniques and he trains us like his warriors. He uses something that he calls 'Ching Gong' on us. We call him Tjing-Tjong. We are very proud of our skill. Our team used to win the rally races. You have to meet him at his office to pay for this."

John went to the door with an 'Office' sign and went in. At the desk he saw a man with black hair and an oriental look.

"How can I help you?"

"I had my car fixed by your mechanics. They gave me a new adjustment bolt for the generator."

"How long did it take?"

"About two minutes I think."

"That was slow."

"Maybe it was because I have an old car. It is from '96."

"Aha! That explains it. It will cost you 800 kronor."

"800! That's a lot isn't it? For two minutes' repair!"

"I think that it is what it is worth, especially on a Sunday. Another mechanics would have taken two hours after several days' waiting and delay for parts."

John could feel the blood rise in his veins but he had to admit that it was worth a lot to have it fixed.

"OK." He opened his wallet and handed the man his credit card.

"But I will be nice to you mister. I will give you a special deal as I understand that you are not from this area."

"What's that deal?"

"You can have it for 400 if you promise not to tell anyone about this. It is kind of our business secret. We don't usually show our talent to foreign people." John had a feeling that this man had a Japanese accent.

"And what is that secret?"

"Don't you understand? We work fast. Fast as lightning. That makes us the winner in the rally races and we make good money in a short time. But so as not to have to share our skill with other car repair shops we keep it to ourselves to gain the advantage of having a lot of spare time."

"And what do you use this free time for? Going home earlier? Sleeping and playing golf?"

"No, not at all. We practise." He smiled and looked very convinced of his superiority.

"I heard that. They said you were practising 'Ching Gong'. I thought that was Chinese but you seem to be from Japan."

Tjing-Tjong was stunned behind the desk. He swallowed. "How do you know … ?"

"I can hear by your accent."

He blushed and looked down at the floor.

"Excuse me, I am very sorry, but I didn't mean to embarrass you. Please forgive me for my rude behaviour. To me being from Japan or China has the same value. I respect Japanese people as well as Chinese. Listen Tjing-Tjong, if that is your name, why

375

do you pretend to be Chinese when you are Japanese, then?"

"My name is not Tjing-Tjong!" My name is Nakumaru!" He stretched his back while he proudly pronounced his name.

"OK. Mr Nakumaru. Why do you hide behind a Chinese mask?"

"How could I explain? It is a long story how I ended up in this place. But when I started here the employees were impressed with something they had seen on video at home and they said to me: 'Hey boss, you are Chinese, can you teach us some Chinese fighting techniques to be better mechanics?' They didn't know the difference between Japan and China so I played the game and became a Chinese expert on fighting techniques. We are good."

"But what happens if you meet another Japanese person? Isn't it very disgraceful to appear under the wrong nationality?"

"I am a bit afraid of that so I have problems with our competition. I can't meet any other team from Japan in person. I usually wait at home for my mechanics."

"And that is just because you think they wouldn't respect you for being from Japan? I think you should go down at once and tell them the truth. I don't think they'll care if your skill comes from Japan or China just because of a video film."

Tjing-Tjong looked very nervous behind his desk.

"How long has this little lie been going on?"

"Seven years."

"Then don't wait any longer! Come with me. Let's talk to them."

Tjing-Tjong followed John out onto the shop floor where the two mechanics were working on a new car.

376

They were acting on the floor like factory robots with sudden changes between movement and concentrated stillness. It looked like they memorized every little move they had just made and prepared for the next move in the next second.

"Hello boys! Your boss wants to speak to you!"

"About what? Is something wrong with our work?"

"No. It's just about where he comes from. You said he was Chinese but he is actually from Japan." Tjing-Tjong looked at the floor waiting for the judgement.

"So what's the difference?"

"You don't think it has anything to do with your respect for his skills?"

"No. Why should it? He is still the same Tjing-Tjong to me, I believe. He looks the same to me. He is great! Can we go on practising now? We want to be the best on this car."

Tjing-Tjong looked up with tears in his eyes.

"Come on," he said. "Let's go into the office again. You left your credit card on my desk."

They went into the office again.

"So much trouble for nothing?" John looked at him. "You are sure that there isn't anything else going on here?" Tjing-Tjong sat quietly behind the desk.

"Well, it could be the reason why I am here and not in Japan. I tried to use this technique in my job at home and I had problems so I had to find another place in the world to live in. That's all. You can have the repair for free if you just forget this. I am very thankful of course for your observation. I hope you will keep this little secret. But you are very welcome back anyway if you want help with your car. But get another one, that one's old. We don't work on that model any longer. Here is your credit card. Please bring cash next time. I have no credit card machine."

"Thanks a lot." John gave him his business card in return. "I promise not to tell anybody. Sayonara!"

"Sayonara!" Tjing-Tjong was smiling again. They shook hands and John went out to Elsa again.

23 - Lost in the Pizza

"How is it going? Can we drive?" Elsa looked up from the iPad. She appeared to be used to it. Now she was playing Sudoku on it.

"The car is fixed and I got it for free. That was great. They are skilled racing mechanics and love to do it fast. Me and the boss became friends so I didn't have to pay."

"I can hear that you are a professional salesman."

"So now we are heading home with a good working car and a full tank. Let's go!"

"Wait! Stop!"

"What? I have not even started the engine yet!"

"I am hungry! I must have pizza. I could read the word 'PIZZA' on a roof!" Elsa sounded like one of his teenagers.

"OK, it's about eleven on Sunday morning. I am not sure we can find a place that's open to eat some lunch."

John started the engine and they went through the city. The radio was playing 'Hey Bartender' by Floyd Dixon. Elsa pointed to where she saw the restaurant sign and she was right. It was there and it was open. John parked the car and they went into the place. It was crowded.

They put in their orders and found a free table close to the door. The customers were mostly young and there was a loud atmosphere. The youths seemed to know each other well and were screaming across the premises at each other. There was a lot of talk and laughing about what had happened the night before.

John had a good time watching the other guests while they were waiting for their food.

He saw two young boys at a table by the window. One of them was rather big and the other one was small and thin. The thin one seemed to be strongly affected by alcohol. Blind drunk was John's classification. They seemed to be waiting for pizza, too. The thin boy had severe difficulties keeping his balance even though he was sitting down. He swayed a lot and was continually close to falling off his chair. His friend was firmly stuck to his chair. "He won't get up from the chair, he'll take the chair off," John was thinking.

John and Elsa were served at the table. They ate in silence as it was hard to speak in the noise. When John was finished the noise had decreased a bit so it began to be possible to talk. He watched the two boys at the window table. The bigger boy appeared to have finished already but the thin boy had not done more to his than make a hole in the centre with his fork. He was completely lost in the pizza. The fork in his right hand pointed out through the bottom side. He raised his hand and tried to lift the whole of it upside down and get a bite of it but failed continually. He tried to grasp the edge of it but his left hand waved the pizza in the air uncontrolledly and the right hand missed once and again. All of the fillings dropped on the table and on the floor. Melted cheese and tomato sauce all over his right arm. It was a really disgusting scene and John wanted to leave at once. When Elsa was finished he asked her if they could move on.

"I would like to have some coffee too, please." John let her go and get two cups.

Again, John watched the thin boy and his struggle with the superior pizza that seemed to be winning the fight: eat or be eaten. He was lying on his right side over the chair beside him now. His face was buried in the pizza wreck on the table. John tried to see if he was eating or sleeping. That boy must be nearly unconscious from alcohol. Had these boys shared a gallon of whisky earlier in equal parts, and the big boy had been able to take the amount much better just because of his bigger body?

"I can see that you have found some interesting object again. Did you drop your fascination over the time in 3D, going back to a pizza in 2D?"

"No, not really, but I am sort of fascinated, yes. I didn't tell you about what happened at the car repair shop. It seems connected with this disgusting behaviour in front of us."

"Do you mean the big guy who ate two pizzas faster than you had one?"

"Two pizzas? Really? I didn't notice that."

"He had two pizzas on one plate. I saw it. It looked like the world's largest hamburger. He folded it and held it with both hands and just crammed it into his face."

"Wow, that must have been a great sight. I was watching the thin guy. Look! Now he has dropped his pizza again. He is still deciding to eat it. All the filling is gone. He would be lucky to hit it at all with his fork. What if he had ordered meatballs?"

"You are right. This is really a waste. It makes me sick. Let's go."

They went back to the car. They had about two hours' drive left to get back to Elsa's. They had food inside them, not in the best form, maybe, but the amount would satisfy them for the rest of the day. Their digestion would break the pizza down into molecules and arrange the ingredients into new valuable stuff like fat, minerals, blood sugar and protein. John started the engine and drove away south.

"Ah, it's so nice to be on the road again. Certainly after this stop."

"I must say that this place made me confused once again."

"It was like being at a school refectory. I mean, I have seen worse."

"Me too. I have a couple of teenagers at home. When they bring their friends home it can be quite wild. But they think it's OK. I think we are just different. No, what I was thinking about is this: at both places it was so much about margins. It makes me so curious, why do they need such a margin?"

"What margin?"

"I did not tell you what happened at the car repair shop. But the mechanics were so skilled and so fast so they were performing, eh, they were acting like artists and did the job in seconds instead of hours. It was really crazy."

"It took no time so you didn't have to pay. That was fantastic."

"No, the boss wanted to charge me for the time it would have taken at a regular place where it would take some hours to do."

"That was shameless, wasn't it?"

"Well, it seemed like they used the time anyway, but not on fixing cars, but on practising fixing cars in advance. They were so well trained that they could fix a car very fast and that gave them time to exercise and learn how to do it even faster the next time. Instead of just taking it easy and working at normal speed. They were heading for the margins."

"What did that have to do with the pizza guys?"

"The big one ate too much and he was overloaded with fat and muscle power. That is a biological way of bettering the margins. The thin guy was just too bad. He just had too much alcohol. More than he needed really. He was so drunk so he needed a whole pizza to be able to hit the food with the fork. But it was too soft to be handled that way. He had margins to hit it but not margins enough to eat it. It is so much about margins these days."

"But these guys were not normal cases were they?"

"No, not in person. They were really odd fellows, together. But all this competition in the world. It is all about cutting the margins from each other. If someone gets too strong in the competitive market that gives him better margins, then the anti-trust lawmen weigh in and try to knock him down from his position. That was what happened to Rockefeller in 1911[28], which forced down the price of the oil for a century. That happened to Microsoft 2006[29]. Windows seemed to be a little too popular, I think.

"People call Big Brother for help when someone has margins that are too good. Or they try to compete with something cheaper because they think they are happy with half the margin. But what is the wealth some people have if it isn't about having very good margins? Is it OK or is it as disgusting as the drunk guy with a hole in his pizza?"

"I don't have that kind of problem anyway so why should I bother?"

"I bother because I am not sure why the rules should be different in the same game. Some people think it is OK to have margins, wide margins, and for other

---

28 http://en.wikipedia.org/wiki/John_D._Rockefeller

29 http://en.wikipedia.org/wiki/United_States_v._Microsoft

people there shouldn't be any margins at all. And after all, the more money you have, the more dependent on the society you are."

"How?"

"If I were rich and had millions and lots of property and all that, I would be very dependent on society. The money is not worth anything at all by itself. It is only numbers on a bank account. The value of the money depends on what I can change them into. To be able to buy goods and duties for the money there must be people that want the money in their turn, people that give the money a value. The worst kind of inflation would be if people dropped their desire for money."

"You said that money was the new religion. Now you say that money can lose its divine value."

"Yes, why not? People's faith in their Gods varies from time to time, doesn't it? By the way, time must be the only absolute value meter. Time does not change speed."

"You said before that value was dependent on relations, that it is relative, now you say that is absolute."

"Oh, excuse me. The value of something depends on its relation to other things. But yes, it is the same! The value of money depends upon the relation between the owner and the presumptive buyer of something. The value of time depends on how much time different things take. Saved time is absolute in one way but relative to something else. We are back where we began. The value of something is different from different points of view. It is this difference that makes business work at all. The value of something compared to something else is the time it takes. If something takes more time to be realized it has to be of higher value."

"I don't understand at all."

"If I have one day to work and I can choose between digging carrots or digging a ditch. The thing I choose to do is the one that has the higher value. The best thing to spend my time on is keeping my general balance between mass, form and meaning. I want to live a good life and if carrots are what I need today then they have the highest value, today, to me. The carrots can have a totally different value to someone else. It is all about how we use our time. I am the one who chooses my way and by choosing I decide what the time is worth to me."

"'I did it my way' … and the rich guy?"

"He has a lot of money but he is still dependent on others for how much of the saved time he will be able to use. He can choose to use his money and hire someone to do a thing or he can use his own time and do it by himself to get things done. The more he earns per hour the more his time is worth. The more it will cost him if he decides to use up his time instead. Gardening work or reading a book will cost a fortune per hour for a person that can make a million per month. To me it is much cheaper."

"It depends on your skill, too, doesn't it?"

"Yes, of course. I am the one that chooses and it is my way of life. A rock can't choose, it is just itself and keeps on existing as long as it has mass, form and value."

"What is the value of a rock?"

"Its characteristics are its value. The space it takes up, the colour, the weight it makes on the ground, the hardness. The value can change quickly if it is combined with the right other object."

"Like what?"

"If you need something to put on papers on a windy day. If you need something to put on a stick to make a club to defend yourself against a bear. A good-sized piece of rock can be worth a life."

"You need some kind of skill for that too."

"Right. We develop our skills all the time. Humanity has been very successful in developing the skill to protect itself from the damaging forces of the nature. The threats from the biological, the organic and the inorganic levels. Viruses, predators, heat, drought, poison and cold. But we have something left to learn about the social level. How to build a better economic strategy."

"Really? I thought we had too much money in the world."

"No. The value behind money is saved time. Too much of the skill is focused on how to compete and cut the margins between the customer value and the cost of production. Instead of concentrating efforts on how to better the margins by increasing customer value, we fight over the remains from the decreasing values that come from overproduction.

"Remember what I told you about oil. Millions of years of saved solar energy that was turned into oil is wasted just because the pricing method of oil has been totally wrong. The judgement from the people of the future on our generation will be hard. Thousands of coming generations will say that. Our time will be seen as the century that spoiled the oil reserves by setting the wrong price on it. Our generation will be remembered as those who left a lot of nuclear waste for the future to take care of but no revenue."

"Even if we're not alive then, I hope they can forgive us. Without the oil we couldn't have done this trip."

Elsa sounded as though she was already planning for a new one.

"OK, but was it worth it?"

"I think so. I am happy!"

"I love you. I love your smile. It is priceless!"

"I love you too. Please hold my hand a little more. I love to watch your joy."

"My pleasure is your pleasure."

The road was wide and straight. They were following the west side of a deep valley that ran south. The mountains were covered by dark green forests while the lower parts were scattered by farms between the pale brown fields of withered grass. Many of the fields were ploughed. The soil was striped in brown and dark violet colours. Waiting for the snow to cover it before next season.

'Bonk!'

"What was that?"

"I don't know. I think we hit something."

"You must stop and take a look!"

John stopped the car by the side of the road and got out to take a look. There was nothing wrong with the car but about 200 yards back he could see a small animal roll around and kick with its legs on the road. Elsa got out and ran to it. John stayed at the car. He could see Elsa pick the animal up. She held it in her arms to her breast. She went from the road out on a field. John saw her disappear into the bushes at the other side of the field. He got into the car, started the engine and backed up to a place where it was possible to stop without interfering with the traffic. He turned off the engine and waited for Elsa to return.

This was not the first time he had hit and killed an animal with the car. "Animals never learn," he was thinking.

"They jump up on the road now and then and get hit by the first car coming by. 'The survival of the fittest' doesn't work well in this case. Some animals learn maybe how to wait for the right moment to cross the road when it is safe but that is a behaviour that is not transmitted to the next generation so every individual animal has to learn how to behave on the road." John had seen so many flat versions of wildlife. Flatness is not a good form for an animal. Life processes don't work if a creature is flattened or mashed and repatterned. There are margins but if the violence is too much the animal will die.

"A biological organism must stay inside the conditional margins for mass, form and value to keep on living. It must eat and drink to preserve its amount of energy and weight. Hunger and thirst forces it to balance the mass.

"It must also stay in the perfect shape to be able to live outdoors in the wild all the year around. The fur must be thick and warm in the winter and thin in the summer." John was sure that an animal couldn't decide when to let the fur grow and fall off. That was more an issue for the function of the individual hair cells. Just as a human can't control the growth of the skin-protecting hair in the armpits. Animals take care of their fur by licking it. They may feel it itching in the spring and find they want to scrub their back against trees and rocks to get rid of the winter wool.

"The value of an individual animal is tested every year at the mating season when bulls and cows perform their instinctive rituals that show how good and important they are for reproduction. Size, actual presence at the same place, and moving patterns that fit together."

Elsa returned from the field.

"What was it?"

"It was a young hare. He was dead so I buried him under a stone."

"It took time."

"He didn't die at once. I held him to my breast. He was shivering from fright. I heard him breathe until the last one that released him from the pain. I felt like it flew away from him. He gave up and became soft in a second."

"So sad."

"Yes, it made me so sorry to see his empty eyes. He was still warm. I had to sit down for a while and cry after I buried him. Powerlessness filled my heart."

John felt tears well up in his eyes. He felt powerless without control.

"It was an accident. No one can prepare for every situation. I feel sorry, too."

"You could have driven more slowly."

"Yes, but that doesn't help every time. I slowed down once for a deer that crossed the road in front of me and then another deer ran into the car from the side and was badly hurt by the rear wheel."

John put on the engine and drove away again. He knew he couldn't have done anything to save the hare but still he felt guilty about its death.

"I am sorry for the hare but we may hope it gives another one a better opportunity to survive the coming winter."

24 - The Magic Flute

"So what do you think is the use of it?" Elsa said after a while.

"The use of what?"

"The 3D perspective of time. The idea that time is made up of three different dimensions: energy, form and value. Is it a way to understand thermodynamics, or what else do you mean?"

"I can't believe that it is the real picture, but it could be a useful model to describe reality as events and processes with an ever-changing value depending on how you look at it. An accountant's graphic description of a company's yield over time or a matrix description in two dimensions is not a real picture. The marks on the wall in the kitchen that show how the kids are growing aren't showing the reality either. Reality is now, the marks shows what happened since they were babies. But these models help us to understand and decide better. By using the 3D-model we can choose anything between 42 different poles of action to keep ourselves in shape."

"Isn't it more like a set of 42 warning lamps?"

"I would call it a set of seven guiding lights in the unknown darkness. Lights showing just any colour, any blend between the three primary colours. Those who don't see it and prefer instead to listen to other people about what is most important in the daily life are walking around in the spiritual darkness."

"Sooner or later they will smack their face into the edge of an open door so they can see stars. So that is why you think it is so stupid to pretend to be normal?"

"Ha ha, yes! But not stupid, a child must have the right to not know anything about adult certainties. This 3D-figure could help scientists with different opinions to understand each other better. They aren't crazy but they have got different bases and perspectives. The fact that there are different dimensions can be the explanation for how people can be so sure of themselves and still have such different opinions from others about the same thing. Einstein and Planck, for example."

"So you think there must be a third view?"

"I have always wondered where the French revolutionary idea[30] about freedom, brotherhood and equality came from but I think I understand it better now. It must have been freedom of our values and individual culture. Brotherhood in the economy, the amount of resources shared as brothers. Equality in the form of society. The structure, the laws mean the same for everyone. We must be able to think in three different ways simultaneously to be good citizens or the revolution will fail. As it did."

"That ideal still lives in France. Red, white and blue."

"Yes, like primary colours. There are three primary colours but an infinite number of blends. But mostly I was thinking about the 3D perspective as a perfect way to be prepared for a close encounter with real aliens from another galaxy."

"You may have to wait for that to happen."

"Yes, I had a good laugh at the idea at first when I saw the film *Close Encounters of the Third Kind*[31]. In that film the army is trying to contact aliens by playing a series of tones and blinking with coloured stage lights

---

30 http://en.wikipedia.org/wiki/Liberté,_égalité,_fraternité

31 http://en.wikipedia.org/wiki/Close_Encounters_of_the_Third_Kind

from a helicopter. I laughed at that scene first of all because I thought it was so ridiculous to presume that aliens would have the same sense for the light spectrum as we have. But later I found out that it was not so stupid at all.

"The visible area in the electromagnetic wave spectrum[32] is the one that is reflected almost perfectly in the physical space. The reflections of the visible spectrum give the best information about the surrounding physical space to an object that is moving in it. Visible light is reflected perfectly to the things in the space and gives precise information about where things are located. The lower frequencies have a longer wavelength and don't give accurate information about the physical details.

"Have you seen a live camera showing infrared pictures that shows how temperature changes slowly in front of the lens? The temperature is still there if you remove a hot object. Thus you can see that it would be hard to be a bird or a fly and orientate between the twigs in a forest if it could only see in infrared. Radio waves that are of even lower frequency don't reflect at all and passes straight through physical material, like walls, for example. The lowest frequencies have the longest waves and they pass straight through the Earth instead of going around it in the atmosphere."

"So you think aliens are listening to the radio?"

"That is possible as electromagnetic waves can transport a lot of information, intellectual concepts distributed over a very long distance and at the speed of light. But I think that, were ever we found aliens in the universe, any evolved life forms that were able to

---

32 http://en.wikipedia.org/wiki/Visible_spectrum

move around in physical space would need correct information for their orientation not to crash into each other. I think they will be equipped with a kind of sight that is sensible of what we call the visible spectrum because that is the most accurate."

"Couldn't they use higher frequencies?"

"I am not sure about that. Higher frequencies have such short waves that they interfere with the atomic structure of the material and the waves gets distorted by it. It gives a warped bounce as if you throw a tennis ball on a bicycle."

"But what would be the use of the 3D-time?"

"The pre-selective Quality process that works behind any event is the means of keeping the balance between energy, form and value. The general purpose is to save time, to continue and to improve the margins. Pirsig's way to describe evolution on Earth, as something that has evolved on four levels: from the inorganic through the organic and the social over to the intellectual, is what has happened on our planet. We have pieces of all four levels already represented in the inorganic but the separate levels are dominated by one of the main functions.

"In the inorganic we have a high grade of repeated static and statistical movements of energy. At the organic level the structures are so complicated that degeneration and depletion are problems and they are solved by making copies of the structure that replace the old. At the social level the organized use of different individuals with different roles in the network, for example as man and woman, small and big members – the advantages from that is used to form a new superior level over the purely biological level. Later the invention of languages that could be

393

inherited and preserved on walls and paper independently of individual or social chains formed its own level above the social.

"Time, however, is present at all stages. In the repeated sequence in atoms and particles, in the inheritance of the code for the next generation by cell division, in the imitation of normative cultural behaviour in social groupings, in concepts like the timeline in a calendar and the GMT system at the intellectual level.

"The evolution on another planet could follow the same path as ours or it could be just about anything else, but with other species and with another pace. It would be quite interesting to discuss their way of evolution with an alien expert."

"I am sure that they don't want to count the years, like we do, from the birth of Christ. And no suit and tie to make a good impression on us."

"Certainly not. The right first question to an alien must be 'How do you do?' I really would like to know what system they use."

"They definitely don't use cassette radios in their cars. I think they have better equipment."

"Hey, listen, this one isn't too bad. I have mounted extra loudspeakers. I wish that I had something to connect this iPad too so I would have a bigger music library. Now I only have space in my box for 10 cassettes."

"What kind of music do you have?"

"I have broad taste, I think. I have a promotional cassette for the sound of stereo equipment. I have some classical music. Handel – Water Music, Mozart. I think there is a Captain Beefheart compilation too."

"How about listening to Mozart?"

"I have the complete *Magic Flute*[33] opera by Mozart. I got rid of some of the talk so it could fit onto a 90-minute cassette."

"I like that love story."

John put in the tape and it happened to be wound to the beginning. The overture filled the car. John turned the volume down to please Elsa's ears.

"No! I like it loud!"

John turned the volume up again. They had almost two hours' drive left to Elsa's. John looked forward to listening. Elsa put down the iPad and leaned back. She closed her eyes and enjoyed the music. She seemed to know every word of it as she moved her lips to the songs.

The dynamic power, the ever-changing tempo, the expression and interaction of intriguing human emotions. The combination, the balance between these three dimensions together made the music. Mozart really knew, he had the right feeling for music. "Salieri[34] was right, it was God who sang through him."

Back at Elsa's, when John had parked the car, there was still some music left.

The choir were singing:

"Triumph, triumph, triumph!

"Oh, noble couple!

"You have conquered all the dangers!

"You are now initiated into the rites of the gods.

"Come, come, enter the temple!"

33 http://en.wikipedia.org/wiki/The_Magic_Flute

34 http://en.wikipedia.org/wiki/Antonio_Salieri

Elsa showed with closed eyes that she wanted to listen to the end so they sat still in the car with the music playing loudly. John closed his eyes and let them rest after the drive. He had listened to this music many times before but hadn't paid much attention to the text. He was more into it for the beauty of the music.

Click. The cassette player turned the direction of the tape again automatically and John turned the key to break the current and automatically turn the player off.

"I'll help you with the things." John got out and stretched his arms over his head to let his body recover. The time was half past two and he wanted to be home before nightfall. He had still about two hours driving to get home.

"Thank you!" Elsa showed him how to carry her bedroll. She could carry her own bags. John left his things and locked the car.

When they were inside her apartment again Elsa looked in surprise at the computer as she had forgotten how it had got there.

"How do you feel now? Are you tired after driving all day?"

"Yes a bit. But I think I'd like to take a shower. I am glad I didn't try to swim in the lake last night."

"You can take a shower and then you can take care of your biology in my bed. I can make some tea and sandwiches for you when you wake up."

John went into the shower. The hot water ran all over him. He washed his hair with Elsa's peach-smelling shampoo. She came into the bathroom.

"Do you want me to wash your back?" John could see her on the other side of the curtain.

"Sure, that would be nice." He opened the curtain and turned his back to her. Elsa buffed him into the

396

cubicle and closed the curtain behind her. She was naked, she didn't want her clothes to be wet while she washed his back. Elsa knew where all the other lotions were located in the boxes outside the curtain and washed his entire body. John washed her in turn from top to toe, twice. There was more room than in Mary's little shower cubicle. The bathroom was steamy and familiar.

John borrowed her pink razor, shaved, found a new toothbrush. Elsa disappeared into the kitchen again. He went to the bedroom and lay down between the violet and grey silk sheets.

He woke up on his left side with his face to the wall. Elsa was breathing into his neck. John felt her right underarm on his belly. He could sense her hand opening and closing at a slow pace. He could hear from her breath that she was still asleep. "There is time. The margins are on my side," he was thinking. It began to get dark outside again.

"Falling asleep is nothing compared to waking up next to you," Elsa whispered in his ear. "This is so lovely."

"Yes, it is. But ..."

"I know. There's just too many buts."

"This will be hard. Painful. I hate to leave you, but I must. I must think about my reputation."

"I've got no reputation but my daughter. You are my fifth man. And for the shortest period."

She caressed him slowly. John turned on his back and caressed her with his left hand.

"I am so glad of this. I will miss you, but I am glad to have got so close. I would have missed it more if I knew ..." John was honest.

"You wouldn't have known this but … If Mary hadn't called … I would have made up something else."

John looked into her eyes.

"You surprise me all the time. I will leave you soon, but I'll be back."

"How soon?"

"I think we can stay here in your bed for at least one more hour if you wish. I think I've got margins for that."

"Oh no, young man! I am the one here that has got margins! I can use my time as I like. Now it's time to get up. We shall play cards before you go!"

Elsa jumped up from the bed. John had to follow her, find his clothing and get dressed again.

Elsa had made tea and sandwiches that were ready on the table. They played two games and John lost both times. She laughed wildly and John was happy to see her so glad.

John had to leave. He held Elsa close with his arms around her. She wept a little. He caressed her neck.

"Don't be sorry. I'll be back. I promise you."

"How soon?"

"I am sorry, I don't really know yet when I will pass this way next."

"I might be dead before then!"

"Then I will cry. I will be happy that I had the opportunity to get to know you before that."

"Now get out! I don't want to be longing for you. I have things to do." She showed him to the door. She did not look angry. But she was not happy either.

"I have to see my granddaughter before she moves to New York. I must teach her how to draw the lifeline."

"Are you going to tell her about me drawing it on you?"

"No, I'll say that I learned it from Chica's grandmother when we attended a conference in Nevada in the fifties. It was about nuclear defence systems. You remember my husband, how he loved the big explosions. I love the small ones.

"Now, please leave before I change my mind."

John said goodbye and closed the door. He waited for a second. He was recalling if he had all his things in order so he had not forgotten anything. He touched his pockets to be sure if he had brought his keys, his mobile and his wallet. He had his glasses on. He turned and could see that Elsa was standing behind the door and watching him through the peephole.

John hesitated. His heart was beating hard. Then he turned again to the door and saw her behind the door in the same position. She didn't say anything. John was quiet. He bit his lips. He tried his pockets again. He turned again and began walking slowly to the elevator. "I could have asked for her phone number," he was thinking.

John got into the car, put in the ignition key and turned it to the right. The cassette player went on when the current was connected and John held his hand still at the last moment just before starting the engine. The Mozart opera began to play from the beginning. It was the overture again. He released his grip of the key and became absorbed in the music. It reminded him of the last few hours. But this was not a repetition of that tour. This must be the beginning of something different. He needed to be alone for a while after this weekend.

He turned the key further to the right, the engine started and he drove away slowly through the easy city. Buildings, high blocks, trees. Parked cars, traffic lights, lamp posts. Advertising, litter, a crow on the ground holding a piece of paper in her beak. A railway station, a hotel, an empty shopping mall. No people anywhere. Everyone at home eating dinner or watching TV. John looked around listening to the music.

"Help! Help! Or I am lost!"

John arrived at the same roundabout that he had passed on his way to Elsa's three days ago. He had to stop to let a heavy-loaded lorry pass from the left. The road home went straight on to the south.

"A fair youth delicate and beautiful!"

John released the clutch and drove into the roundabout.

"More beautiful than I have ever seen!" He listened to the words and missed the exit for the road to the south. He continued circling. Passed another exit.

"Yes, yes, certainly beautiful enough ..." The next junction was back north to Elsa again.

He passed it again and took the next road heading west. John had already forgotten the past, his mind was clear, clean and white like snow. He passed a couple of crossings with traffic lights and after a while he crossed the edge of the city. He changed to a higher gear and breathed out. He got tired of Mozart and changed the cassette to the *Stereo Spectacular 3* again. 'Dreaming the blues' by Bert Kaempfert was cleansing his ears.

John held the steering wheel with his left hand and his right foot gently on the accelerator to keep the car straight around 50 mph. He was alone in the car and on the road. At the end of the straight he could see a bend to the left. He looked forward to what he would find there.

www.ingramcontent.com/pod-product-compliance
Lightning Source LLC
La Vergne TN
LVHW011319080426
835513LV00006B/126